UNCOMMON SENSE

unCOMMON SENSE

INVESTMENT WISDOM *since*
THE STOCK MARKET'S DAWN

MICHAEL KEMP

WILEY

First published in 2016 by John Wiley & Sons Australia, Ltd
42 McDougall St, Milton Qld 4064
Office also in Melbourne

Typeset in 11.5/13.5pt Bembo Std by Aptara, India

© Kemp's Nominees Pty Ltd 2016

The moral rights of the author have been asserted

National Library of Australia Cataloguing-in-Publication data:

Creator:	Kemp, Michael E., author.
Title:	Uncommon Sense: Investment wisdom since the stock market's dawn / Michael Kemp.
ISBN:	9780730324249 (pbk.)
	9780730324256 (ebook)
Notes:	Includes index.
Subjects:	Stocks.
	Stock exchanges.
	Investments.
	Finance, personal.
Dewey Number:	332.6322

Cover design: Lizzie Deller and Wiley
Cover image: Paper Tear © Lizzie Deller
Cover and internal images: The Old Exchange of Amsterdam
© Job Adriaensz Berckheijde; Wall Street New York Stock Exchange
© iStock.com/LUNAMARINA

Printed in Singapore

Disclaimer

To Sandra, Andrew and Jessica

CONTENTS

FOREWORD

'Where do I find a good investment analyst to hire?' I asked a close friend.

'Well, there's one guy I know. He's brilliant, but he's kind of... intense.'

That man was Mike Kemp.

The first time we met, I felt like Mike's eyes were burning into the back of my brain.

To prepare for our casual chat he'd read my book cover to cover, and watched two seasons of my show, *The Barefoot Investor*, on CNBC, back to back.

I'm also pretty sure he didn't blink for the entire 30 minutes we spoke.

I count that meeting as one of the luckiest moments of my professional life.

Mike and I have worked together daily for over three years now, and in that time I've learned that there's another trait that Mike has in equal measure to his intensity: integrity.

In an industry full of wonks and shonks, Mike's the real deal.

I've never met anyone who's more committed to rigorously uncovering the truth. And, as this book attests, if that means he has to go back to the dawn of capitalism to prove his point, so be it.

When you begin dipping your toe into the wonderful world of investing, you're instantly bombarded with all sorts of opinions that are rolled up and presented as investment 'laws'.

It's almost impossible for the new investor to separate fact from fiction. Who could blame them? After all, as this book shows, the same investment delusions that were whispered by shoe-shine boys on Wall Street are polished up and presented as facts today on the internet and cable TV.

So let's cut to the chase. If you're standing in the bookstore reading this, let me give you three reasons why you should pony up to the counter.

First, Mike will show you just how hard it is to convincingly beat the market over a long period of time. However, he'll also give you the intellectual building blocks to start you off on your quest to do so.

Second, this book is like a guided history through high finance—and it's surprisingly saucy: from the invention of the stock exchange, to Evangeline Adams (a spiritual mystic who was giving the holiest stock tips in the lead-up to the 1929 Crash), to the cheesy-but-true story of rat trading (seriously, a number of hedge funds got interested in the idea of rats delivering market-beating returns from trading stocks and currencies).

And finally, it'll dramatically slim down your future reading list. That's because *Uncommon Sense* takes a knife to the most common investing illusions held dear.

The end result is that you'll never look at charting, market timing or valuation in the same way again. In fact, I'm convinced that after you read this book you'll begin to see just how close CNBC is to the Comedy Channel.

Scott Pape
The Barefoot Investor
January 2015

ABOUT THE AUTHOR

Dr Michael Kemp completed an MBA before embarking on a career in corporate finance during the mid–1980s bull market. As a young financier he was awarded the Ian Roach Prize for achieving first place nationally among employees of the Australian Securities Exchange studying for the Graduate Diploma in Applied Finance and Investment.

Michael Kemp graduated from Melbourne University and has subsequently gained two master's degrees, including an MBA from Monash University.

His financial career has included working in the Treasury Department of the Australian Wheat Board, as a trader for Bankers Trust and in the Corporate Finance department of stockbroking firm Potter Warburg (both in Australia and London).

Today Michael spends his time investing on his personal account, writing articles for the Australian Securities Exchange and analysing and writing about stocks for the *Barefoot Blueprint* newsletter.

To Michael, finance has always been a passion, never a job. *Uncommon Sense* is his second investment book.

ACKNOWLEDGEMENTS

Writing this book has been a fascinating journey, one I'm sad is now over. And like any journey its completion allows me to reflect on those who I shared it with. Thanks to friends and family who showed an ongoing interest in the process. And a special thanks to those who read the first manuscript: Colin Nicholson, Robert Miles, Scott Pape, Michael Wall and my two children, Andrew and Jessica. Their respective critiques helped sculpt the final product.

Part I
THE LIMITS OF REASON

0.9

START THINKING FOR YOURSELF

First up, that's not a typo. I wanted this to be chapter '0.9'. If I'd called it 'Introduction', 'Prologue' or 'Preface' you'd probably have skipped it. But it contains stuff I want you to read. So here it is: chapter 0.9.

My passion for the stock market became obvious when I was in my early to mid twenties. Problem was, by then I was already a dentist. What's more, I'd studied dentistry for all the wrong reasons. Those who thought they knew me best used to say, 'Hey Mike, you're getting great grades. You're really good at science. And since you can get into any university course you want, you should study medicine.' But I didn't want to be a doctor, so I chose dentistry on the rebound. Seemed like a good idea at the time. After all, doesn't everyone choose dentistry when they decide not to study medicine? Wrong. As I later found out, dentistry is what you study when you don't get the grades for medicine.

I should have noticed the warning signs earlier. Like when I was six years old and told my mother I wanted to be a bank manager. I mean, what six-year-old wants to be a bank manager? Most six-year-olds want to be a pilot or a fire engine driver.

My mother knew all along that I'd made a mistake doing dentistry. I should have listened to her when, halfway through my degree, I broke the news that I was thinking of tossing it all in. I thought she'd break down and start crying, tell me I was giving up the chance to have a great career and earn good money. And through her sobs she'd ask, 'Does this mean I have to stop telling my friends my son's going to be a dentist?' But she didn't do any of that. Instead she broke out into a big smile and said, 'Well, thank God for that. Now you can study economics and become a stock broker like I always thought you would.'

I got there eventually, after working briefly and very unhappily as a general dentist. Fortunately, when I finally started looking for a job in finance it was the mid eighties. The stock market was on fire and anybody in a pinstriped suit who had a pulse could get a job. I'd just finished an MBA because I thought I needed some economic credentials on top of the dental degree before fronting up to my first interviews. Turns out I'd wasted my time — Bankers Trust took me on regardless. I remember my future boss, Bruce Lugton, telling me at the interview: 'You should have come and seen us a couple of years ago. You didn't need the MBA.' He was right. A few weeks later I was in the dealing room in Sydney and the FX trader behind me had just tossed in a job delivering pizzas.

I was green to the game and needed to establish some credibility. Talking about teeth just didn't cut it on a money market dealing desk. So I learned the jargon. The Reserve Bank wasn't putting up interest rates, it was 'tightening monetary policy'. You weren't about to sell, you were 'going short'. And you weren't taking advantage of the other guy, you were making a 'good spread'.

I had trouble with the whole economics thing. It wasn't like science. Science is pretty much black and white, and I'm a black-and-white sort of guy. But that brand of thinking doesn't work with economics. While everyone around me reeled off economic commentaries like they were one job application away from becoming Chairman of the Federal Reserve, I was still trying to work out why the Reserve Bank would raise interest rates if a flood in Queensland had caused the price of bananas to go up.

For those who learned to play the game, a good economic spiel came in very handy. Econospeak goes something like this: First come up with a few terms like 'fiscal deficit', 'monetary policy' and 'quantitative easing'. Next wrap a good story around them. And finally tell it like you're dead certain you're correct. It doesn't matter if you throw in a few predictions, because no-one will ever check whether they come true or not. People will just remember you as that smart guy who had all the answers.

But enough about financial economics—there's plenty more of that later in the book. I want to introduce the reason for writing this book. To me the financial markets present the most fascinating environment I've ever interacted with. Thought-provoking, stimulating, yet an environment most people approach in an entirely illogical way. This book seeks to question commonly held beliefs about the financial markets by putting them through a sieve of logic. And in the process I hope it helps you develop a set of investment principles that works well for you.

One thing you'll notice as you read this book is that there are lots of quotes. And for that I make no apology. Quotes are great. They're an efficient use of words, distilling great ideas into pithy messages. But I know not everyone shares my enthusiasm. When I was writing this chapter I spotted a newspaper article in which the writer was condemning the use of quotes. He said their use stemmed from a lack of original thought...and then he used a quote to strengthen his case.

I particularly love old quotes. The older the better. The fascination for me is that they show how investment principles transcend time. Century-old investment books contain exactly the same stuff as books written today—that's right, the very same principles modern writers want you to believe they thought up all by themselves. Old quotes about investing also show that investors in the past held the same fears, hopes and dreams that investors hold today. So I hope you share my passion for quotes and financial history, because you're going to get a decent dose of both in this book.

Also this is not a 'how to' investment book. The world is full of them, and in the wrong hands they are extremely dangerous. Successful people don't blindly accept everything they hear; they work things out for themselves. So if you want to be a great investor, leave the recipe books in the kitchen. As Johann Goethe wrote in *Maxims and Reflections*, 'There is nothing so terrible as activity without insight.'

So steer clear of books with titles like 'A Sure-fire System to Beat the Managed Funds by 15%' or 'How to Trade Like a Pro'. Successful investing just isn't that easy.

I want to spread some good news early on. Solid returns are there to be had if you develop a basic knowledge of how the stock market works, and mix it with a good dose of common sense. For example, simply leaving your money in an index fund and letting it compound over time will serve you well. Average stock market returns can be great returns. Problem is, people don't like 'average', and they don't realise that it takes work to become 'above average'. The famous stock trader Jesse Livermore once put it this way:

> Over a long period of years I have rarely attended a dinner party including strangers, that someone did not sit down beside me and after the usual pleasantries inquire: 'How can I make some money in the market?'

> It is difficult to exercise patience with such people. In the first place, the inquiry is not a compliment to the man who has made a study of investment and speculation. It would be as fair for the layman to ask an attorney or a surgeon: 'How can I make some quick money in law or surgery?'[1]

To beat the market you need a deep understanding of everything that investing can throw at you. That understanding is hard earned. I haven't met a good investor who wasn't driven by the need to learn and to keep learning.

Now there's an irony to all of this: the more you learn about investing, the more you appreciate how simple the process needs to be. I'm not saying that financial markets are simple, or that, given enough time and education, one day you'll find them simple, or that you can treat the process casually and win. Quite the opposite on all three counts. I'm saying that as your appreciation of financial markets develops it will become clear that they are too complex to be completely understood. So our only hope is to interact with them in a simple way. This was a truth understood by Charles Dow, the founder and first editor of *The Wall Street Journal* and a great investment thinker. He summed up how experienced Wall Street operators felt in his editorial of 20 November 1901: 'The more they actually know, the less confident they become.'

But until you appreciate the complexity, until you get your mind around the complications, intricacies and difficulties the market can throw at you, you won't have the capacity to undertake this simplification. In Goethe's words, you would be acting 'without insight'.

Despite the complexity and contradictions of financial markets, there's no shortage of people who claim to see order where there is none. You see them every night on TV offering concise explanations for the inexplicable. This does no more than perpetuate the myth that financial markets can be easily understood and described.

The aim of this book is to get you thinking. To become a serious investor you need to question and doubt; to challenge every word delivered by articulate men in pinstriped suits; to appreciate where the limits of reason lie. Then you'll be better placed to make your own investment calls.

Investment great Warren Buffett has stated that he sees little point in writing a book on investing, that everything one needs to know has already been written. There's truth in what he says. But it's also important how those insights are arranged. And I hope the words in this book are arranged in a way that both captures your interest and focuses your thinking.

Most words eventually fall from the public eye. The books that contain them either are destroyed or remain unread for years, gathering dust on bookshelves. Before this book becomes another collector of dust or lost digital imprint, I hope it leads someone, somewhere, to make better investment decisions.

As a postscript, I should add that I've pitched this book to readers who already have some knowledge of how the financial markets operate. But if you're still relatively early on that journey, you might find the glossary of financial terms at the back of the book helpful.

Now on to chapter 1!

1

THE PIED PIPER

Several years ago, while at an investment conference, I got to thinking about why people act blindly on the advice of others. Why do they bestow guru status on their favoured adviser, whether that trust is earned or not? It's a phenomenon I call the 'pied piper approach to investing'. What got me thinking was a presentation I attended late that afternoon. The guy on stage was trying to convince the audience that all you needed to become a stock-picking superstar was a ruler and a pencil. I'll give you a taste of what he was saying:

> Now let's all get trendy. Just hold the ruler against the squiggly lines on the stock chart. Now draw a straight line with the pencil. It's so simple I could get a six-year-old doing this. If the line points up, it's a buy. If it points down, it's a sell. There you go. Now you know how to beat the market.

I don't know how many in the audience accepted his message, but there were plenty taking notes. I'd suggest that few even knew who he was. What then gave this speaker legitimacy? Was it his polished delivery and his tailored suit? I wondered if the audience would see things differently if he spoke with a stutter and dressed like Ronald McDonald. Was his argument strengthened by the simple fact that he was the one on stage, that somebody, unknown to the audience, had considered him enough of an authority to present to us that afternoon?

The reality is that we should always question 'definitive' financial advice. The mere fact that so much of it is contradictory should alert us to that. And in the case of this presenter I knew there were plenty of views to counter his. Let's start with investment great Ben Graham, who wrote:

> Rather extensive studies that we have made of the subject lead us to conclude that reversals of trend in every part of the financial picture occur so frequently as to make reliance on a trend a particularly dangerous matter.[2]

Or this, again from Graham:

> Never buy a stock because it has gone up or sell one because it has gone down.[3]

Not only did Graham's advice run counter to that of our 'trendy' presenter, but Graham delivered it in his book *The Intelligent Investor*, described by Warren Buffett as the best book ever written on the subject of investing.

This example of diametrically opposed advice is just one of many to be found in the finance industry. Why do they exist? If one of two views can be proven to be correct, then only the correct view should be held. And if neither has been proven, then neither should be held passionately and to the exclusion of other views. Where doubt exists nobody should hold any view too strongly. Yet they do.

The problem stems largely from the fact that in the world of finance most things are difficult to prove beyond a shadow of a doubt. And where doubt exists, however small, there will develop a divergence of opinion. The conflict this creates is confusing for those new to investing. We have a natural aversion to contradiction, so to resolve it we choose a single view. Once we've chosen it, we support it with a fervour befitting the one-eyed support of a football team. That's why outspoken pied pipers are so dangerous to follow. They've chosen their team and, armed with their definitive answers, they've become the font of all financial wisdom. But there are two types of people who run a heightened risk of losing money in the stock market: those who know nothing and those who know everything.

Let's extend the whole line-drawing/trend-following argument a bit further.

Drawing straight lines on stock charts supposes that stock prices trend. There are plenty of great minds who've researched trend-following techniques only to find they've come up short. Louis Bachelier, Alfred Cowles, Maurice Kendall, Harry Roberts, Maury Osborne, Holbrook Working, Paul Samuelson, Eugene Fama—the list of researchers who've looked at this issue is nearly endless. All of the aforementioned concluded that 'getting trendy' is a waste of time. None found enough of a link between historical price data and future price direction to deliver trading profits.

And what about the following comment from Jesse Livermore? His speculative brilliance allowed him to pull millions from the market (and sadly later deliver it all back). Although he died in 1940, Livermore remains a cult hero among traders today. Ironically, this hero of charting zealots had the following to say about charts: 'Personally, charts have never appealed to me. I think they are altogether too confusing.'[4] Which means you would never have found a pencil and ruler guiding Livermore's stock trading decisions.

It seems to me this whole investment game is terribly confused. Professional disciplines such as science and law assume nothing until proven. Yet most 'investors' are prepared to accept anything stated by someone standing on a stage or presenting on TV.

WHY THE CONFIDENCE?

Why is it that pied pipers appear so confident of their views? Is it an act aimed to establish public acclaim, or do they believe deep down that what they're saying is correct?

I raised this one day with a friend who had an interest in behavioural finance. 'Why', I asked, 'do you think those in the public eye hold such definitive views in such a "grey" area as investing?' He couldn't offer a reason.

So a week later I put the question to another friend, a financial adviser with decades of experience. He, too, struggled to deliver an answer. I don't think he'd ever really given the issue much thought.

A plausible answer was delivered just weeks later. I was reading *Thinking, Fast and Slow*, by psychologist and Nobel laureate Daniel Kahneman.

Kahneman referred to the illusions of skill and validity supported by a powerful professional culture. He commented:

> We know that people can maintain an unshakable faith in any proposition, however absurd, when they are sustained by a community of like-minded believers. Given the professional culture of the financial community, it is not surprising that large numbers of individuals in the world believe themselves to be among the chosen few who can do what others cannot.[5]

Or as Demosthenes said, 'Nothing is easier than self-deceit. For what each man wishes, that he also believes to be true.'

There it is. I reckon Kahneman's right. Put someone on a pedestal, shove a microphone in their face, and they believe they've got the answer to every question asked of them.

Deep down we're all born suckers, which is a problem, because it means many of us are pied piper bait.

Remember *War of the Worlds*, that early sci-fi book by H.G. Wells? In 1938 his near namesake, actor and director Orson Welles, decided to broadcast part of the book as a radio dramatisation. Orson thought it would be a bit of fun to throw this story about a Martian invasion out onto the airwaves. Unfortunately he hadn't factored in how gullible the public can be.

Welles' trick was to deliver the broadcast in the form of live news bulletins, as if the events were unfolding as he spoke. The reaction was phenomenal. *Time* reported that in Newark, New Jersey, 20 families wrapped their faces in wet towels in anticipation of the Martian gas attack. Fifteen people were treated for shock at Saint Michael's Medical Center. A Tennessee newspaper recalled all its editorial staff and began to prepare a special edition on the bombing of Chicago and St Louis. A Pittsburgh man was barely able to stop his wife from swallowing poison. The angry mayor of a midwestern city telephoned the radio station to report mobs in the streets of his city, violence, looting and masses seeking safe haven.

Now if people could swallow this stuff, they'll swallow pretty much anything. When Joe Citizen is sitting in his lounge room with his TV dinner on his lap and Eddie the Economist tells him how things are going to be, he's sure to believe it.

It doesn't even need to be an economist or a stockbroker who's spinning the fiction. At the tail end of the Global Financial Crisis (GFC) in early 2009, a friend of mine was watching one of those tabloid 'current affairs' shows on TV. You know the type—they sneak into dental surgeries with a hidden camera to get footage of the dentist returning from the bathroom without washing his hands.

For this show they'd consulted a psychic about where the stock market was heading. I have no idea whether it was the cards, the tea-leaves or how Jupiter and Mars were aligned, but the psychic delivered some pretty bad news. After watching the show my friend became worried sick about her stock portfolio.

Even hardened investment professionals can get suckered in. On 11 April 1997 a *Financial Times* story reported that a fund called Czech Value Fund (abbreviated to CVF) had invested in fraudulent companies and was facing big losses. The news, upon reaching the US, caused Castle Convertible Fund (stock ticker symbol CVF) to plummet. Trouble was, Castle Convertible Fund had no relationship with Czech Value Fund beyond the chance sharing of the three letters 'CVF'.

And what about this one? In the late 1890s a Baptist minister, Prescott Ford Jernegan, claimed he'd received a 'heavenly vision' that enabled him to extract gold from seawater. Jernegan saw the opportunity to convert his God-given skill into a profit-making scam. But first he needed to give it some credibility, so he enlisted the aid of lifelong friend and confidence trickster Charles Fisher, who was a professional sea-diver.

Jernegan had constructed a box he called the 'Accumulator'. He claimed his invention could collect gold when dropped into the sea. It supposedly worked by sending a current of electricity through wires, resulting in detectable deposits of gold forming in the box within 24 hours. Jernegan then invited an unwitting jeweller, Arthur Ryan, to test his 'gold from seawater' claim.

Ryan and an associate dropped the Accumulator off the end of a pier at Narragansett Bay, Rhode Island. While Ryan was waiting for the gold to 'accumulate', Jernegan's accomplice, Fisher, donned a diving suit, swam under the pier and slipped a few gold nuggets into the submerged box. Ryan retrieved the box and confirmed the gold was genuine. Word of Jernegan's magic Accumulator spread quickly.

Off the back of his now legitimised business model, Jernegan set about establishing a listed company. Stock in the Electrolytic Marine Salts Company was offered at $1 per share. The first tranche of 350 000 shares sold out in three days, and investors demanded more. Within weeks $2.4 million worth of stock had been subscribed.

To keep the scam rolling, Jernegan and Fisher commenced the planning and construction phase for a new commercial facility based on Accumulator technology. But they didn't stick around to supervise construction; they shot through with the $2.4 million from the capital-raising without so much as a goodbye. And if you think that couldn't happen today, that hardened professionals are too market-savvy to fall for con men and tricksters, I'll give you just two words — Bernie Madoff.

If it makes you feel any better, this whole rip-off thing isn't always about trying to outsmart the common punter. Anyone is fair game. Sometimes investment professionals even turn on their own kind.

Nineteenth-century Wall Street stock trader Daniel Drew was renowned for plenty of scams, but one that served him particularly well was his handkerchief trick. Drew famously once used it to pump up the price of Erie Railroad stock. After dining with fellow stock traders at a New York club, Drew wrapped a note in his handkerchief. It was a list of (fictional) reasons why Erie was a great buy. He placed the handkerchief in his pocket, then, when pulling it out, allowed the note to fall to the floor. After Drew had left, the traders swooped on the discarded note. Acting on Drew's false tip, they bought Erie stock and in the process pushed its price north. Drew was on the other side of the trades, madly selling at the inflated prices.

While Drew might have been cunning, he can't claim that his handkerchief scam was original. Author and businessman Joseph de la Vega traded stocks on the Amsterdam Exchange back in the 17th century, and in his 1688 book *Confusion de Confusiones* he writes:

> If it is of importance to spread a piece of news which has been invented by the speculators themselves, they have a letter written and [arrange to have] the letter dropped as if by chance at the right spot. The finder believes himself to possess a treasure, whereas he has really received a letter of Uriah which will lead him into ruin.

Hey, we live in the digital age now. No longer the need for notes scribbled on pieces of paper. Just find a thinly traded stock and get to work on the internet. Enter 15-year-old Jonathan Lebed, the first minor ever to fall foul of the US Securities and Exchange Commission (SEC) on charges of stock manipulation. From late 1999 into early 2000 Lebed made hundreds of thousands of dollars using the time-honoured technique of 'pump and dump', also known as 'buy, lie and sell high'.

Lebed bought shares in small-cap stocks where he had a chance of moving their share price. Then he'd use multiple fictitious names to post hundreds of messages on Yahoo Finance message boards recommending the stock as a strong buy. After the price moved up, he'd offload his holding. No different from Drew or the 17th-century Dutch traders.

Lebed settled out of court with the SEC but kept a fair proportion of his ill-gotten gains, which probably explains why he kept using the internet to hype stocks. In an interview with Fox Business's Cody Willard long after his scuffle with the SEC, Lebed admitted to running a business where he was paid by small caps seeking promotion on his website. Stock research be damned—if they paid up, they scored a buy recommendation.

DRAWING THE LINE OF CREDIBILITY

There is so much information out there. What should we believe? Where do we draw that line separating fact from fiction? It's a pretty important line to draw when investing. Problem is, everyone draws it in a different place. And who's to say you've drawn yours in the right place?

Take 19th-century English economist William Stanley Jevons, who came up with a novel way to predict the business cycle: he linked it to sunspot activity. Jevons wasn't a crackpot. In fact he was a highly respected economist, having presented views on marginal utility theory and the application of mathematical logic to the study of economics—which meant his sunspot idea gained some traction.

While Jevons had observed a loose correlation between sunspots and the business cycle, correlation doesn't prove causation. Bald men are more likely to wear hats, but that doesn't mean hats cause baldness.

But this whole sunspot thing mightn't seem so stupid if you are a 'Gann trader'. William Gann died back in 1955 but his stock trading techniques are still being used by current-day disciples. They use, among other things, astrology, which means Gann traders are very easy to spot. They're the guys trying to read *The Wall Street Journal* with one eye while the other is shoved hard against the lens of a telescope.

But Gann wasn't the first trader to look skyward for inspiration. Nearly 500 years ago Christoph Kurz, a commodities trader on the Antwerp Bourse, referred to the stars when forecasting the prices of pepper, ginger, saffron and bills of exchange.[6]

And what about the proposed link between women's hemlines and the stock market? Both the Roaring Twenties and the Swinging Sixties saw hemlines and world stock markets reach new highs. What does that mean? Absolutely nothing. But a correlation between the two was an idea that gained traction with some punters. Pick women's fashion trends before the rest of the market and you could be on a winner. Next we'll have stock insiders working at Yves Saint Laurent and Giorgio Armani trying to get the inside running!

Now we've got some momentum up, let's stretch the limits of reason even further.

In 2009 controversial Austrian entrepreneur, artist and ex-trader Michael Marcovici tried to sell the concept of 'rat traders'. He claimed he could breed and train rats to trade financial securities. He offered these rats for sale to wealthy investors, hedge fund managers, brokerage houses and banks. On his webpage he claimed to have filled orders of up to 1000 rats for trading floors in large financial institutions.

Unlike Colonel Sanders, who kept his 11 herbs and spices a secret, Marcovici told all on how he trained his rodents. So if you don't want to shell out any cash, and would rather train your own rats, here it is.

He reckons he converted historical market price data into 10- to 20-second sound bites referred to as 'ticker tracks'. These matched the past price movement of the relevant security. As prices went up, so did the pitch of the sound. The ticker tracks would then be played to the rats. Based on what the rats heard, they would execute a buy or sell order. If the rat chose to buy, it would hit a green button positioned inside its box. If it chose to sell, it would hit a red button. Get it right and the rat scored a food reward. Get it wrong and the rat was hit with an electric shock. They were effectively 'reading' the charts with their ears.

Marcovici claimed the ability to train specialist traders in currencies, Treasury bonds, stock options, gold, oil—whatever. Rats were given names such as Lehman (since deceased), Morgan and Kleinworth (maybe he meant Kleinwort). When Marcovici was promoting these furry financiers, a *Financial Times* blog suggested that his company, Rat Traders, had 'come up with an economic and efficient solution, available from any zoology department, pet shop or nearest sewer'.

So you want a piece of the rodent action? Marcovici can be contacted through his Cayman Islands address. Just Google rattraders.com.

If you think no-one would take Rat Traders seriously, then consider this: I was contacted at the time by a friend who spends much of his time sitting on a beach in the South Pacific. He provided me with a link to the website and asked me: 'Do you think this would really work?' Now I said earlier that everyone draws their investing credibility line in a different place. I'll admit this guy's line was drawn a few standard deviations from the mean, but it does prove the point. One man's joke is another man's trading gem.

And before you totally dismiss the ability of rats to trade claw to toe with humans, consider a study outlined by US psychologist Philip Tetlock. It might be that rats have more of what it takes to become successful traders than humans do.

Tetlock described a study that pitted the predictive powers of a single Norwegian lab rat against a classroom of Yale undergraduates.[7] The study was set up so that food appeared on either side of a simple maze in which the rat was housed. On each occasion, the side on which the food appeared was largely randomly determined. But there was an underlying bias: it would appear on the left side of the maze 60 per cent of the time and on the right 40 per cent of the time. Statisticians call this a random binomial process.

Sven, the rat, quickly worked out that if he hung around on the left side he'd win more often than he lost. The undergrads insisted on trying to work out patterns and sequences, chasing the randomness with futile explanations. They performed worse than the rat.

I don't want to talk too much now about what's coming up later in the book, except to say that humans can learn a lot from this rat's behaviour. Successful investing is not about always being correct; that's only ever going to happen in your dreams. Investing is about operating in a world that's largely characterised by randomness. Like the rat, successful investors lose plenty of times. But, also like the rat, successful investors set out to win more than they lose. Like Sven, they've worked out ways of tipping the odds in their favour. And the whole time they're doing it, they're watching most other investors behaving like the Yale undergraduates — looking for and often believing they've found patterns where they don't exist.

It's now time to make a powerful point.

Every story in this chapter has described a person or group of people who truly believed they were onto a winner. Whether it was drawing lines on stock charts, studying sunspots or buying specially trained rats, each believed they possessed a market-beating method. Each drew their 'credibility line' in a position they believed was correct. You might have been amused at some of their beliefs, but remember they weren't laughing at themselves.

So where is your line drawn? You probably reckon it's in the right spot. Chances are it isn't.

The reality is, investing is not like most people imagine. Options aren't clearly defined, even to those with years of market experience. It's not a predictable or decipherable puzzle solved eventually by attending enough investment conferences, reading the best-selling investment books or following the best financial guru.

Most of the gurus that you believe have the answers are really just like you — wearing a blindfold in a room full of blindfolded people. Fundamentally they possess more chutzpah than market intelligence. They declare to the world, 'I know where I'm going, just follow me'. And because everyone is blindfolded, no-one realises the guy making all the noise is simply taking them all on a trip to nowhere.

If you don't want to be one of the guru-following multitude, you must read, learn and, most importantly, start thinking for yourself. Then, just like Sven, you'll have the tools to work the odds in your favour. But the tools have to be rationally based. They have to be repeatable. Only then can you hope to beat the market — that is, of course, unless you beat it by plain dumb luck.

Chapter summary

- Question all advice, particularly when it's delivered in a dogmatic way. While chance dictates that it might predict an outcome, often it won't.

- Not everything you believe to be true actually is.

- In the field of investing, success doesn't rely on always being correct. Rather, success is achieved by pursuing logical methods that tip the odds in your favour.

2

THE ART OF PREDICTION

It was an unusually warm day for a Melbourne winter, one of those sunny days July occasionally delivers—not a breath of wind or a cloud in the sky. I was crossing the pedestrian bridge over the Yarra River that connects Flinders Street Station to the Southbank business precinct. In 10 minutes I would be addressing the clients of a large financial advisory firm. Despite my iPod pumping out Led Zeppelin, my mind was busy running through the presentation.

My presentation was largely about prediction. Audiences love hearing about those big, and very wrong, predictions—the bigger the gaffe the better, and the higher the profile of the 'gaffee' the better. TV personality economists, presidents, chairmen of the Fed, CEOs—they all make dumb predictions that leave them with egg on their faces. There are books full of their dumb predictions, so there's little point in repeating them here.

Okay then, just a few.

In July 2007 Ben Bernanke, then Chairman of the Federal Reserve, stated: 'Employment should continue to expand…The global economy continues to be strong…financial markets have remained supportive of economic growth.'

Bad call. The US economy collapsed into recession five months later.

On 17 May 2007 Bernanke had said: 'We do not expect significant spillovers from the subprime market to the rest of the economy or to the financial system.'

The following year the fallout from subprime triggered the world's worst financial crisis in 80 years.

The irony is that Bernanke was a student of the 1929 Crash. And below is an extract from an editorial published in *The Wall Street Journal* on 3 September 1929. The Dow Jones Industrial Average had just closed at its all-time peak of 381.17:

> Wall Street entered the autumn financial season in a definitely optimistic frame of mind. With railroad traffic showing steady gains, and production in the major branches of industry continuing at a high rate, the earnings prospects of the principal corporations with shares listed on the Stock Exchange were looked upon as extremely promising. Sentiment regarding the credit outlook was reassured by the activities at the Federal Reserve authorities in placing funds at the disposal of business through bill purchases in the open market. With trade and credit conditions favorable, buying orders accumulated in large volume over Labor Day, and the forward movement in the main body of stocks was vigorously resumed in the early dealings... Bullish enthusiasm was stimulated by the return of United States Steel to leadership in the industrial division.[8]

Like a boat full of oblivious oarsmen rowing towards Niagara Falls, there's not a single hint of imminent danger. The next month the 1929 Crash hit, and less than three years later the Dow had collapsed by 89 per cent.

At the epicentre of 2008's GFC were mortgage providers Fannie Mae and Freddie Mac. On 16 July 2008 Bernanke said that Fannie and Freddie were 'adequately capitalized' and 'in no danger of failing'. Just weeks later the US Treasury committed to a $200 billion bailout to save the two insolvent institutions. Financial markets and economies around the world went into a tailspin.

Okay, enough of that. If I keep going we'll be here all day. Back to a more general discussion, starting with those who believe prediction is possible—the Nostradamus set. This type of thinking is exemplified by Harry S. Dent, Jr., who states in his book *The Next Great Bubble Boom*: 'Today there is an attitude that nobody can predict the future... that there are too many complex variables that can impact it. But this is obviously nonsense.'[9]

Could I suggest that what's obviously nonsense is the statement itself? Dent's book doesn't offer any prediction methodology, nor have his own powers of prediction been particularly impressive. For example, in 1998 he forecast the Dow would be between 35 000 and 40 000 by late 2008 or 2009. The time he chose for the peak was slap-bang in the middle of the GFC. By then the Dow had actually plummeted to a low of 6470.

The problem is that we can't deny some degree of prediction. Prediction is central to investing; it's what investors do. They invest money today predicting they'll be delivered more back in the future. So we need to explore the subject of prediction further. Let's start by looking at 'game theory'.

GAME THEORY

I saw a documentary a few years ago called *The Next Nostradamus*. It featured political scientist Professor Bruce Bueno de Mesquita, from New York University. He'd developed a predictive computer program based on game theory. While Bueno de Mesquita didn't come up with the idea of game theory, his name has become closely associated with it.

Game theory is the study of strategic decision making. It aims to predict outcomes by first identifying who the big movers and shakers are in any deal. Then it identifies the outcome each player is looking for. That's relatively easy. Put yourself in their shoes: humans are driven by self-interest, so what benefits each is the outcome they're driving for. Next, assess how much influence each player brings to the table. The biggest mover and shaker has the greatest influence on the outcome. Then throw all the variables into a computer and let it spit out the answer.

But Bueno de Mesquita reckons his technique isn't applicable to all situations, the stock market being one of them. He applies it principally to the political arena. Is Iran going to produce an atomic bomb? Is the President going to be re-elected?

So if it can't be applied to stock markets, why have I mentioned it? The reason is that Bueno de Mesquita is an intelligent guy who has devoted his career to making a science out of prediction. He believes in prediction. And even he is ruling out the stock market as something that's predictable.

In February 2009 he delivered a presentation on game theory in Long Beach, California, as part of the popular TED series. He told the audience that the use of game theory didn't facilitate stock market prediction. But he immediately followed with a tongue-in-cheek stock market prediction of his own: 'Okay, it's not going up any time soon.' He was spot on with his 'inability to predict' comment: 12 months later the Dow was up by 21 per cent.

But in the same TED presentation Bueno de Mesquita proposed that the power base of Mahmoud Ahmadinejad, the President of Iran, was being eroded and that he would soon cease to be a force in Iranian politics. He was correct on the first point but wrong on the second. Ahmadinejad was re-elected to a second term just four months after the TED presentation. But there were cries around the world that the election was rigged — the only way Ahmadinejad could regain office. Now you could argue that the model couldn't be expected to predict foul play. But on the other side of the coin the model is based on consideration of the political influence each player brings to the game. Clearly Ahmadinejad possessed more influence than Bueno de Mesquita had dialled into his model.

While game theory presents nuances upon subtleties upon uncertainties upon judgements, Bueno de Mesquita reckons he gets a 90 per cent strike rate when using it in the appropriate arena.

One very interesting aspect of game theory is the number of potential interrelationships between the players in the game. Bueno de Mesquita explains it this way: if you're considering a problem that involves five participants, there are 120 different ways in which those five can interact. This figure is calculated by using the following factorial operation:

Factorial $5! = 5 \times 4 \times 3 \times 2 \times 1 = 120$

Adding extra factors or participants sees this number expand dramatically. For example, consider 10 players. The potential number of direct interrelationships is 3.63 million. One hundred players (defined by factorial 100) is a staggering 9.33×10^{157}. That's nine (and a bit) with 157 zeroes on the end!

You can start to see why game theory can't be applied to financial markets: the number of variables in the stock market is mind-boggling. There are unknown factors that impact unknown factors that impact unknown factors that impact the unknowable outcome—multiple layers of unquantifiable complexity that are impossible to imagine, let alone measure.

As if that's not enough complexity, yet another layer needs to be added. The system is dynamic. The factors and the relationships between them are forever changing. There are no constants.

Bueno de Mesquita is the first to list the limitations of game theory. He doesn't hold it out as a tool for long-term prediction under any circumstances. The players must actually be in the act of playing the game when the call is first made. I know it's a fine point, but this means he isn't really making absolute prophecies; rather he's predicting outcomes. But, despite its limitations, game theory is one of the more credible 'prediction tools' around.

So is Bueno de Mesquita's model similar to those used by economic forecasters—the ones politicians, economists and stock brokers use to formulate their bold claims regarding our economic future? Let's investigate.

ECONOMIC MODELLING

Economists spend a lot of time developing models to predict our economic future. Businesspeople and politicians then use the output from these models to make plans and to deliver bold statements about the future.

One night in 2012 I was listening to a popular economics podcast called Planet Money, and the topic of discussion was economic modelling. Mark Zandi, chief economist with Moody's Analytics, was being interviewed. He is an economic researcher with a strong interest in macroeconomics and financial markets.

Zandi gave an interesting insight into the problems faced by economists who use computer models as an aid to framing economic policy. He'd spent 20 years building and tweaking his model of the macroeconomy. It comprised 1700 variables—the inflation rate, interest rates, employment level, oil prices, consumer confidence, national debt and so on. Combined they painted a complex picture of economic interrelationships affecting each other in either a positive or a negative way. Want inflation to fall by half a per cent? Fiddle with interest rates. Want retail sales to pick up? Play around with consumer confidence. But changing one variable doesn't mean just one other variable changes; it unbalances many, many others.

Zandi's model is the result of 20 years of unrelenting hard work. It attempts to take 1700 economic variables into consideration. Does it work? Who knows? Not even Zandi knew the answer.

UNLIMITED POSSIBILITIES

Remember the movie *Sliding Doors*? For those who didn't see it, Gwyneth Paltrow plays a young woman who just misses boarding a train on the London Underground. The film then splits into two universes. The first is based on how her life actually worked out and the second on how things would have been had she boarded the train. The film switches between each of her parallel lives, showing how a seemingly inconsequential event, like missing a train, can have a profound effect.

Here's a real example of the same thing. At the outbreak of World War I a young Austrian painter volunteered to fight with the German army in the trenches of Europe. He served as a dispatch runner with the Sixteenth Bavarian Infantry Regiment, never rising above the rank of lance corporal. He was awarded six medals for regularly putting himself in the path of enemy fire. His regiment was decimated in battle, rebuilt and decimated again, yet he escaped serious injury. The only injury he sustained during his military service was a wound to his leg inflicted by a stray shell fragment during the Battle of the Somme. It was an injury from which he fully recovered. If the shell had caused a mortal blow, world history would have been altered. The man was Adolf Hitler.

Had Hitler been killed during World War I, as could so easily have happened, the demographics of the world's population would be profoundly different today. Not only would six million Jews who died at his dictate have had the benefit of living, but so too would their never-to-be-born descendants. Total World War II civilian and military deaths were around ten times that figure. That's millions of people who were never given the opportunity to create a family lineage of their own, hundreds of millions of people who might have lived but never did. It's a world so different it's impossible to imagine.

And of course on the other side of the ledger are those living today who otherwise wouldn't be. I'm the son of an Australian Lancaster pilot who met his English bride in London during World War II. It has crossed my mind that if Hitler had copped a bullet in 1915 then I wouldn't be here today, and nor would millions of others.

One small event would have had a profound effect on the population of the world, not just today but to the end of human history.

One simple, unpredictable event—a chance bullet. Yet there are those who suggest the future can be predicted.

A few years ago I was told the true story of a young Australian woman who was fleeing an encroaching forest fire. Having left her threatened home, she was faced with a fateful decision when driving through a nearby town. Should she turn left or right at the end of the main street? She turned left, while the three cars immediately in front of her turned right. She escaped the fire, while the next day the three cars in front of her were featured on the front page of newspapers around the country. The image of those three burnt-out car shells left no doubt as to the fate of their unfortunate occupants.

Finally (although the examples could be practically endless) consider how the rock band The Rolling Stones came together. More than 50 years after their formation, British officials arranged to honour the spot where Mick Jagger and Keith Richards first met in 1961. Their lifelong association started with a chance meeting on a platform at Dartford railway station.

Life is a constant unfolding of chance events over which we possess a degree of control, but it's far from absolute. Yet this is *not* the way most people see things. Typically they view events through a rear-view mirror. Looking back, they see life as a series of events and imagine that was the only way it could have been. It's this flawed perception of how events unfold that delivers the false sense of predictability about the future. But future certainty is a delusion, and those who deliver a message of certainty should never be allowed onto the public stage.

Economic and stock market predictions are typically delivered as a single narrative. And they sound pretty convincing. Sometimes I'm asked by worried or excited friends, relatives or associates to comment on these predictions, particularly when they're extremely optimistic or pessimistic, as they so often are. My typical answer is: 'Yep, that could happen. Doesn't mean it will. Probably it won't.'

Let me use an analogy. Imagine you are on the top branch of a massive tree. To see how you got there, run your eye back down your line of ascent all the way to ground level. Your eye will follow one pathway, from the tip of the branch you're on down to the base of the trunk. Now stand on the ground looking up into the tree. Imagine all the branches you could end up on. Making a prediction is more like being on the ground looking up than it is being on the top branch looking down. There isn't one single course of events leading to one particular outcome. There are many ways things could turn out, and you don't know which will materialise.

This is the real environment within which you make investment decisions.

Chapter summary

- If an 'expert' is on TV delivering predictions on the future direction of the economy or the stock market, then use the time productively: go and make yourself a cup of tea.

3

WHY ECONOMICS WILL NEVER BE A SCIENCE

My education and much of my working life have been split between science and finance. It's been interesting, as each requires a different way of thinking. The science came first, which meant that when I initially came to finance I mistakenly assumed it would conform to the laws of scientific logic. It doesn't, and I'm certainly not alone in recognising this. This is the opening sentence of Samuel Armstrong Nelson's 1902 book *The ABC of Stock Speculation*:

> The question whether there is such a thing as scientific speculation is often asked. Various answers of a somewhat affirmative character have been given but they have generally been hedged about with so many qualifications as to be nearly useless for practical purposes.[10]

'HYPOTHESIS NON FINGO'

It's time to address the whole science/economics/logic question. So let's begin by describing the scientific process. It starts with an observation. There's usually something about the world that captures a scientist's imagination, so he or she starts asking questions. What's the cure for a particular disease? Why do the planets appear in the sky with precise regularity? Why do objects fall to the ground when they're released? Next they propose a possible explanation for their observations—a hypothesis. And finally they set out to test their hypothesis experimentally.

The gold standard for experimental study is the controlled study. Two systems are set up that differ in only one respect—the variable being tested for. Both systems are put into effect so the scientist can observe and measure the outcomes resulting from differences in just that single variable. Data is then collected from a series of experiments and tested for statistical significance to establish whether there's a high probability of a cause-and-effect relationship. If other researchers produce similar results when they repeat the experiment, the hypothesis is considered likely to provide an explanation for the observed outcome.

You can't perform these types of experiments in economics. A simple example will help explain why.

Let's say you're testing for the pull of gravity on objects of different mass. To do this you release a feather and a lead ball from the same height at the same time. Which one hits the ground first? Answer: it depends. If you perform the test in your living room, there's no doubt the feather will hit the ground long after the lead ball has punched a hole in your shagpile. But that's because there are two forces here. As the Italian physicist Galileo demonstrated four centuries ago, you aren't testing for gravity alone. There's also the opposing force of air resistance, and air resistance slows down the feather much more than it does the lead ball. It hasn't been a fair contest.

Now perform the experiment in a vacuum, where the effect of air resistance is eliminated. This time the feather and the lead ball hit the ground at the same time. You are now testing for just one variable—their mass. And you have been able to determine the relationship between mass and acceleration under gravitational force. Apollo 15 commander David Scott performed this test in 1971 on the surface of the moon. He dropped a feather and a hammer, and, due to the lack of aerodynamic drag, they hit the lunar surface at the same time. But what if you hadn't been able to test in a vacuum or on the surface of the moon? The effect of gravity on objects of different mass wouldn't have been clear at all.

That's the problem in testing economic relationships. There are too many variables in the real economy—not just one or two but a near infinite number. And you have no way of isolating them in order to test the impact of changes in each. Simply put, you'll never be able to set up an economic laboratory to test for changes in trade flows, fiscal stimulus, population or any other economic variable you wish to study.

Which all means economics never gets much past the storytelling stage. The problem is that a story, repeated often enough, starts to sound like a fact. Economist Milton Friedman warned us of how many different stories can be fabricated to explain any set of circumstances when he said: 'If there is one hypothesis that is consistent with the available evidence there is an infinite number that are.'

This must have been on Sir Isaac Newton's mind when he was describing the law of universal gravitation. Newton outlined his gravitational formula in *Philosophiae Naturalis Principia Mathematica* ('the Principia'), first published in 1687. And in the second edition, published 26 years later, he added the declaration 'hypothesis non fingo', which translates as 'I feign no hypothesis'. Newton had observed gravity and proposed an equation enabling the prediction of how objects would move under its influence, but he had no explanation of what actually caused it. He chose not to guess what might be behind it all for risk of being proven wrong later on. He didn't want to risk having proverbial egg left on his professorial face.

What about the branch of economic study called econometrics? It applies statistics to economic data. That's a bit like trying to accurately measure the physical dimensions of smoke. Which reminds me of that old economic adage: there are two things you don't want to see in the making—sausages and econometric estimates. But for those of you looking to explore econometrics further, I refer you to Ed Leamer's 1983 article 'Let's Take the Con Out of Econometrics'.

Science is by no means perfect either, but it's harder to get away with as much artistic licence as in economics. But, hey, I'm not the only one who thinks this way. If you want to do some further reading, look out for *The Pretense of Knowledge* by Friedrich August von Hayek or 'Science as Falsification' by Karl Popper.

A SOCIAL SCIENCE

Another monumental difference between economics and science is the human factor. Scientific laws are unshakeable but economic outcomes are influenced by human sentiment and behaviour. The imagined future can affect the present, and thereby influence how the future turns out, which means economic researchers are studying themselves. I've heard it said that this makes economics a bit like studying the movement of 'billiard balls with eyes'. The rules of physics describe how two billiard balls interact as they crash into each other and the cushions of the billiard table. But consider how a billiard ball would move out of the way if it was capable of seeing another ball approaching!

In deference to others, I acknowledge that my views are not held by all. Consider these words taken from *The Next Great Bubble Boom* by Harry Dent Jr, published in 2004, containing cover-to-cover stock market and economic predictions:

> Today in economics and in many fields of politics, sociology, and science, there is an attitude that 'nobody can predict the future past a certain point'… But this is obviously nonsense as more and more fields of science have become capable of predicting more phenomena for centuries as our knowledge of the universe has grown exponentially.[11]

Clearly this author is confused. He argues that our ability to make economic predictions has improved as a result of progress in the 'fields of science'. Interestingly, this book was released not long before the GFC, yet it failed to predict it. (No doubt this will be fixed in the next edition.)

Famed US economist John Burr Williams was working as a security analyst when the 1929 Crash decimated stock portfolios around the country. He later told of the experience, noting the price movement in a stock called American & Foreign Power. Pre-crash it traded for 199 ¼* (100 times historical earnings). Post-crash it plummeted to a low of 2. Like pretty much everyone else, Williams hadn't seen the Crash coming. He felt this was due to an inadequate appreciation of the forces driving the economy. It prompted him, in 1932, to enrol at Harvard to obtain a PhD in economics. Someone, he figured, must be able to explain to him what had caused the biggest collapse in stock market prices ever seen and the ensuing Great Depression. He later reported that he never found the answer he was seeking.

Want to summarise the whole macroeconomic question in a few lines? Economics presents an interesting study. It assists us in thinking about and articulating important issues that impact our lives. It measures and reports on historical information in an interesting way. But economic models fail abysmally in either describing or predicting the real world.

---

*Stock prices used to be quoted using fractions of a dollar. In this example, ¼ means 25 cents.

Chapter summary

- Economics doesn't lend itself to experimental rigour. Therefore most economic concepts can be neither proved nor disproved.

- Economics is largely a social science.

4

FORECASTING THE STOCK MARKET

I want to start this chapter by saying that everything I've stated so far regarding our inability to predict applies to the stock market. I'll say it again. Everything I have stated so far regarding our inability to predict applies to the stock market. I could repeat that sentence a hundred times. But most people would forget it the minute they closed this book. Why?

Because people believe that a different set of rules applies to the stock market—that making forecasts is a rational activity.

I'll give you an example. If you had a friend who constantly walked around making predictions about anything and everything that was going to happen in the world, you'd think he was pretty crazy. On the upside, he'd be easy to buy for at Christmas—a set of tarot cards or a ouija board would be just the thing. Let's think of some tags we might give him: psychic, supernatural, psychogenic, telepathic, clairvoyant, occult, palm-reader, crystal-gazer, whacko.

In the world of finance they'd call him an economist.

Let's wind the clock back to March 2009. The world's financial markets were in turmoil, had been for months. The mayhem was triggered by the fallout from the US subprime crisis. For years US financial houses had been packaging billions of dollars of dodgy mortgages and flogging them to banks, hedge funds, insurance companies and municipalities around the world. The problem with these mortgage-backed securities was that they were based on loans granted to people who were incapable of servicing them. With no payments by the mortgagees there was no return to the bondholders. The reason dealers had been able to shift them so easily in the first place was because rating agencies Moody's and Standard & Poor's had unjustifiably been slapping triple-A credit ratings on them.

The whole mess was further complicated by the extensive distribution of credit default swaps (CDSs). These were effectively bets on a business, as defined within the contract, going bust. Some were used as they were initially intended — as insurance. But most were naked CDSs — straight-out bets on an unrelated party failing. It was a bit like taking out life insurance on a stranger and then wishing them dead. By the end of 2007 there was over $60 trillion worth of CDSs circulating the world's financial markets.

Eventually things blew up. And with all the mortgage-backed securities, CDSs, collateralised debt obligations and other synthetic derivatives and financial instruments out there, no-one knew exactly who owed what to whom. The world's financial markets went into a blind tailspin, which leads me into a story I want to tell you.

During the darkest hours of the GFC, on the evening of 5 March 2009, I arrived at an auditorium to address a large group of battle-weary investors. They were guests of a large stockbroking firm. The brokers who'd invited me staged the event each year to reward their clients for their loyal custom. March 5th is a particularly relevant date since the next day the Australian stock market hit its lowest point during the entire GFC. Of course, I didn't know the next day would mark the bottom. But I did know the extreme panic of recent months had been delivering some pretty cheap stock prices.

That evening I took it upon myself to calm frayed nerves — to take a journey back through the centuries and deliver a historical overview of past crashes and subsequent bear markets. I posed questions and framed the answers within the context of how things had panned out following past panics. Was the market cheap now by historical standards? How long did past bear markets last? What had been the market's pattern of recovery following previous crashes, etc., etc. My presentation was peppered with quotes. One I remember was from financier Nathan Rothschild, who said: 'Buy when there's blood on the streets, even if the blood is your own.' As I've said, I had no idea the next day would mark the low point of the market, but I left the audience in no doubt that stocks were cheap. I also suggested that markets typically bounce strongly from the bottom and that it was quite possible, although by no means certain, that markets could be significantly higher this time next year.

These were the statistics I delivered that night: The nine bear markets the Australian stock market had experienced in the previous 50 years had averaged 15 months in duration. We were already 16 months into this one. Historically the average fall of the general index from top to bottom had been 34 per cent, and the worst had seen a fall of 59 per cent. In this bear market the index was already down 55 per cent.

And here's the clincher: the average percentage gain in the first 12 months after the bottom had been reached was a very healthy 32 per cent. In other words, the market (not always, but typically) climbs strongly and quickly from the bottom.

Now I wasn't claiming to be Nostradamus, but I did place some faith in George Santayana's advice that those who cannot remember the past are condemned to repeat it. I simply figured the odds were becoming increasingly short that we were about to experience a big bounce. The pessimism out there was just so overpowering.

There was a second speaker that night—a high-profile economist regularly seen on cable TV. His presentation started with a brief apology. It turns out he'd stood in the same spot 12 months earlier and told the same group of investors that the market would rise strongly over the course of 2008 and into 2009. Alas, since his last presentation, rather than powering ahead, the market had collapsed by 45 per cent.

Unfazed by the inaccuracy of the previous year's call, he wound up his presentation with a renewed outlook for the year ahead. He confidently declared the market would be flat all year. So how did he go this time? Rather than remaining flat the market actually climbed 53 per cent in the 12 months following that night. The crazy thing is he was invited to present again the next year.

This economist's failed predictions in no way reduced his appeal to audiences. Several months later I attended another seminar where he was voted the best presenter of the day. As I stated earlier, presenters are judged on how confidently their message is delivered rather than on its content.

A popular form of TV entertainment is to pit two economic 'experts' with opposing views head to head. Who wins the debate? Answer: the articulate, silver-haired, pinstripe-suited gladiator who beats his chest the hardest. Problem is, just as with pro wrestling, there are viewers who actually believe it's all for real.

All this reminds me of a night just before Christmas last year, when I was sitting watching a business show on ABC TV. Over the course of the year the show had run a competition. At the start of the year four leading economic experts and one schoolboy had been asked to predict where the broad stock market index would finish at the end of the year — that is, now. The lowest call by a long shot was from the 'perma-bear' of the group of economists. This doomster had long been known for his never-changing declaration that the market should be lower. It's an interesting strategy: stick to the same script. In a cyclical game you're going to be correct every now and again. It's a bit like the broken clock with hands that don't move — it delivers the correct time twice a day.

That night they were announcing the winner of the competition, the one who was closest to predicting where the market index would be at year end. And the outcome? The four industry heavyweights were trounced by the fifth contestant, schoolboy Luke Adams.

Now I'm not suggesting that Luke had superior powers of prediction; clearly he was just lucky. But it was interesting to hear the responses from the four so-called experts. I mean these guys were supposed to be intelligent people. Asked why their predictions were so far off the mark, not one of them came up with a legitimate reason (something like, 'Well, that's just the way the dice rolled this year', or, 'It's all just a crapshoot anyway; have a Merry Christmas'). No. Each responded with a defensive barrage of econospeak.

All four had been around the financial markets for decades. The question is, shouldn't that have given them an edge over the schoolboy when it came to 'seat-of-the-pants' judgement? Seems the answer is no.

Finance psychologist Daniel Kahneman, whom I introduced back in chapter 1, has investigated this whole seat-of-the-pants judgement issue. He collaborated with researcher Gary Klein to investigate when skill and experience actually make a difference. They concluded that you need two basic conditions for acquiring a skill: an environment that is sufficiently consistent to be predictable, and plenty of practice.

Experienced sportspeople, surgeons, tradespeople and musicians are able to sum up situations very quickly. They've spent thousands of hours doing the same thing over and over. Their world is governed by a fair degree of consistency, which lends itself to skill development by repetition. They develop an ability to swing, cut, hit or pluck without thinking too hard about it.

But consistency is not a word that describes the financial markets. Today's market is different from yesterday's, which was different from the one the day before. And the reason it varies day to day is varying as well—no consistency, no pattern, no repetition. So it's not an environment that is conducive to skill development. The stock market is not an arena where time and practice convert into an ability to make reliable predictions.

It seems the only people who believe (or pretend) it is such an environment are ingenuous members of the public and a number of economic and market 'experts' who are duping either themselves or the public.

BABSON'S BREAK

At the peak of the euphoric 1929 bull market, a single comment made by economist Roger Babson caused the US stock market to drop 3 per cent in a blink. On 5 September 1929 Babson was addressing a luncheon at the annual National Business Conference in Boston. It must have been a slow news day, because his comments were flashed across the country within minutes of being delivered.

Here are Babson's words: 'Sooner or later a crash is coming which will take in the leading stocks and cause a decline of from 60 to 80 points in the Dow-Jones barometer.'[12]

The market reacted immediately. It dropped due to the prophecy of just one 'expert'.* Some others were not happy with Babson's comments, so they presented their own expert willing to express the opposing view. At 2 pm that same day, high-profile Yale professor Irving Fisher announced publicly that Babson's comments were groundless. Now there were two experts at loggerheads. What a dilemma for followers of experts!

---

*On 5 December 1996 a similar event happened. Alan Greenspan, Chairman of the Federal Reserve, described stock market investors as behaving with irrational exuberance. Major stock markets around the world fell by between 2.3 and 4 per cent.

The fact is these guys were in the dark just as much as those reacting to their predictions. Which begs the question: why do we bother listening to stock market prophets at all?

Alfred Cowles, founder of the Cowles Commission for Research in Economics, came up with a great explanation for why we seek 'expert' opinions, even when we're repeatedly reminded they're worthless. After extensive research, which failed to find any useful advice in numerous popular stock tipping and prediction sheets, Cowles had this to say:

> Even if I did my negative surveys every five years, or others continued them when I'm gone, it wouldn't matter. People are still going to believe that somebody really knows. A world in which nobody really knows can be frightening.

Cowles is right: people are driven to know. And since they have absolutely no idea themselves, they look for someone who might.

The take-home message after combining the concepts of Kahneman and Cowles is that we have apparently confident experts delivering their message from a platform of self-delusion to an audience listening from a platform of blind, accepting ignorance. And neither truth nor reason need at any stage interfere with the message.

It reminds me of a comment made by Robert Rhea, a pioneer of Dow theory (which I'll explore in later chapters), about predicting stock prices:

> Those who try to profit from the advance and decline of security prices are perplexed perhaps 90 percent of the time. And it seems that perplexity increases with experience... Unvarying cocksureness on the part of traders or investors is a badge of incompetence. There is, nevertheless, a time and a place for certainty where the market is concerned, but such times and places are few and far between.[13]

I agree with Rhea. And I would add that those times of (near) certainty are roaring bull and gut-wrenching bear markets. But even then not everyone sees these situations for what they are. They get caught up in the mood of the moment and fail to recognise how polarised the market is at the time.

It's interesting to see what Charles Dow thought of those claiming to know where the stock market would be next week or next month. Here are Dow's words from a *Wall Street Journal* editorial of 20 November 1901:

> People who trade in stocks can set down as a fundamental proposition the fact that any man who claims to know what the market is going to do any more than to say that he thinks this or that will occur as a result of certain specified conditions is unworthy of trust as a broker.

And if you think I'm being a bit harsh, I've barely warmed up. Let me share with you the story of Evangeline Adams.

EVANGELINE ADAMS

Evangeline Adams was a celebrity astrologer. Her fame peaked just prior to the spectacular 1929 Crash. Her specialty was predicting where the market was heading. Not surprisingly, making bullish calls in a bullish market was serving her well at the time. That was until October 1929, when the stock market imploded—and with it her reputation.

The Crash and its aftermath remains the most shocking stock market collapse investors have ever experienced. In just two trading days, 28 and 29 October, the Dow Jones Industrial Average collapsed by 23 per cent. It triggered a grinding bear market that, by July 1932, saw the Dow down a chilling 89 per cent from its September 1929 high. It sent thousands of banks to the wall, bankrupted countless businesses and investors, and triggered the worst depression in American history. Of course, as it always does, the stock market eventually recovered, but it was 25 years before the Dow regained the dizzying heights of its pre-Crash peak.

Let's wind the clock back to the first half of 1929, the period just before the Crash. There was a carnival atmosphere in Wall Street. The Dow Jones was up threefold from the start of the decade. Making money in the stock market had been easy—just own stocks, any stocks. But some people were beginning to feel uneasy. They knew the market couldn't climb at this rate indefinitely. The question in their minds was, when to sell? People were looking for someone who could deliver the answer.

Enter Evangeline Adams—a national celebrity, a superstar of prediction, someone people could look to for guidance.

Adams wasn't a newcomer to the game of prediction. By 1929 she was already 70 years old and had been reading stars, palms and tarot cards for years. In 1914 she had been placed on trial for practising astrology, widely considered a questionable activity. She was acquitted after winning over the judge by delivering an accurate character description of his son based purely on his birth date.

But it was the years immediately leading up to 1929 that saw Adams' fame skyrocket, and with it her bank balance. At the peak of her fame she employed several assistants and stenographers to generate her monthly stock market forecasting newsletter. She typically received about 4000 letters a day from fans and followers. And from her rooms above Seventh Avenue's Carnegie Hall, she consulted to the rich and famous at $20 a sitting. This was a massive fee considering US factory workers were paid about 60 cents an hour at the time.

Among her many clients, two names stand out: Charles Schwab and John Pierpont Morgan.

By 1929 Schwab was a battle-hardened 67-year-old steel magnate. He'd experienced a long and successful career, first at Carnegie Steel and later at Bethlehem Steel. At the tender age of 35 he'd been appointed president of Andrew Carnegie's steel production powerhouse, and in 1901 he was instrumental in rolling Carnegie Steel into the newly created US Steel. Unfortunately, his capacity as a deal-maker was more than matched by his capacity to spend. Down to his last millions in 1929, Schwab was on his final roll of the dice. He threw what remained of his once-great fortune into the stock market, a gamble he was about to lose.

Evangeline's other high-profile client, J.P. Morgan, was a real surprise. Morgan died in 1913, but during the course of his career it's said he consulted with Adams, and there are claims he asked her for stock market predictions. That's possible, but it's difficult to understand given the hard-nosed financier that Morgan was. His credentials were even more impressive than Schwab's. While Schwab was a deal-maker, Morgan was that and much more. He was, without peer, the most powerful and highly respected financier Wall Street had ever produced—a financier's financier.

Is it plausible that 'Jupiter', the supreme god of finance, was seeking financial direction from the heavens? And, for all her fame, what was Evangeline's track record?

On the evening of 2 September 1929, just weeks before the Crash, New York radio station WJZ broadcast a prediction made earlier that day by Evangeline. She'd told a WJZ reporter that 'the Dow-Jones could climb to Heaven'. The fact was it was nearly there already. The Dow peaked the next day, 3 September, then commenced its now famous descent. By 24 October the market had fallen by 20 per cent from the time of Evangeline's prediction. Strike one against Evangeline.

But as market sentiment changed, Evangeline switched her call.

By the time the first of the big single-day corrections hit on 24 October, she'd done a complete about-face and was predicting a crash.

Black Thursday, 24 October 1929, gave investors their first taste of the fury that would be remembered as the 1929 Crash. The highlight of that day looked to be the visit to the exchange by Winston Churchill, who had recently lost his position as Britain's Chancellor of the Exchequer. But Churchill's arrival was overshadowed by the frenzy of activity occurring on the trading floor. Trade started fast and furious from the opening bell. Selling pressure dominated. By lunchtime the market had plunged by over 10 per cent on heavy trading volume. And, while the afternoon saw the market steady and even regain much of its earlier losses, the bear had been unleashed.

The number of shares traded for the day was nearly 12.9 million, a staggering 4.6 million higher than the previous record. Paper profits built on margin were lost in an avalanche of margin calls. Nerves were frayed. The last remaining shreds of confidence had been severed. Fear had become endemic.

So it was in Evangeline's office that her clients congregated that Thursday evening. They all sought direction: Where was the market heading? Should they sell? Should they hang on?

What Evangeline told her clients that night was a classic case of the pied piper leading her followers over the edge of the cliff. On the eve of the most horrific stock market rout the world has experienced, she advised her clients that the conjunction and interrelation of certain planets were creating 'spheres of influence over susceptible groups, who in turn will continue to influence the market'.

She went on to say that the market would recover strongly over the next two trading days. But it was advice she wasn't prepared to take herself—her own stock portfolio was haemorrhaging. The next morning, worried about sustaining further loss, she telephoned her broker and told him to sell everything. Strike two against Evangeline.

Evangeline's third strike came when the market hit rock bottom in 1932, having fallen 89 per cent from its 1929 peak. But her opportunity to redeem her poor market record was over. She died only months later. Her story of ill-timed advice explains why you never see a newspaper headline that reads 'Psychic Wins Lottery'.

In November 2012 stock markets around the world were celebrating a five-year anniversary—five years since markets were at their pre-GFC 2007 peak. To mark Australia's five-year anniversary, the TV news aired an interview recorded five years earlier on the very day Australia's stock market reached its zenith. The interview was with a high-profile stockbroker, but it might as well have been with Evangeline Adams.

How did the stockbroker go? Did he foresee the imminent market decline? No, he didn't. In fact his commentary didn't contain a hint of caution. Phrases such as 'strong market momentum', 'high earnings' and 'good underlying value' spilled freely from his lips.

Remember the words I used at the start of this chapter: 'Everything I have stated so far regarding our inability to predict applies to the stock market.'

JESSE LIVERMORE

I've already mentioned Jesse Livermore's name twice, so it's time I formally introduced him. Many recognise him as the greatest stock trader who has ever lived. And by *trader* I mean one who aims to profit from the short to medium movements in stock market prices rather than the long-term returns an *investor* expects by owning stocks for longer periods.

Livermore was born on 26 July 1877 in Shrewsbury, Massachusetts. His father was a poor farmer, the antithesis of what Jesse was to become. Jesse was a bright boy, excelling in mathematics at school.* Yet his father pulled him out of class at age 14, handed him a pair of overalls and announced it was time he started working for his keep.

---

*An aptitude in mathematics is a common characteristic among skilled traders and investors.

Jesse's mother didn't want her son to spend his life eking out an existence from the New England soil. So, with her blessing and five dollars in his pocket, Jesse set off for Boston. At the tender age of 14 he found himself a job at stockbroking firm Paine Webber posting stock quotes on a chalkboard. The stock market was a natural home for Jesse, a medium where he could express his aptitude with numbers. He searched for meaning in the stock prices he was posting on the board. He made notes in a pocket book and developed theories on how to beat the market. Despite his youth, he started frequenting 'bucket shops' to test his ideas using the cash he'd earned from his job.

Bucket shops were nothing more than betting shops where patrons bet on stock price movements rather than racehorses. Physical stocks were not exchanged; rather, movements in stock prices formed the basis of the bet. The betting stake was made on margin against the house. Jesse became so successful he was progressively banned from all the bucket shops in Boston. He earned the nickname 'Boy Plunger'.

It was inevitable that Livermore would end up on Wall Street. Ultimately he carved out a career in stock trading that spanned four decades. He shorted the 1907 Panic, netting $3 million in trading profits. He did it again during the chaos of the 1929 Crash, netting $100 million. He became a household name. The press loved him. *Time* described him as the most fabulous living US stock trader.

Livermore's life wasn't always characterised by financial success, however. He filed for bankruptcy in 1934, for example, and it wasn't the first time that trading in stocks had wiped him out. He was broke three times by the age of 30, and he suffered from chronic depression. These demons ultimately caused him to take his own life. On 28 November 1940 he walked into the cloakroom of the Sherry Netherland Hotel on Fifth Avenue, New York, placed a .32-calibre Colt automatic pistol behind his right ear and pulled the trigger.[*]

Was it skill or luck that delivered Livermore a millionaire's life? We'll never know. But one thing is for sure: he was an extremely intelligent man who devoted his life to studying the stock market. Draw your own conclusion.

---

[*]There is a strange addendum to this story. At the time of his death Livermore was married to Harriet Metz Noble. Livermore was her fifth husband. All of Harriet's five husbands committed suicide.

History has thrown up some brilliant and insightful investors and traders. De la Vega, Dow, Livermore, Graham, Buffett—they've each brought their own trading and investing methods to the market. On the surface these methods appear to be totally different. Yet when you dig deeper it becomes apparent these men possessed three common characteristics: intelligence, insight and intensity of application.

Given that Livermore profited from shorting the 1907 Panic and the 1929 Crash, did he possess an ability to forecast the market? Not according to Livermore himself; he no more had a crystal ball than the rest of us. What he did was take a view—a view based on how he expected people to react to news. The following are his words:

> Speculation is nothing more than anticipating coming movements. In order to anticipate correctly, one must have a definite basis for anticipation, but one has to be careful because people are often not predictable—they are full of emotion—and the market is made up of people.[14]

So Livermore undertook his trades with both feet placed firmly in the present. He waited for the first signs that his view might be played out before acting. In his words: 'Don't back your judgment until the action of the market itself confirms your opinion.'[15]

Livermore regularly got it wrong. But he (usually) got out of his position quickly before too much damage was done. Despite his being one of the most revered traders of his time, and still for many people today, these are not the actions of someone who could reliably forecast the future direction of the stock market. Livermore was one of the world's most famous traders, but a trader who didn't claim an ability to predict the future and didn't use charts!

I'd like to finish this chapter with a great quote from Warren Buffett, the world's most successful investor: 'Forecasts may tell you a great deal about the forecaster; they tell you nothing about the future.'

Chapter summary

- The stock market is no different from any other forum. Like all others, it cannot be accurately predicted.

- The power of prediction eludes even seasoned stock market participants because two basic conditions for acquiring a skill can't be met: the market isn't sufficiently consistent, and therefore it doesn't allow for practice.

- There always has been, and likely will continue to be, no shortage of participants who claim an ability to predict.

- Neither the world's greatest trader nor the world's greatest investor have claimed a capacity to predict the movements of the stock market.

5

DOES THE STOCK MARKET FORECAST THE ECONOMY?

So far I've posed the question 'Can the stock market be predicted?' Can economic forecasts, for example, be used to predict where the stock market is heading? I hope by now you've come to the same conclusion as me: they can't.

Now I want to turn things around. Rather than asking whether economics can predict movements in the stock market, let's ask whether movements in the stock market can predict the economy. That's right. Can what was previously being predicted deliver a prediction on what was being used as the vehicle for the forecasting? The logical question is, how is it possible that each could forecast the other? It sounds ludicrous but that's exactly what many people propose and believe.

Here's a comment I recently read in the investment journal *Equity* in 2012:

> Technical analysis is particularly useful in providing underlying information about the market perception of the health and probable future price movement of a stock. This technical approach also applies to a national stock index which gives a forward glimpse in the economic activity of a country perhaps up to nine months into the future.

Let's consider whether there's any basis to this belief. Firstly, the stock market is nothing more than a mixing pot of the combined beliefs of the multitude of individuals interacting with it. They back their conviction with their chequebooks, and the weight their vote carries depends on the size of the cheque they write. Intuitively this questions how the market could be expected to have predictive powers. We know that the individual investors and those who influence the investors—the analysts, the fund managers, the brokers, the market commentators, and even the politicians and the economists who choose to deliver economic commentary—have little idea where the economy will be in six to nine months. So how can their combined consideration deliver what they can't individually? Surely individual ignorance can't be transformed into collective wisdom.

Yet the popular belief that the stock market is a forecaster of the economy has been around for a long time. I don't know who first proposed it, but Thomas Gibson had this to say back in 1910: 'Security prices always move ahead of basic developments, never after or in connection with such developments.'[16]

It's not an unrealistic observation that stock market crashes tend to precede economic downturns, or that stock market recoveries tend to precede better economic times. But does this demonstrate a capacity to forecast, or is it simply an association? For example, could it be that a stock market crash is the initiator rather than the predictor of an economic downturn? Or maybe the stock market upturn initiates a sense of improved economic wellbeing, which then leads to an economic recovery.

This was the view held by author Henry Hall. Early last century Hall wrote that, while the stock market appeared to precede economic conditions, it could be that the stock market was causing the economic effect rather than predicting it. He stated: 'It is to be noted, as a distinct and logical phenomenon, that a decline in stocks antecedes an actual turn downward in business, and sometimes brings about the crisis.'[17]

It seems Hall's conclusion that a decline in stocks 'sometimes brings about the crisis' was nothing more than his personal opinion. Nevertheless it ran counter to the belief of many people in both his day and ours. In my mind Hall's view remains a highly credible one. Which comes first, the economy or the stock market? Which is the horse and which the cart?

Another who considered this issue was unemployed securities dealer turned author Julian Sherrod. Sherrod took to writing in the wake of the 1929 Crash after losing his job as a bond salesman for National City Bank. In his 1931 book *Scapegoats*, Sherrod lambasted the Wall Street excesses leading up to the 1929 Crash. He wrote: 'To say that the Depression has caused the things which I have been discussing is not only putting the cart before the horse, but it is turning the horse around also and facing him north while driving south.'[18]

Sherrod felt the 1929 Crash and the Great Depression were the direct result of the excesses preceding the Crash. The Crash didn't predict anything. It was a catastrophe just waiting to happen.

In September 1930, around the time Sherrod was writing *Scapegoats*, Richard Whitney, the President of the New York Stock Exchange, delivered an address to the Merchants Association of New York. His topic was 'Trade Depressions and Stock Panics'. Whitney blamed the unfolding business slump on the excessive production and artificially high prices prior to the Crash. Like Sherrod, he used the horse-and-cart analogy, stating: 'To attribute business depressions to stock market panics is to place the cart before the horse.'*

He proposed that stock prices were merely a barometer of business conditions and a response to, rather than a cause of, economic conditions. In his mind there was nothing predictive about the Crash since deteriorating business conditions preceded the Crash by five months. On that point Whitney was right. In the months leading up to the Crash, steel output and auto production were falling.

But if stock prices respond to the real economy rather than predict it or affect it, why can subtle shifts in the economy result in such dramatic shifts in stock prices? And why is the deterioration in economic conditions typically amplified in the wake of a significant crash, not before it? Why did the Long Depression** of 1873 to 1879 follow the Panic of 1873? And why did the Great Depression of the 1930s follow the 1929 Crash?

---

*You might have expected the President of the New York Stock Exchange to say this. Besides, Whitney was a master of spin. Consider a presentation he gave to the Philadelphia Chamber of Commerce in April 1931. His subject was 'Business Honesty'. He described the fraudulent security dealer as a coward and declared that the Exchange was doing everything in its power to ferret out such criminals. Seven years later Whitney was locked up in Sing Sing after being convicted of embezzlement.

**For five decades the depression of 1873 to 1879 was referred to as the 'Great Depression'—until the Depression of the 1930s stole the title.

Charles Dow had expressed his thoughts on this matter 30 years earlier. In his editorial of 10 May 1900 he said:

> The stock market discounts tendencies. Stocks went up before the improvement in business became pronounced. Stocks will discount depression before depression actually exists, but this discounting quality in stocks makes them run to extremes. They discount shadows as well as substances and often anticipate that which does not occur.

Dow is suggesting here that the stock market reacts both to expected and to current alterations in the economy. But, equally, markets can overreact. So a very large correction can result from subtle shifts in economic data. I might add that an overreaction is more likely when the market is substantially overpriced to start with, as it so obviously was in 1929.

So we've now come full circle. The cart is chasing the horse. And so it goes around and around.

Let's see what Jesse Livermore, the cunning and perceptive reader of shifts in market sentiment, had to say on the matter. Livermore published his share trading secrets just before his death in 1940. In *How to Trade in Stocks* he wrote:

> It is therefore foolish to try and anticipate the movement of the market based on current economic news and current events … these facts were not facts I could ever use to 'PREDICT' the market.[19]

Prominent economist and US fund manager John Burr Williams was interested enough in the horse-and-cart issue to devote an entire chapter of his 1938 book, *The Theory of Investment Value*, to the subject. His views were similar to those of Dow and Whitney. He pointed out that the stock market did not issue the first signal. Shifts in the volume of orders for new goods in the real economy preceded the stock market's reaction. This meant the first investors to react were merely responding to what they sensed, read about or could see for themselves — that is, real shifts in economic activity. All the other investors then just responded to the price moves that resulted from their selling. These price moves began as a trickle but ultimately became a flood. The early economic signs from the real economy, and the downward drift in share prices from their peak, are effectively the 'canary in the coalmine' preceding the main brunt of a crash. But it's the crash that grabs everyone's attention. Williams concluded the stock market had no capacity for prophecy at all.

This line of thinking is akin to that of modern-day investing marvel Warren Buffett. Buffett has often stated that the economic statistic he would choose if he were stranded on a desert island for a month and could get only one set of economic numbers would be railway freight car loadings. The Association of American Railroads reports the amount of raw materials, inputs and supplies moving around the country every week. And since the inputs transported by rail eventually get processed into inventory, final output and goods for sale, freight loadings should help flag early shifts in the direction of the overall economy.

So let's do a stock take at this stage. It's been observed by some that the stock market moves ahead of the economy. Others have said it doesn't. Some say the stock market is a predictor of economic change. Some suggest it's not a predictor of change but rather the catalyst. And some suggest that the stock market does no more than respond to current economic conditions, but in doing so can overshoot in either direction.

All clear now?

This whole issue has never really been put to bed. Many investors today still believe the market possesses predictive powers. I think a big part of the problem is the general inability of people to distinguish between association and cause. At university my epidemiology* lecturers used to ram down my figurative throat that simple association does not prove cause and effect. To repeat an analogy I made earlier, bald men are more likely to wear hats but that doesn't mean hats cause baldness. And even if an association can be demonstrated, it could be a classic case of—dare I say it again—putting the cart before the horse.

So let me finish the discussion this way. The popular belief is that the stock market is capable of predicting the future. That's wrong. The stock market is people, and people can't predict beyond their next coffee break. The reality is that stock market participants *attempt* to predict the future. The difference is night and day.

The relationship between the real economy, stock market prices and participants in the stock market is far more complex than simple statements such as 'the stock market forecasts the state of the economy six to nine months ahead'. How participants in the stock market respond

---

*Epidemiology is the statistical study of disease within a population. It often leads to a deeper understanding of the causes of particular diseases.

to economic signals is complex. How the economy reacts to the signals issued from the stock market is complex. There are a multitude of variables. How significant is the economic news? How sensitive are participants to that news? How overstretched are stock prices?

Stock market crashes can trigger economic downturns. Stock market crashes very rapidly strip people of wealth, destroy confidence and seize up lines of credit. They lead to bankruptcies, which lead to job losses and factory closures. If that isn't enough to bring on an economic downturn then I don't know what is. I'm proposing that stock market crashes have the capacity to *bring on* significant economic downturns, but not to predict them.

The problem is that people observe that crashes often precede downturns, and they assume the crash 'predicted' the economic downturn. But the dictionary shows us that the words *preceding* and *predicting* have very different meanings.

Chapter summary

- There appears to be a relationship between the real economy and the stock market.

- Despite the popularity of the belief, it's unlikely the stock market operates as an instrument of prediction.

- The relationship between the economy and the stock market is complex and ever changing. While a multitude of factors are at play, important ones include perceived economic and market conditions, general investor sentiment, and the prevailing relationship between stock market prices and underlying values.

- The observation that market crashes tend to precede economic downturns more likely reflects a cause-and-effect relationship than it does a capacity for prediction.

6

CAN CHARTS PREDICT?

Investing is all about the future — invest your money now and the returns will be delivered later. So it isn't surprising investors are constantly trying to divine the future. Fundamentalists do this by studying business models and financial statements. Technical analysts use charts, moving averages and price trends to identify momentum and trading volume. This chapter is about the tools used by traders, particularly charts. Do they tell us anything about the future? Or do they simply paint a pretty picture of what has already happened but is unlikely ever to happen again?

Traders believe their charts deliver useful information. Many academics and fundamentalists say they don't. But think about it. There's a character bias coming into both sides of the argument. Academics are typically a conservative bunch; they're unlikely either to trade stocks or to use the trading tools and charts that support the habit. So it's easy for them to condemn something they see as of no use to them.

Traders are an entirely different beast. They're more willing to take on risk in their search for a quick buck. Traders want action. Unlike the academics, they need tools that feed their sport. And they definitely don't want to sit on their hands for months or even years like value investors, who undertake their own valuation and only buy when they think a stock is underpriced or sell when they think it's overpriced. Many traders expect to double their money quickly, and they see activity as the only way to do it.* Since market prices are constantly changing, it seems crazy to them not to be in the middle of the action much of the time. So they look to tools that will regularly deliver the buy and sell signals they need to maintain their activity.

Researchers have been asking for more than 100 years whether historical stock price movements deliver any useful signals regarding future price movements. But no-one has yet come up with a definitive answer. If they had then today either there wouldn't be any traders using charts or there wouldn't be any reason to doubt those who are. So let's take a journey through time to see what past researchers have found.

LOUIS BACHELIER

Let's kick off our review of the evidence by going way back to 1900. That's when a young French mathematician, Louis Bachelier, was undertaking a doctorate in mathematical sciences at Paris's Sorbonne University. Bachelier was studying how the market prices of options on government bonds behaved. After gathering his findings he cut and diced them mathematically and then presented them in his doctoral thesis. These words are from the introduction of the thesis:

> The influences that determine the movements of the Exchange are innumerable; past, current and even anticipated events that often have no obvious connection with its changes have repercussions for the price ... The determination of these movements depends upon an infinite number of factors; it is thus impossible to hope for mathematical predictability.[20]

Bachelier concluded that the market can only be beaten by luck. Here's another quote from his thesis: 'At a given instant the market believes neither in a rise nor a fall of the true price.' And another: 'Evidently a player will be neither advantaged nor disadvantaged if his total mathematical expectation is zero.'

---

*Nineteenth-century Gilded Age industrialist and stock trader John W. 'Bet-a-Million' Gates is said to have spent a rail journey betting with an associate on the outcome of raindrops running down the window of his railway car—at $1000 a race.

So he pretty much kicked the game off by describing the financial markets as a gamble. As with roulette, you can't pick the next spin of the wheel. He's saying price trends are a myth because security prices move in a random, unpredictable manner.

Bachelier argued that for each quoted price there existed both buyers and sellers. In any trade, who's right and who's wrong? And he has a point. You may be full of conviction, but so too is the guy on the other side of the trade.

ALFRED COWLES

Alfred Cowles III was born in 1891, the grandson of the founder of the *Chicago Tribune*—which means he was born into money. In an effort to find this money a home, Cowles developed a strong interest in the financial markets. He subscribed to several investment newsletters that, as today, claimed to provide their readers with an investing edge. From 1928 to 1932 Cowles tracked the tips provided by the two dozen most popular sheets. It was an interesting period since it covered the overheated bull market preceding the 1929 Crash, the Crash itself and the crushing bear market following it. Cowles felt, in retrospect, that any tipping sheet worth its salt should have been able to flag the big market moves before they occurred.

Over the four years of Cowles' review, the Dow reached its giddying heights of September 1929, sustained a 23 per cent plunge over two days (28 and 29 October 1929) and fell by an unprecedented, and yet to be surpassed, 89 per cent between September 1929 and July 1932. These were massive events but, just like the general public, the tipping sheets didn't see them coming.

Cowles became intrigued by the question of whether stock prices are predictable. He wrote to Yale professor Irving Fisher, President of the Econometric Society and an old friend of his father. There was a certain irony here since Fisher will be forever remembered for making what proved to be one of the most ill-timed market predictions of the 20th century. Two weeks before the 1929 Crash he stated that stock prices 'have reached what looks like a permanently high plateau'. With egg still running down his face, it's likely Fisher was also interested in the answer to Cowles' question. In January 1932 Cowles established the Cowles Commission for Research in Economics. The commission spawned the respected journal *Econometrica*, which carried an article in July 1933 entitled 'Can Stock Market Forecasters Forecast?' Its conclusion: 'doubtful'.

In 1950 Cowles published a very interesting study in *Econometrica*. He was looking at the potential for markets to trend. It made intuitive sense to him that if stock prices trended then there would be a greater proportion of price sequences than reversals. He had published a study along similar lines in 1937, but in response to criticism he revised his statistical method for the 1950 paper. He found that there was a slight tendency for prices to sequence, but that it could easily be explained away. For example, there is a tendency for general stock market prices to change over time anyway.* Alternatively, a move in interest rates is sufficient to explain the degree of change Cowles observed. Stock yields adjust to changing interest rates, and shifting yield expectations deliver changes in underlying stock prices.

More importantly, even if a correlation did explain the results observed in Cowles' study, it wasn't significant enough to deliver a trading profit.

HOLBROOK WORKING

In 1934 agricultural economist Holbrook Working published the results of a novel study that looked at price changes in commodity markets.[21] He started by acknowledging that patterns existed in historical price charts. And clearly he wasn't alone in thinking so — for years chartists had been drawing conclusions from the paths these charts traced out. But Working's question wasn't how the charts appeared but whether there was any justification in drawing conclusions from their appearance.

Traditional price charts show consecutive market prices wandering across the page, but Working used these price charts to produce a different type of chart. He measured and then showed graphically the quantum of successive price changes, and he found that, instead of being pattern-like, they took on a totally random appearance.

---

*The tendency is for stock markets to increase over time, which means that if you want to predict the future direction of the stock market you can. General market indices, given enough time, have never failed to reach new highs. So you are safe in saying the market will be higher in the future. It's the 'exactly when that will happen' part of the question that gets everyone unstuck.

He tested the concept further by producing graphs 'in reverse'. First he generated a series of random numbers; these he treated as the quantum of successive price change. Then he used them to construct what appeared to be traditional price charts. He compared these randomly generated charts with real commodity price charts, and couldn't tell the difference. He even showed the charts to professional commodities traders down at the Chicago trading pits — they couldn't tell the difference either.

Holbrook's findings were a blow to traders who were confident that historical price charts delivered insightful information.

RALPH ELLIOTT AND MAURICE KENDALL

Ralph Elliott told the world in 1938 that market prices unfold in clearly discernible patterns. His concepts have been distilled into a stock trading technique called Elliott Wave Theory. Elliott stated in his book *The Wave Principle* that:

> ... because man is subject to rhythmical procedure, calculations having to do with his activities can be projected far into the future with a justification and certainty heretofore unattainable.[22]

Let's look at how Elliott's concept stacks up against the evidence.

Fifteen years after *The Wave Principle* was published, London statistician Maurice Kendall put Elliott's claims under the microscope. His article, published in the *Journal of the Royal Statistical Society*, shot holes in Elliott's claims. After analysing copious volumes of data covering 19 different stock groupings over a 10-year period, as well as 50 years of price movements on wheat and 135 years of price movements on cotton, he found no evidence of association between consecutive commodity prices. And he had this to say about stocks:

> [Trends were] so weak as to dispose at once of any possibility of being able to use them for prediction. The Stock Exchange, it would appear, has a memory lasting less than a week.[23]

In other words, in debunking Elliott, Kendall found himself agreeing with Working.

HARRY ROBERTS

Six years after Kendall's paper, the *Journal of Finance* published a paper by Chicago statistician Harry Roberts. Like Working and Kendall, Roberts felt that proponents of technical analysis were being fooled into believing price charts were supplying information that simply wasn't there. Technical analysts had long argued that embedded within price and volume data lay everything you needed to know about a stock—market sentiment, future prospects, value and risk.

But, like Working and Kendall before him, Roberts felt that the shortcoming of traditional price charts was that they displayed successive price levels rather than quantum changes in price. This, he felt, gave the artificial appearance of a pattern or trend. Roberts' methodology was similar to Kendall's but he based his study on US companies. And, like Kendall, he concluded that chance outcomes produce patterns that invite spurious interpretations. Roberts made particular reference in his study to the appearance of one randomly generated chart—it showed a pattern that any technical analyst would have clearly identified as a 'head-and-shoulders' top.

Roberts declared that the main reason for producing his paper was to call to the attention of financial analysts empirical results that seemed to have been ignored. He reminded them of Working's and Kendall's earlier findings as well as describing his own. When you read Roberts' paper you can sense his frustration. That was 1959. Roberts lived until 2004 and, despite his pleas, few people listened. They continued to trust what the charts were 'telling' them.

Roberts felt that the appearance of a trend was an easy concept to challenge, because chance outcomes are often successive in nature. A coin tossed a hundred times doesn't come up heads, tails, heads, tails, and so on for 100 tosses in a row (in fact this outcome is so unlikely you should feel comfortable betting your life savings against it happening). But successions of heads or of tails will occur, and if you plot the outcome it *will* look like a trend—even though it's not.

Yet how often do you hear someone playing a game of chance claiming to be on a 'hot streak'? The hot streak is merely their interpretation of a string of chance events. Or the person who has tossed heads four times in a row and announces there's a greater chance that tails will come up next because 'it's time it did'. In both cases chance events carry no predictive power whatsoever, yet people dearly believe that they do.

The reality is that the interpretation of past stock price movements can be equally deceptive.

WHAT ABOUT BULL AND BEAR MARKETS?

Let's now consider this issue from another angle—one that isn't research based and that appeals to intuition.

Market prices are driven by perceptions of value—many people's perceptions of value. Some base their perceptions on estimates of future earnings, but not everyone reaches their value judgement so analytically. For many, sentiment alone drives their perceptions of value. So what happens if sentiment becomes the predominant force shaping perceptions, such as occurs in bull or bear markets? Sentiment can become self-fulfilling. Isn't it possible that if most investors believe a market should rise, and it does, that this will reinforce their belief and the market will rise further? And while that view can't be held forever, isn't this causing the market to trend for a while at least? In other words, are the findings of the researchers—that market prices don't trend—inapplicable when sentiment is polarised, as in bull and bear markets?

People get drawn into crazes—bike riding, Pilates, yoyos, Sudoku puzzles, Pokemon cards, the stock market. It's simply part of being human. A bull market is just another craze, and it's tempting to believe that bull markets trend. As more and more people get caught up in the craze, the price movement gains momentum. Increasing prices attract more participants. Anticipated price rises become self-fulfilling as more people join the craze.

One of the problems here is that few people recognise a bull market, which means that, even if it can be shown subsequently that bull markets trend, most participants don't know when to start looking for that trend. And there's a bigger problem: even assuming the capacity to recognise a bull market, how is one supposed to know when it's going to end? A failure to recognise that is like walking blindfolded towards a cliff.

Outside of a bull market it's more difficult to argue the case for trends. What about a bear market? Bear markets typically start with a crash or a significant correction, which is then followed by a period of enhanced price volatility. Attempting to find a trend among that lot is unlikely to be either productive or profitable.

PUTTING RANDOMNESS INTO PERSPECTIVE

I want to put this whole randomness issue into perspective, because it's easy to come to the wrong conclusion. It's not that share prices are driven solely by chance; that would be nonsense. A stock consistently earning $2 per share is clearly worth more than one earning 50 cents. Real forces do drive share prices over time. But the forces guiding current prices are based on perceptions of the future, and these perceptions are constantly changing. It's this that leads to the observed randomness.

To help explain, let's consider a hypothetical company. Like most companies it generates profits. It pays a proportion of these profits to its shareholders in the form of dividends and retains the rest to reinvest into the business. Over time the underlying value of the business increases and so its share price follows—but not in a straight line. If fundamentals justify an increase in the underlying value of the company of 6 per cent over a 12-month period, you won't see the share price increase by a geometric average of 0.112 per cent every week over the course of a year. No stock ever has or ever will trace out a perfectly straight share price graph. Instead, market prices jump around in an unfolding long-term revaluation.

Given the multitude of other factors that also drive share prices—including investor sentiment, interest rates and economic conditions (and changing perceptions of all these factors)—market prices must be viewed as a *reflection* of the underlying value of a business rather than an exact measure. Share price movements map out a course like a drunk walking from point A to point B. For significant periods of time he'll probably be heading in the wrong direction but eventually he'll arrive at his destination. So it's wrong to judge where the drunk's final destination is simply by observing the direction he's walking at any point in time. Similarly, it's wrong to judge a stock's true value by either the current market price or the direction the stock price is heading at any particular time.

Using another analogy, the relationship between a stock's real value and its market price can be likened to a rubber band. Sometimes market price and underlying value are close; sometimes extremes of human emotion and misperception pull them far apart. But, like the rubber band in various stages of extension, the connection is self-correcting.

Misplaced sentiment and misjudgement can cause prices to move in the wrong direction, but not forever.

This underpins one of the fundamental problems I see in relying solely on technical analysis. Technical analysts draw conclusions from market price and volume data, but this information is provided without any distinction between rational and emotional influences on the data. This all-inclusive method of measurement—the supposed strength of technical analysis—I see as a weakness. To take your cue solely from the actions of the market means you'll probably find yourself following the drunk as he's trying to find his way home.

Chapter summary

- Research has shown that charts of randomly generated numbers are indistinguishable from real stock price charts. And while that doesn't lead to the conclusion that stock price charts always describe random events, it does place doubt on the information they deliver.

- The benefit of using historical price charts to determine future stock prices is therefore questionable.

- It's feasible that prices trend in bull markets, but it's difficult to apply this information in a practical manner.

7
MARKET TIMING

Many people claim they can time the stock market—to sense when the market is about to change mood, to get in before it climbs, to switch into cash before it falls. Evidence is thin on the ground that even experienced players can do this, yet there's no shortage of novices who believe it's the way to generate superior returns. I'll give you an example.

At the time I was researching stocks for an investment newsletter I was working on. I received an email from a new subscriber who was keen to roll $200 000 from a managed fund into his newly created self-managed superannuation fund (SMSF). He was planning to make his own stock selections for the first time in his life. He'd been reading all the back issues of our newsletter containing recommendations made well before he joined. We tagged our stock recommendations with a 'buy below' price based on our valuations. Most recommendations were performing well and were now trading well above our recommended buy price. His email was aimed at getting our 'permission' to buy those stocks at prices above our recommended buy price. He reassured me that it was okay for him to pay high prices for these stocks because 'no doubt they'll keep rising and I'll just sell them before the market starts to fall'.

It's interesting to consider how people believe they're endowed with this sixth sense. Astrologer Lynn Hayes describes how she knew the 2008–09 GFC was just around the corner:

> A study of astrological cycles reveal the ebb and flow of the psychology of the masses, these cycles can provide clues that are useful in financial investing. For example, while Pluto was traveling through Sagittarius, the sign of expansion and optimism, there was a seemingly endless flow of consumer confidence that drove the stock and housing markets in an unending upward direction. As soon as Pluto entered Capricorn in January of 2008, the reality check that Capricorn requires caused investors to realise that they were standing on a house of cards and with the fall of confidence came the fall of the markets and the rest of the economy. Short-term planetary cycles can give some clues as to the twists and turns of the markets, but it is difficult to predict specific investments with any precision because of the huge number of variables: the cycles of the individual investor, the particular company, its CEO, etc.[24]

I guess to Lynn's credit she stopped short of suggesting astrology is useful for picking individual stocks, but I think you get the picture.

These ill-founded beliefs are frighteningly common, but the question remains: are similar beliefs held by battle-hardened stock market campaigners? Is the capacity to successfully time the market a legitimate skill? Some claim so. Many say it's impossible. So let's look at the evidence.

IS IT PREDICTION OR A STUDY OF CYCLES?

I have already argued that the prediction of short-term movements in market prices is not possible. It's a view that was also held by the famous financier J.P. Morgan. I like the response Morgan provided to an inquisitive reporter more than 100 years ago: when asked where the market was heading Morgan replied, 'It will fluctuate.'

But what about long-term changes in the stock market? In 1902 a book called *Financial Crises and Periods of Industrial and Commercial Depression*, by Theodore Burton, was published. As old as this book is, the title implies something people had already known for a long, long time: there's a relationship between the state of the economy and the health of the stock market. Both cycle. As night follows day, each swings successively from boom to bust, which means there's a pot of gold waiting for the investor who can successfully read the stock market cycle. And here's the beauty of it. Forecasting in the sense of matching events to times isn't necessary. If it's possible to identify the stage of the cycle at any time, then all that's necessary is to buy in bad times and wait patiently. The cycle will do the work for you.

Let's look at some of the tools that have been proposed as market cycle indicators.

DOW THEORY

Many market timers use 'Dow theory', which isn't so much a single theory as a collection of ideas packaged together and called a theory. Dow theory is named, naturally enough, after Charles Dow, of *The Wall Street Journal* and Dow Jones Industrial Index fame.

Dow was an intense man—understated, unassuming, but a great thinker. Long-serving *Wall Street Journal* reporter Oliver Gingold,* who worked under Dow, commented: 'I recollect Mr. Dow as a tall, portly, imperturbable man with a beard, rather stooped. I never recollect his smiling and he did not talk much to anybody.'[25]

Dow was intent on understanding how the stock market works, what forces make it move and how investors can best interact with it. Many of his ideas were revolutionary for the time—some so insightful they form the bedrock of contemporary investment philosophy.

Dow died in 1902 at just 51. It was the editorials he wrote in the years immediately preceding his death that form the basis of Dow theory. (Interestingly, Dow didn't propose Dow theory, and didn't even coin the term; it developed by others following his death.) Dow theory is a mix of Dow's ideas, interpretations by others of his ideas, and a number of concepts Dow himself never articulated. It was shaped, developed and successively added to over a period of decades by William Hamilton, Robert Rhea and George Schaefer.

---

*It's reported that Gingold was responsible for the term 'blue chip'. Apparently Gingold coined the phrase in the 1920s while standing next to a stock ticker at a broking house. He was drawing an analogy to the colour of high-priced casino chips as he noted the large number of high-priced stocks recorded on the ticker tape. Gingold's original interpretation of blue chip has been altered; today it refers to high-*quality* stocks.

There is a common misconception about Dow: many believe he was a hardcore technical analyst. He wasn't, but neither was he a hardcore fundamentalist. His original editorials demonstrate that he drew from both disciplines. But there is one overwhelming feature that comes through in his writings—his appreciation that successful investing is based on the search for value. Value, he believed, was the fundamental driver of market price. And it was this core belief that drove Dow's concept of market timing. Dow never believed market timing was about prediction. He believed it was about developing an appreciation of whether the market was cheap or expensive at any point in time, acting on that information, and then waiting patiently for things to change.

Dow hasn't been alone in holding this belief. It's one many other great investors, past and present, have held as well. Warren Buffett presents a good example. He is constantly in search of undervalued stocks, knowing that if he buys and holds them they will eventually rise to fair value. The following Dow quotes demonstrate the similarity between his and Buffett's views:

> It is always safer to assume that values determine prices in the long run. Values have nothing to do with current fluctuations. A worthless stock can go up five points just as easily as the best, but as a result of continuous fluctuations the good stock will gradually work up to its investment value.[26]

> An investor who will study values and market conditions, and then exercise enough patience for six men will likely make money in stocks.[27]

These comments underpin the activity of the investor who uses value as the bedrock of investment decisions—to independently value a stock and then wait for the market to present a favourable price to either buy or sell. Real opportunities for this don't present often, so the concept of patience is extremely important here. That this characteristic is essential to success is echoed by traders and investors both past and present, such as Jay Gould, Ben Graham and Warren Buffett. You need patience for the cycle to move in your favour, which means long periods of inactivity are a hallmark of true investors.*

---

*Famous stock trader Jesse Livermore believed that speculation also needed to be an intermittent process characterised by extended periods of inactivity. He said a trader shouldn't be in the market every day or week. He believed there are only a few times a year—possibly four or five—when a trader should be active.

As an aside here, I want to expand on the importance of patience. Warren Buffett's daughter, Susie, was once asked, 'What two words best describe your father?' She replied without hesitation: 'Patience and integrity.'

As a practical example of the degree of patience required by an investor, Buffett has often stated that an investor's career should be limited to 20 carefully considered decisions. He recommends the use of a hypothetical punch card to keep a record. In the knowledge that after the card has been clipped for the twentieth time no further investment decisions can be made, we are constantly reminded that each needs to be made with great deliberation.

Investment should be limited to the very best deals we come across in a lifetime.

Back now to Dow theory, and the various followers of Dow who have developed the theory. It covers several areas, but it's not my intention to explore them all here. I'll limit discussion to that part of Dow theory that relates to market timing.

Samuel Armstrong Nelson

Charles Dow's good friend Samuel Armstrong Nelson released his book *The ABC of Wall Street* in 1900. Following its publication Nelson received many requests to write another book dealing specifically with investment principles. Nelson urged Dow to take on the project but he refused, so Nelson wrote it himself. The resulting book, *The ABC of Stock Speculation*, was released in 1902.

Nelson had a great deal of respect for Dow so he incorporated a lot of Dow's ideas into the book. He drew heavily from Dow's editorials, acknowledging this in footnotes throughout the book. Each footnote simply states 'Dow's Theory', and so the term was born.

Although this was the first time the term appeared in print, Nelson's references did not distil the concepts we recognise today as Dow theory. The words were simply used to acknowledge that Charles Dow's ideas were woven into the book.

William Peter Hamilton

William Peter Hamilton was the fourth editor of *The Wall Street Journal*. He joined the journal in 1899, at age 32, and was its editor from 1908 until he died in December 1929. Hamilton got the whole Dow theory thing moving. He outlined his version of Dow theory in his *Wall Street Journal* articles, his writing for *Barron's* magazine and his best-selling book *The Stock Market Barometer*.

It was Hamilton who developed, refined and explained much of what we now refer to as Dow theory. Essentially, the theory was born from the intertwining of the beliefs of Dow and Hamilton.

Dow saw the stock market as having three forms of movement. He described an underlying long-term movement in either an upward (bull) or a downward (bear) direction. This 'primary movement' is typically sustained for a long time, usually years. He believed that within this large directional move there are two further movements, which can run against the underlying long-term market direction without changing the fact the market remains in a long-term bull or bear mode. These other two movements are a medium-term 'secondary movement', typically running between 10 and 60 days, and a 'daily movement', characterised by random, erratic moves of no significance at all—in other words, market noise.

Dow warned against reacting to secondary movements and daily movements. He saw them as irrelevant. He said the first thing an investor needs to do is identify whether it is a primary bull or bear market; this should guide investment decisions.

The following is from Dow's editorial of 4 January 1902: 'Losses should not generally be taken on the long side in a bull period. Nor should they be taken on the short side in a bear period.' In other words, if your stocks have fallen in a bull market, don't sell. It sounds like good advice, but how is an investor supposed to know whether it's currently a bull or bear market? And even if the investor gets that right, how can they tell whether a reversal signals the end of the bull or bear market or is just a short- or medium-term move that will revert back to the long-term underlying condition? Dow covered this in the same editorial:

> It is a bull period as long as the average of one high point exceeds that of previous high points. It is a bear period when the low point becomes lower than the previous low points.

Okay. That covers the primary movement, but it still doesn't tell you when it's going to end. Dow acknowledged this is a difficult question:

> It is often difficult to judge whether the end of an advance has come because the movement of prices is that which would occur if the main tendency has changed. Yet it may only be an unusual, pronounced secondary movement.

In other words, it seems it's impossible to distinguish short-term and medium-term noise from a fundamental shift in the market's long-term direction—until you review it all with the benefit of hindsight. Living in the market day-to-day is like not being able to see the wood for the trees. So what can you do?

Well, this is an area in which William Hamilton contributed to Dow theory. He said that to determine whether the long-term market direction remained unchanged it was necessary to check whether 'the two averages corroborated each other'.[28] By 'the two averages' he meant the Dow Jones Industrial Average and the Dow Jones Transportation Average. He said, 'there is never a primary movement, rarely a secondary movement, where they do not agree'. Unfortunately for us today, Hamilton's comments relate to a different era. The railroads once represented a significant part of the stock market, and while the Transportation Average still exists it doesn't carry the influence it once did.

Does Dow Theory work?

So is Dow theory a useful tool for timing the market? Does a bull period exist as long as the average of one high point exceeds that of previous high points? Is it a bear period when the low point becomes lower than the previous low points? Seems like an easy thing to test. After all, Dow theory was proposed a long time ago, which means we have plenty of data for back-testing.

Alfred Cowles, whom I've mentioned already, was also interested in this question. Cowles studied 255 of Hamilton's editorials from 1903 to 1929, comparing the percentage gain or loss achieved by acting on his calls against the returns achieved by simply staying fully invested in the broad market. He took the study period up to 9 December 1929, the date Hamilton died. Cowles calculated that Hamilton's market timing would have resulted in a 19-fold growth in capital from 1903 to 1929, which doesn't sound too bad. But Cowles also calculated that a buy-and-hold strategy would have achieved more than double that return over the same period. He performed similar studies on recommendations provided by a number of other tipping sheets and found they fared no better than Hamilton.

Later research undertaken by Richard Durant came to a different conclusion. Durant studied the outcome by applying Dow theory from 1897 to 1956. He found that over this period it outperformed buy-and-hold more than tenfold. And in 1997 William Goetzmann, from the Yale School of Management, published a paper refuting Cowles' study methodology and conclusion. He claimed that Hamilton's calls would have actually yielded positive risk-adjusted returns over the period Cowles studied when compared with a buy-and-hold strategy.

Confused? You'd think the facts were there to see, that they'd be irrefutable. Seems not. The problem is that Dow theory relies, in part, on subjective judgement. So researchers carrying bias into their studies will come up with erroneous conclusions, not only from data selection but also in the way they interpret it. Seems the jury's out on Dow theory.

BEN GRAHAM AND THE COMMITTEE ON BANKING AND CURRENCY

The bottom line is, picking the market cycle isn't that easy. One of the biggest barriers we face is social influence. Whether it's a raging bull market or a crushing bear market, the airwaves will be always be filled with voices justifying the current stock prices. Words like: 'Sure the stock market is up, and so it should be. Corporate earnings are at record levels. The economy is strong. The outlook is great. Things won't be changing for a long time.' Yet a year later you'll hear: 'Sure the stock market is down, and so it should be. Corporate earnings are depressed. Workers are being laid off. Things won't be changing for a long time.' The best thing you can do with this fickle blow-by-blow commentary is shut it out. A difficult thing to do, I know, but it's something Ben Graham managed to do.

Ben Graham was a great Socratic thinker. In March 1955 he appeared before the Committee on Banking and Currency. It was the first session of a hearing looking into the factors that affect the buying and selling of shares. An answer Graham provided to the committee shows he didn't rely on market commentary:

> Chairman: I wonder if you could give us your views in a broad sense about the economic future of the next few years.
>
> Graham: I will do it with the proviso that these views should not be taken too seriously...As a matter of fact I have never specialized in economic forecasting or market forecasting either. My own business has been largely based on the principle that if you can make your results independent of any views as to the future you are that much better off.

In addition to his verbal comments Graham also prepared a statement for the committee. It provided an insight into how he gauged the state of the market at any point in time. The following are excerpts from that statement:

> The true measure of common stock values, of course, is not found by reference to price movements alone, but by price in relation to earnings, dividends, future prospects and, to a small extent, asset values.
>
> As a guide to identifying the present level of stock prices in the light of past experience, I have related the present prices and the high prices in 1929, 1937 and 1946 to earnings of the preceding year, the preceding five years and the preceding ten years. The Dow-Jones industrials are now at a lower ratio to their average earnings in the past than they were at their highs in 1929, 1937, and 1946. It should be pointed out also that high-grade interest rates are now definitely lower than in previous bull markets except for 1946. Lower basic interest rates presumably justify a higher value for each dollar of dividends or earnings.

Graham felt that stock prices were neither cheap nor expensive — they were about fair value. He went on to say it was quite possible prices could rise further, and that in times of optimism markets can move well above fair value.

So was Graham's assessment of the market at that time correct? Of course, we now have the benefit of hindsight. The hearing was held in March 1955. At that time the Dow was just above 400 points, double what it had been at the start of the 1950s. The market continued to rise, more than doubling again over the following 10 years. That took it into the 1960s, the exuberant 'Go-Go Years' — a period when the market became significantly overpriced. But 17 years later the Dow was at the same level it had been in 1965. By then not only had earnings caught up with prices but they had overshot the mark, which meant that in 1982 the market was cheap. From there the market took off again, increasing 13-fold over the next 18 years.

So there can be extended periods of significant inequity between price and value. As Graham reported to the committee, the true measure of common stock values is not found by reference to price movements alone. Yet this is what most people do. They use price as their single measure. They take their investment cues from movements in stock market prices without ever relating these prices to value.

Graham told the committee how he valued the market objectively at any particular time:

> I have found it useful to estimate the central value of the Dow-Jones Industrial average by the simple method of capitalizing 10-year average earnings at twice the interest rate for high-grade bonds. This technique presupposes that the average past earnings of a group of stocks presents a fair basis for estimating future earnings, but with a conservative bias on the low side. It also assumes that by doubling the capitalization rate presented by high-grade bonds, we allow properly for the differential in imputed risk between good bonds and good stocks. Although this method is open to serious theoretical objections, it has in fact given a reasonably accurate reflection of the central value of industrial common stock averages since 1881.[29]

Graham then went on to discuss something quite interesting. From the 1929 peak until the lowest point in the ensuing Great Depression, the Dow collapsed from a high of 381 to a low of 41 points. Using his method the fair market price for the Dow in 1929 was 120.

BOB SHILLER'S CAPE

The price earnings (PE) ratio is one of the most popular ratios used by investors. It is calculated by dividing the current market share price by the most recently reported annual earnings attributable to each share (earnings per share). It is one of the many tools investors use to judge whether the market price of a stock represents good value. The logic goes that the lower the PE ratio the better the value on offer. (In chapter 13 I will discuss in greater depth whether this is true.)

Typically the PE ratio is applied to individual stocks, but US economist Bob Shiller, in a similar fashion to Graham, has adapted the PE ratio in order to gauge the relative value of the general stock market at any point in time. Shiller's market measure was popularised in his 2000 book *Irrational Exuberance*. Referred to as the cyclically adjusted price earnings (CAPE) ratio, it is regularly updated on the web at www.econ.yale.edu/~shiller/data.htm.

Shiller's CAPE ratio delivers a relative value of the entire S&P 500 index. For the 'P' in the numerator Shiller uses real (inflation-adjusted) monthly averages of daily S&P closing prices. For the 'E' in the denominator he uses the average of real S&P composite earnings for the preceding 10 years. So it's effectively a 10-year moving average. He derives monthly aggregate earnings data from the S&P four-quarter totals by using 'linear interpolation' to derive the intervening monthly figures. Linear interpolation is a method for deriving data for a particular time or period even though an actual measurement hasn't been taken. A line is drawn connecting measured and known data points, then a reading is taken from the line at the interim time point(s) required.

The long-term average for the ratio over the 140-plus year period from which Shiller has drawn data has been 16.6. It reached its highest levels in 1901, 1929, 1966, late 1999/early 2000 and 2007. Spot the pattern? These years were all bull market peaks.* So it looks like Shiller's ratio is telling us something: there appears to be a relationship between his composite market PE and stock market extremes.

While Shiller's ratio is not predictive, it does allow for a relative judgement of market value. The relative judgement is made by comparing the current ratio with both the long-term average of 16.6 and past stock market periods. It's an objective grounder, a reality check that allows prevailing market conditions to be questioned, particularly during times of value polarisation, as occurs during extreme bull or bear markets. This reality check is particularly useful for investors who are easily influenced by *groupthink* (and that probably means most people). Shiller's ratio reminds us of the concept of 'mean reversion'—that as market prices become more extreme, on either the upside or the downside, the chances of an imminent reversion also increase.

Shiller's research has also shown that in the wake of high PE peaks investors should expect prolonged periods of poor returns—for years, and sometimes decades. The data has even been used to calculate an

---

*Interestingly, at the time of writing (May 2015), Shiller's CAPE was higher than two of these historical peaks and was approaching a third.

implied market return over the ensuing years and confidence levels for alternate outcomes.

Despite the apparent benefit of periodically reviewing Shiller's CAPE ratio, it's worth mentioning that it isn't without its critics. Their main concern is that the earnings component of CAPE is lower now than it has been historically. This has resulted from the introduction of new accounting standards, changing how earnings are measured and justifying a higher CAPE ratio now than the long-term average of 16.6. In 2013 Deutsche Bank's David Bianco went so far as to construct his own modified CAPE ratio, which he claimed adjusted for the changes in accounting standards and modified the way the ratio was adjusted for inflation. At the time Shiller's ratio indicated that the S&P was more than 50 per cent overvalued compared with its long-term average. Bianco's ratio judged it to be close to fair value.

Others argue that Shiller's CAPE needs to be considered in combination with the prevailing long-term interest rates. That's because there is a strong relationship between interest rates and the discount rates analysts and investors use when calculating formula values for stocks. The lower the discount rate, the higher the calculated stock value.

For example, in May 2015 Shiller's CAPE was sitting at 27.38, about 65 per cent above its long-term average. But long-term interest rates were close to their lowest levels in the 144 years that Shiller's CAPE data covered. Some saw the high CAPE as justified given the low interest rate environment. I saw the situation differently. To me the historically low interest rates were an atypical discount rate indicator and when interest rates did rise, stock prices would likely fall.

Shiller expressed his thoughts about his own ratio in an April 2012 interview with *Money* magazine: 'Things can go for 200 years and then change. I even worry about the 10-year P/E — even that relationship could break down.'

JAMES TOBIN'S 'q'

In February 1969 the *Journal of Money, Credit and Banking* carried an article that was to have a profound impact on the issue of stock market timing. The article, written by highly respected US economist James Tobin, was titled 'A General Equilibrium Approach to Monetary Theory'.[30] It wasn't specifically about market timing, nor did it have much to do with the stock market. But buried within the 15-page article was a reference to a factor he called 'q', and stock market watchers have since adopted q as an indicator of fair market value.

This is how the reasoning goes. Tobin started by considering the market price of capital goods, the tangible assets used by companies to produce whatever it is they produce, such as buildings, equipment and machinery. This was referred to as 'p'. And the market price of the business was referred to as q times p, or 'qp'.

Proponents of q argue that there is a strong relationship between the cost of these capital items and the market prices of the businesses using them. This applies to both unlisted companies and companies listed on the stock exchange. This relationship exists for the following reason. If an operating company is achieving a good return on the capital required to conduct its business, then competitors will be attracted to that business space. If low barriers to entry exist, then it is unlikely that a new entrant would pay an inflated price to purchase an existing business—they'd just set up their own. Therefore competitive forces will tend to drive market prices for businesses down towards the cost of purchasing the tangible productive assets required to undertake the business. That is, qp will tend to move towards p, which means q tends to mean revert to one.

If qp represents the market price of capital goods already in use, then, using Tobin's own reasoning, q represents a factor by which the value of existing capital goods diverges from their current replacement cost. Tobin adds: 'An alternative interpretation of [the model] requires that capital be valued at its reproduction cost i.e., that q=1. This may be regarded as a condition of equilibrium in the long run.'

The argument has then been taken several steps beyond Tobin's paper, and it goes something like this. Some businesses have what is commonly referred to as an enduring competitive advantage. That commonly means they have the capacity to maintain a high return on assets employed. Considered in isolation they would tend to maintain a high q. But when q is applied to the aggregate price of the stock market it tends to mean revert; that is, it reverts to one as the market price reverts to the replacement cost of the capital employed by all the companies in that market.

We accept that stock markets are prone to mispricing; they can be overpriced at times of exuberance and underpriced at times of pessimism.

What q provides is an indication of how overvalued or undervalued the market is at any point in time. Like Shiller's CAPE, q is not predictive, but indicative. The further it moves from one, either in an upward or a downward direction, the higher the likelihood it's about to commence its reversion back towards one.

Andrew Smithers and Stephen Wright have applied this reasoning in their book *Valuing Wall Street*.[31] They highlight the strong historical correlation between q and general stock prices. When *Valuing Wall Street* was written (just prior to the dot-com crash), q was approaching 1.8, the highest recorded level over the course of the 20th century—even higher than the 1.4 it reached just before the 1929 Crash. The authors suggested the stock market was a very dangerous place to be at the end of the 20th century.

As Smithers and Wright note, the Dow did come down strongly, dropping by more than 35 per cent from its January 2000 high to its October 2002 low. But by 2006 the US market had fully recovered those losses and it subsequently reached even higher levels as it approached the GFC of 2008. What was q indicating just prior to the GFC? It was travelling at about one. So if you were relying solely on q you wouldn't have suspected the GFC was coming. It's important to realise that indicators aren't infallible.

So instead of relying on just one indicator, use several. Together they paint a picture. For example, Shiller's CAPE would have caused greater concern than Tobin's q leading up to the GFC. At its pre-GFC peak in October 2007, the US market had Shiller's CAPE sitting at 27.31, around 65 per cent above its long-term average.

WARREN BUFFETT'S FAVOURITE METRIC

Warren Buffett's preferred general stock market indicator is not dissimilar to Tobin's q but it's income based rather than asset based. It's derived by dividing the total market capitalisation of the US stock market by the US gross national product. Buffett describes it as 'probably the best single measure of where valuations stand at any given moment'. Historically there has been a strong correlation, with levels above 100 per cent coinciding with periods of overvaluation of stocks and levels around 50 per cent representing great buying opportunities. In a 2001 *Fortune* magazine article Buffett stated: 'If the percentage relationship falls to the

70% or 80% area, buying stocks is likely to work very well for you. If the ratio approaches 200% as it did in 1999 and a part of 2000 you are playing with fire.'[32] At the time of writing (May 2015) it measured 126.8 per cent, which is best described as significantly overvalued. The Dow was 18 232 points.

It's important to add that Buffett doesn't base his investment decisions either on this metric or on his view on the general index. He's the first to admit he's not a market timer; in fact he doesn't believe market timing is possible. Like every value investor, he looks for disparities between price and value for individual stocks at all stages of the market cycle. It's just that when the general market is depressed there are more stocks being offered at attractive prices. It's therefore likely the experienced value investor can sense the state of the market by the number of undervalued stocks on offer at that time. Buffett's favoured metric simply serves as another 'grounder' at times of market extremes.

THE COPPOCK INDICATOR

One particularly difficult judgement for investors to make is when to re-enter the market in the wake of a stock market crash. At these times the mood is always one of severe pessimism. It's a time when most commentators are delivering strong warnings not to re-enter the market 'just yet'. Many continue making that call until the market has recovered 40–50 per cent. So in keeping with the theme that objective market indicators are better than subjective commentary, let me introduce you to the Coppock Indicator.

Edwin Coppock developed his metric as a way to determine the beginning of a new bull market following a significant market decline. Coppock was the founder of the Texas-based Trendex Research Group, and he has produced several market publications based on trend-following principles. He was asked by the authorities at the Episcopal Church for a practical long-term buy indicator for the stock market and responded by developing the Coppock/Trendex Indicator. That was in 1945. It became known to the broader investment world in 1962 when *Barron's* magazine carried an article describing it.[33]

Coppock's general philosophy was to turn stock market numbers into stock market charts. He didn't see charts as cold or mathematical, he saw them as painting a picture of human behaviour. As he described it, he was undertaking a process of 'emotional indexing'. He saw mass selling on the stock exchange as very much an emotion-driven process, which meant that once the selling process began it became self-fulfilling. The selling gained momentum because people took their cue from the actions of those around them. Selling created selling. This resulted in the market over-correcting on the downside.

Coppock felt that after a big market fall, particularly one fuelled by panic selling, many investors would be reluctant to buy back into the market. Their behaviour could be likened to a person who has recently been burnt by an open flame and is reluctant to get close to a fire again. But Coppock knew that over time this emotion dissipates, and he set out to develop an indicator that would tap into these shifting emotions. So he developed an analogy, likening the emotion experienced following a market collapse to a period of bereavement. He asked the bishops at the Episcopal Church what the typical time was for someone to recover emotionally from the loss of a friend or relative; he was told 'between 11 and 14 months'. Coppock used this information to develop a weighted moving average of the Dow Jones Industrial Average. This is how it's calculated:

1 Calculate the percentage change between the index at the end of the most recent month and 14 months prior.

2 Do the same for the recent month-end value and 11 months prior.

3 Total them.

4 Derive a 10-month weighted moving average of this total.

A 10-month weighted moving total is calculated by multiplying the current month's figure (the sum of the 11- and 14-month changes) by ten, the previous month's figure by nine, the month before by eight, and so on until you get to the tenth-last month, which is multiplied by one. Add the result of these multiplications to achieve the weighted moving total for the current month. When this data is produced in the form of a graph, it shows a line that swings from positive to negative—that is, it moves above and below a horizontal zero line. A signal to re-enter the market is delivered when the Coppock line is below zero and turns upward from a trough.

Of course the most important question is: does it work? Before we explore this question, it's important to note that Coppock himself said there were a couple of things he didn't expect his indicator would tell us:

- It wouldn't work well for individual stocks or sectors. Rather it was designed for the index (he applied it to the Dow Jones Industrial Average).

- It wasn't a precise timing method. It was designed to indicate a condition of low risk for new long-term stock commitment.[34]

Without conducting any research on the effectiveness of the Coppock Indicator, it's easy to pass one obvious judgement from the way it's mathematically derived. Namely, it will deliver false positive signals: sometimes it will signal a new bull market is underway when it isn't. The Coppock Indicator will turn upwards as a depressed market improves, but if the market quickly runs out of steam so too will the indicator. This lack of dependability obviously trips people up. And, depending upon their personal experience in using it, they'll carry different views on how useful it is. I've heard opinions vary from 'it's reliable' right through to 'it's no better than a coin toss'. Its strike rate probably lies somewhere in between these two extremes. That is, it's better than even odds the signal will be correct.

Which begs the question of whether there's any benefit in using it at all. The answer is probably yes—if it suits your investment style. Remember there is no tool, applicable to the financial markets, that provides a 100 per cent hit rate. Success in the financial markets is very much about managing risk and stacking the odds in your favour. Having said that, in the wrong hands the Coppock Indicator is a bit like playing Russian roulette. If you rely on it totally and place big bets, it's like having one chamber loaded in a six-chamber pistol. It's only a matter of time before you blow your brains out.

Coppock of course realised this. So he recommended its use under the following conditions. Firstly, don't rely upon it as your sole analytical tool. And, secondly, use stop losses: if the signal it delivers proves to be wrong, bail out before too much money is lost. What the Coppock Indicator doesn't do is deliver a packaged answer. Like every other tool, if it did it would have made a lot of people rich by now with very little mental effort.

The Coppock Indicator is a tool for those who believe that markets both trend and can be successfully timed. But it doesn't address the most fundamental question in investing: what stocks do I buy? It's not a tool for stock pickers. The tools stock pickers use don't rely on an assessment of the market cycle.

MARKET TIMER OR STOCK PICKER?

It's commonly said that there are two ways to achieve superior returns in the stock market—by market timing or stock picking. That is, either buy when stock market prices are generally depressed and sell when they are generally inflated, or buy great companies that are underpriced independent of the market cycle.

Many confuse the two activities, and a conversation I had several years ago with a friend of mine shows how.

'Buffett's a market timer', my friend announced. 'Don't know why he says he isn't.'

'What do you mean?' I asked.

'Well,' he replied, 'whenever the market collapses he pulls out his chequebook.'

It was an easy one to respond to. I replied: 'Sure he does. Because that's when there are plenty of great stocks around that are cheap. But he's still a stock picker through and through, not a market timer. He's not indiscriminate in his buying. He knows beforehand the companies he wants to buy. Once chosen he waits and, when they're offered to him at the price he wants to pay, he acts on the opportunity.'

The simple truth is that stock pickers don't need to be market timers. They can cast their net at any stage of the market cycle. It's just that they catch more fish when stock market prices are down across the board. Buffett isn't sitting there saying, 'The Dow has fallen enough now, I think I'll buy some stocks.' He's saying, 'The price of ABC Ltd has now fallen to a price I see as attractive.' It just so happens that the odds of ABC Ltd, or any other stock on his wish list, hitting its buy price are greatly improved in a bear market. And conversely it becomes increasingly difficult to find stocks at attractive prices in a bull market.

In 1956 Buffett formed an investment partnership, effectively a hedge fund. He was extremely successful at investing the partners' money, achieving an annual geometric rate of return of just below 30 per cent over the 13 years of its existence. It's interesting then that he wrote to its members on 29 May 1969 announcing his intention to retire from the partnership at the end of that year. He commented: 'Opportunities for investment that are open to the analyst who stresses quantitative factors have virtually disappeared, after steadily drying up over the last 20 years.' In other words, he could no longer find any stocks worth buying. Buffett didn't come to this conclusion by drawing on any general market timing skills or tools; he just couldn't find any undervalued stocks.

There are apparently experienced market commentators who fail to understand this simple principle. I heard a broker, who regularly appears on Australian TV, once declare that investors who rely solely on stock picking possess only half the jigsaw, the other half being the capacity to time the market cycle. Interestingly, during the GFC the same commentator declared that it was too dangerous to re-enter the market. In the ensuing 12 months the market climbed more than 50 per cent.

I read this recently in an investment newsletter:

> While fundamental analysis tells the investor which stocks represent value and might be the best stocks to buy, technical analysis by contrast gives the investor some insights into the emotions of market participants and can tell the investor when to buy.

While this comment acknowledges that emotion can result in a discrepancy between price and value, investors don't need to gauge the level of that emotion in order to act. They merely need to identify solid companies for which a significant gap exists between market price and value.

As a further example of the contradictory advice existing in financial markets, Coppock had this to say about buying stocks in recently depressed but recovering markets:

> Do NOT try to buy a depressed stock. Instead, buy ... stocks even though you may feel you are paying too much for them. At that moment, you can test whether or not you are on the road to becoming a realist. You see, a novice tries to chisel the market, while a pro knows from experience that the better bargain, at the time of such a major bottom signal, is the stock

that is then at a new high for the past several months! Does this sound foolish to you? If you answer with a yes, you are still in the kindergarten of the stock market world.[35]

Interesting, isn't it? Advising investors *not* to buy depressed stocks, and that to do so demonstrates you are still in the kindergarten of the stock market world. These would be difficult words for experienced, market-hardened (and, might I add, wealthy) value investors to accept. Coppock believed in market timing and picking trends; he placed less weight on selecting stocks based on their business merit and value. It's not that he felt these issues were unimportant, just that he felt there was no advantage in acting on financial information that's freely available to all investors.

It's tempting to believe this, and for many investors it's probably true that they can't profit from publicly available information. But successful stock pickers are like elite sportspeople. Champion golfers, cricketers and baseball players use the same sports equipment that's available to the masses, yet they excel in its use. Great investors use the same information as the masses, yet they too excel in its use.

Chapter summary

- The stock market cycles through boom and bust.

- No-one has demonstrated a consistent ability to forecast when future stages of a cycle will occur.

- Efforts at timing the market are better directed towards judging what stage in the cycle the market is at any point in time, acting accordingly, and then waiting for the market to move into another stage in the cycle.

- Metrics that have been developed to indicate the current stage of the market cycle include Dow theory, Shiller's CAPE ratio, Tobin's 'q', total market cap/GNP and the Coppock Indicator.

- No single tool should be relied upon, since none has a 100 per cent success rate.

- Stock pickers are less concerned with timing the market cycle than they are with constantly searching for differences between price and value.

8

ARE COMPUTERS
THE ANSWER?

Investors have been trying to beat the stock market since stocks first traded over four centuries ago. But achieving superior returns isn't so easy, and it seems the frustration stems from two big problems.

The first problem is that our brains struggle to take in, process and interpret the near infinite number of permutations and combinations the future is capable of delivering. Our brain needs to be a Formula 1 racing car; nature delivered us a Model T Ford.

The second problem is emotion. We are riddled with it, some people more than others.

Could it be that both problems have now been eliminated? Today we have cheap and powerful computers that work at speeds our brains can't, and they deliver answers untainted by emotion.

Computers are increasingly being used to build all sorts of models. Models to predict the state of the economy. Models to determine appropriate fiscal and monetary policy settings. Models to guide trading decisions in financial markets. Models to select the best stocks. Models to aid all sorts of decisions. But how much do computers really contribute to the investment process? Maybe less than you think.

ALGORITHMS

Computers are driven by rivers of logic called algorithms. Algorithms aren't new — Persian astronomer and mathematician Muhammad ibn Musa al-Khwarizmi described them in the 9th century. What they do is break big problems down into small steps called 'binary decision trees'. Yes or no? If no, then left. If yes, then right. This simple process moves down a path until an answer is derived — pure logic, black and white, perfect for computers.

Algorithms solve linear problems, just as our brains do. They are a reflection of the way we think. But, unlike us, when a computer uses algorithms the answers come fast. All inputs are considered, calculations are delivered accurately, emotion is totally absent.

Algorithms sat around for centuries waiting for electronic computers to come along. This time lag between the origination of a potential tool and the means for its effective use is typical in many areas of human endeavour. Long before technology converted their ideas into reality, great minds dreamed of what might one day be possible. Jules Verne dreamed of men landing on the Moon more than a century before Neil Armstrong and Buzz Aldrin actually did so. Leonardo da Vinci dreamed of the automobile four centuries before the internal combustion engine made it commonplace. And three centuries ago German mathematician Gottfried Leibniz dreamed of solving complex problems by breaking them down into extended sequences of binary code, but his theorising wasn't fully realised until the development of the modern computer.

HIGH FREQUENCY TRADING

There's been a debate raging over recent years and it's gaining momentum. It's all about high frequency trading (HFT). HFT involves loading a computer with trading algorithms and setting it loose to compete against other, similarly loaded computers. No humans, just one computer's algorithms versus another computer's algorithms. They trade fast. They don't take coffee breaks. They trade in huge volumes. And if they do their job well, they transform pennies into fortunes.

So quickly has HFT been adopted that some reports say it now constitutes about 60 per cent of all stock trades in the United States. Other reports place the figure higher: a 2012 Morgan Stanley report cited by the *Financial Times* put HFT at 84 per cent of total US equity trading. And it's not just in the US that it's taken off. The use of HFT is growing in financial markets around the world.

Supporters of HFT argue that it has brought increased liquidity to the markets, lowered commissions and narrowed buy/sell spreads. Others say the extra liquidity is a mirage. They argue that, because high frequency traders display their buy and sell orders for such a brief time, it doesn't help mum and dad investors. And there's a powerful argument that HFT destabilises the markets — occasional computer glitches can cause prices to go crazy.

New Jersey–based investment house Knight Capital Group lost a small fortune through such a glitch. On 1 August 2012 an unproven algorithm developed by Knight incorrectly bid for $7 billion of stock, which rival computers were only too prepared to offload. Knight lost $440 million in a single trading session. And while public sympathy might be thin on the ground for profit-centric trading houses such as Knight, two years earlier there had been an event with a much broader public impact.

In the early afternoon of 6 May 2010 an avalanche of spurious computer-generated activity caused the Dow Jones Index to embark on a wild, 1000-point ride since referred to as the 'Flash Crash'. The prices of individual stocks went haywire, with some trading for pennies and some for thousands of dollars. Twenty minutes later the crisis was over, like a passing storm, and everything returned to normal.

The US Securities and Exchange Commission (SEC) deliberated for five months before issuing a 104-page report on what caused the Flash Crash. Academics, traders and market participants didn't totally accept its findings, and disagreement on the cause continued to fuel debate.

A further development occurred in April 2015 when a 36-year-old solo trader, Navinder Singh Sarao, was arrested on charges of fraud and market manipulation. Regulators claimed that Sarao was responsible for one of every five sell orders placed during the frenzy. Commentary has been strong that Sarao's activity contributed significantly to the Flash Crash.

Whatever the cause, one thing is for sure: without HFT it wouldn't have happened.

So when did the story behind this whole high frequency thing begin? Believe it or not, when a 21-year-old Hungarian immigrant stepped off a boat onto the shores of New York back in 1965.

THOMAS PETERFFY

Fifty years ago, when Thomas Peterffy first arrived in New York, he was penniless and unable to speak English. Today he's worth more than $5 billion, making him the 60th richest person in the US. He made it all through his ability to get computers talking to each other.

Peterffy's brain was genetically wired for writing computer code, and this innate skill was unlocked when he landed a job as a draftsman at a New York engineering firm. Just two years later he got his first taste of Wall Street.

In 1967 Peterffy switched jobs to Aranyi Associates, a company that set up computer systems for finance houses. With his skill at writing code rapidly developing, Peterffy left Aranyi after three years to write trading algorithms for one of Wall Street's big players, the Mocatta Group. By now it was the early seventies, and Wall Street was getting very interested in computers. Peterffy's skills were about to make him a wealthy man.

In the late seventies pure computer-to-computer trading didn't exist. Humans were still required on the exchange floor to execute stock trades, which meant traders stood toe to toe barking out buy and sell orders. The decisions driving those orders were made by analysts and traders sitting in quiet offices plugging numbers into hand-held calculators and desktop computers.

But Peterffy was destined to change this world forever. He didn't think in terms of markets filled with people. His vision was a market where computers communicated directly with other computers. His was a world of financial markets dominated by code-writing geeks, not testosterone-driven traders.

Peterffy had developed a very successful trading system at Mocatta. And while he was well paid for writing code, he could see how much money his employer was making from his efforts. With no prospect of a business partnership at Mocatta, he decided to strike out on his own, and in 1977 he left the security of his salaried job. Armed with a $2000 computer and a seat on the American Stock Exchange, he set out to beat the market single-handed.

Peterffy knew that financial markets were inefficient at setting prices. After all, they were merely a product of human thought, and humans have deficiencies: they can't maintain focus, they're poor at communicating with each other and they're swayed by emotion. Peterffy knew that by eliminating these inefficiencies he could maintain an edge over the market. He just had to keep finding new ways of replacing humans with machines.

He started by taking a look at the options markets. For hundreds of years, first in Europe and later in the US, options had been priced inefficiently. Calculation was absent, with prices set by a mix of market forces and emotion-fuelled gut feel. But this was all about to change.

In 1973 Fischer Black and Myron Scholes published their now-famous option-pricing formula. While today their formula underpins every option price, the markets were at first slow to adopt it. This was great for Peterffy. He'd developed his own option-pricing model, which meant that, until the rest of the market adopted Black–Scholes, he traded with a distinct advantage. His computer, loaded with option-pricing code, generated fairer than market prices for each of the option series. Armed with pages of printed option price data, Peterffy stepped out onto the trading floor and made a killing. He stood silently waiting for mispriced options to be offered either on the buy or the sell side. When they did, he struck. No-one could work out why this little guy with the strong Hungarian accent was making so much money.

In 1982 Peterffy pushed this advantage even further. He worked out a way to feed market data directly into his computer. Now he didn't have to scour the market for opportunities and manually key information into his computer, a process that was slow and bound to miss plenty of opportunities.

Peterffy leased a Quotron, a machine that delivered stock prices. The operator simply keyed in a single stock code and its stock price would appear on the screen: one code, one price. But Peterffy knew the live feed was capable of delivering multiple prices on multiple stocks; he just needed to hack into the machine to access the information flow. So he pulled the wires from the back of his Quotron and spliced them directly into his computer. Now market data was flowing into his computer like a flood-engorged torrent. The code within his computer sifted rapidly through the multitude of security prices and spat out trading opportunities faster than any room full of analysts could.

Peterffy knew he could make the system even more efficient. After the computer alerted him to profitable trades, he still had to execute them on the trading floor. His dream was to remove the human factor altogether.

If he could only get his computer to suck in the market prices, identify profitable trades and then execute them as well, it would all happen so fast that other players in the market wouldn't know what hit them. His opportunity came in 1987, and it was none too soon, because the rest of the market was starting to work out what he'd been up to.

In 1987 the National Association of Securities Dealers Automated Quotations (NASDAQ) stock market made human traders redundant. Phone trading was replaced by an electronic feed. Someone wanting to make a trade simply read the market price from the screen and then keyed in their order via a keyboard. This is exactly what Peterffy had been waiting for. Now trade execution didn't rely on a phone call or a trading floor. He simply wired his computer directly to a NASDAQ terminal sitting in his office and his computer could suck in information, process it and make the trade. The entire process was done without any human input. No-one but Peterffy had thought of doing this. With no human involvement slowing down the process, he now had the goose that could lay him plenty of golden eggs.

Peterffy was playing the game of arbitrage, and this game is won by speed. It involves seeking out mispricing and then acting on it. If the same security is offered at different prices in two markets, then buy in one and sell in the other, and pocket the risk-free difference. Play it well and you become rich. Trouble is, everyone else is trying to play the same game, which means you need to act on an opportunity before the next guy does. Get there late and you may as well not be in the game at all.

Peterffy's speed meant that in 1987 he made $25 million. In 1988 he made $50 million. Today he is worth $5.4 billion. He is not a speculator — he built this fortune on low-risk and no-risk trades. He's not an investor — he doesn't look for undervalued stocks like Warren Buffett does. Nor has he ever used charts. In fact, he didn't bring any financial insight to the marketplace. He built his fortune by developing new technology — he's a computer geek. His edge came from technologically driven speed, and yet he's not the first to have done it.

THINGS HAVEN'T ALWAYS BEEN SO FAST

Investors in the 18th and early 19th century didn't have Quotrons, telephones or even the telegraph. For more than two hundred years in Europe, and several decades in the US, financial markets operated without the telegraph or the telephone, which meant investors had to congregate to facilitate the rapid transfer of stock market information. Early stock investors typically met in coffee houses, where they had access to newspapers and stock pamphlets. They could also trade information by word of mouth.

So it was coffee houses, not stock exchanges, where many of the world's first stocks were traded. The most renowned were Jonathan's and Garraway's coffee houses in London and the Tontine Coffee House in New York.

When the English stock market began, in the late 17th century, the literacy rate among adult males was about 45 per cent, which meant that for many players the pamphlets and newspapers they could pick up in the coffee houses were of little use. So the news they carried had to be read aloud. An observer of the day commented:

> ... the greatest part of the people do not read books, most of them cannot read at all, but they will gather together about one that can read, and listen to an Observator or Review (as I have seen them in the streets) ...[36]

Communication over long distances was difficult. Over water it relied on ships, and it remained this way until 1866, when the first successful transatlantic cable was laid. The cable reduced communication time between New York and London from at least a week to minutes. Not only had ships been slow but they were also unreliable. In the days before steam even the relative proximity of Europe to England wasn't without its problems. The London-based journal *Tatler* observed that a news blackout between England and the Continent could result 'when a West wind blows for a fortnight, keeping news on the other side of the channel'.

Samuel Morse's telegraph represented a monumental leap in technology, not just for transoceanic communication but also for relaying news across land. Prior to its commercial rollout, which occurred in the 1850s, stock market news was transmitted across land by foot, carrier pigeon, horse and semaphore (a system of flag-waving between men on hilltops). It took half an hour to relay a semaphore message the 150 miles between the stock exchanges of Philadelphia and New York. It meant flag-bearing men spent their day on high ground, telescopes pointed to the adjacent manned vantage points, on the lookout for the next message to pass on.

When the relayed semaphore message finally reached the stock market precinct it was fast, young, athletic messengers (referred to as 'pad shovers') who then moved the information around. One of the most celebrated of Wall Street's pad shovers was William Heath, better known as 'the American Deer'. If Heath were alive today he'd likely be an Olympian. Six foot six inches tall, gaunt and angular with a prodigious drooping moustache, he cut a conspicuous figure on Broad Street and Wall Street as he raced between the Exchange floor and the broking houses. According to an article in *The New York Times*, he was 'as quick in his locomotion as in his operation'.[37]

But Heath's speed was eventually displaced by technology. In late 1867 the first stock ticker, invented by Edward A. Calahan, was placed in the office of broker David Groesbeck & Co. Even within the parameters of the financial district, the superior speed delivered by the electric impulse supplanted that previously delivered by human muscle.

When this new stock ticker was installed, the Groesbeck brokers gathered around in amazement. This quickly changed to amusement at Heath's expense as Wall Street's fastest pad shover burst into their office. In his panting voice he reeled off the prices of recent trades on the stock market floor. But he was too late—ticker tape bearing the same information had already spewed from the stock ticker onto the office floor.

HOW FAST CAN IT GET?

From semaphore to telegraph, from stock ticker to Quotron, from telephone to internet—how fast can things get?

It's easy to imagine the flow of information can't get any faster from here, but that conclusion has been reached before. An amusing quote is this one, written over a hundred years ago by British journalist Francis Wrigley Hirst:

> As a centre of speculative activity New York has no rival. The publicity of its quotations is only matched by the rapidity with which they are circulated to the most distant towns of the American continent. This is all due to the tape machine, called 'the Ticker', an American invention which has been developed in an extraordinary way during the last thirty years ... It is difficult to see, now that the tape machine and the telephone have been perfected, how the invention of aids and facilities to speculation can go much further.[38]

Few people of Hirst's day could have foreseen the development of personal computers, the internet, and fibre-optic and microwave data transmission. You might say, 'That's the point. It was foolish of Hirst to make such a prediction back in 1911.' But to be fair to Hirst, the quantum increase in speed delivered by the telegraph and telephone was on a scale that won't be repeated. Improvements in transmission speed are now being measured in millionths of a second and centre on getting signals travelling in as direct and unhindered a manner as possible. Improvements in microwave technology present the current challenge but where we go from there is uncertain.

Fibre optics took over from copper wire years ago as the preferred method of carrying signals over long distances. Fibre-optic technology sees an electrical signal converted into an optical one and fired down a cable at the speed of light. At the other end it's converted back into an electrical signal. Users of fibre-optic cable seek 'dark fibre' as the gold standard of speed; that's a fibre-optic cable not being utilised by any other users. Once obtained, an investment house seeks to maintain exclusive use of the cable. Before dark fibre can be used, the line needs to be illuminated, which means several million dollars of expenditure on lasers. And that's on top of the millions already committed every year to leasing the line. It's expensive but it guarantees high speeds. And once the line is set up, you hook up your computers loaded with cutting-edge algorithms, step back and watch the trading profits flow.

To give you an idea how far the race for speed has come, consider Dan Spivey and the story of Spread Networks. Spivey dreamed on a big scale, planning to lay a $300 million fibre-optic link between Chicago and New York. Sounds reasonable, until you realise there was a pre-existing fibre link in place. For Spivey's link to be faster than the existing line, it needed to be shorter. Despite fibre-optic signals travelling at the speed of light, it still takes time for light to travel from A to B.[*] Spivey's cable was 100 miles shorter, achieved by laying it along a straighter route than the existing cable. It reduced the transmission time between the two cities by three milliseconds; that's $100 million of expenditure for every one-thousandth of a second shed. The point was, Spivey knew market players couldn't afford not to use his line. Three-thousandths of a second behind the game means you aren't in the game at all.

---

[*] It's actually about two-thirds its theoretical speed because the light signal bounces between the walls of the cable.

Some have quipped that even Spivey's 'as the crow flies' cable could be bettered. One driven through the Earth's crust could be laid straighter because it wouldn't have to follow the Earth's curvature!

THE TAKE-HOME MESSAGE

So far I've described the use of computers in forecasting geopolitical outcomes as per game theory, and I've also described their application in terms of high frequency trading (HFT). But it's important to stress that neither of these applications has delivered a deeper understanding of the workings of the stock market. To date computer, fibre-optic and microwave technology have delivered us speed in execution, but not investment insight.

Will further advances in technology deliver improvements in investment decision making? What about artificial intelligence? Renowned Canadian-American economist John Kenneth Galbraith was sceptical. He wrote:

> The rule is that financial operations do not lend themselves to financial innovation … The world of finance hails the invention of the wheel over and over again, often in a slightly more unstable version.[39]

To date Galbraith remains correct but maybe he was being too dismissive of future possibilities, particularly AI.

What then about those black-box trading and investing tools that are so commonly available today—the ones loaded with software and backed by claims that they will make you rich? I'd strongly recommend that you don't place your faith in commercially available software. Acting blindly on the output of black-box technology means placing your trust in another person's trading or investment philosophy. Most likely it has been developed with the aim of making money for its developer, not for you.

Computers are great for accessing your broker's webpage and placing orders, and they're good for constructing spreadsheets to keep track of your investments. But unless you can hook yours up to a multi-million-dollar fibre-optic cable, and become a high frequency trader, that's about where it should end—for the time being anyway.

Oh, and yes, it's true that you won't find a computer on the desk of the world's most successful investor, Warren Buffett.

Chapter summary

- The adoption of computers by the finance industry delivered hope that the human traits of emotion and incapacity to accurately process and interpret large quantities of information could be overcome.

- Computers have contributed significantly to processing information quickly and to trading on those findings, but advances in technology have been delivering similar benefits for more than 150 years.

- To date, computers have delivered the finance industry speed but not insight.

9

THE EFFICIENT MARKET
HYPOTHESIS

A discussion about investing wouldn't be complete without considering the Efficient Market Hypothesis (EMH). And if, after reading more about the EMH, you reckon it makes sense to you, this might be the last book on investing you ever need to read, because it comes as close as you can get to refuting the arguments in support of market timing, stock picking or technical analysis. The take-home message of the EMH is this: it's not possible to beat the market except by luck, so you may as well invest in an index fund and go on a long vacation. It's a belief held by many people, but I'm not one of them.

Let's start our discussion of the EMH by briefly considering what drives stock prices. After all, they aren't just numbers on automated electronic boards in stock exchange buildings around the world. No, there are forces driving those numbers. These forces are the distillation of multitudes of judgements made by both buyers and sellers of every stock. The buy/sell spread is a stand-off between those buyers prepared to pay the highest price and those sellers willing to sell at the lowest price. It represents investors standing either side of a metaphorical price trench picking each other off as their prey comes close enough to tempt them to strike.

But it's not just the active participants who hold a view on price. Falling in behind them, in the battlefields on each side of the trench, are plenty of potential buyers and sellers who have declared their bid and offer prices. The bids of the inactive buyers aren't high enough, nor are the offers of inactive sellers low enough, to elicit trades until the market price moves. Their hopes are stacked up behind those of the frontrunners in anticipation of the trading front moving towards them.

So who has the best handle on value? Is it the buyers or the sellers? These thoughts were running through the mind of Louis Bachelier when in 1900 he wrote: 'It seems that the market, the aggregate of speculators, at any given instant can believe in neither a market rise nor a market fall, since, for each quoted price, there are as many buyers as sellers.' Or in other words, as Bachelier also said, 'The mathematical expectation of the speculator is zero.'[40]

But I'd suggest that the expectations (as described by Bachelier) of many small investors aren't based on much consideration at all. Some may be selling to raise cash for a new car or a vacation. Others may have developed negative feelings towards the stock they're selling after reading an unfavourable newspaper report, hearing something down at the golf club, or becoming fearful after a recent drop in the share price. Few have necessarily based their decision to sell on a value judgement. So at what price should these investors sell? Since they haven't developed their own view on what the stock is worth, you'd think the most rational thing to do would be simply to sell at the price the market is bidding. That should be as good a price as any to them. But no, many want to sell at higher than the current bid price; they want to wring out an extra cent on the deal. It makes them feel better, like they've won, if the buyer comes to their price. So they set their offer price just above what the buyers are bidding. Then they sit and wait, sometimes only to watch the market move away from them!

And there will be buyers on the other side of the trading trench behaving in a similar manner. Their decision to buy the stock might be based on a different newspaper report, something they heard down at the golf club, or the simple and often unwarranted assumption that because the share price has recently dropped it must be offering good value. They haven't put in a buy order at market, they've just joined other low-ball buyers on the bid side of the spread. No conviction, just the unrealistic belief that squeezing out an extra cent or two will deliver them a great bargain. Whether they get set or not is now in the realms of chance—the chance that the fluctuating stock price will fall to the price they're prepared to pay.

It all sounds like a recipe for disaster, doesn't it? Thousands of people are throwing money into the market without a rational view on what they're buying or selling is actually worth. Fortunately, whatever the process investors go through in deriving these prices, there seems to be a group of guardian angels protecting them from making too many silly decisions. Well, most of the time anyway! Let's explore.

They are being protected by the actions of another group of investors, the 'guardian angels' who spend time considering value. Fortunately, there appears to be enough of them (most of the time) to influence stock prices and so generate fair trading prices. The process by which these prices are established by the better informed investors is called the Efficient Market Hypothesis.

ORIGINS OF THE EMH

While the term was coined in the 1960s, the concept of market efficiency predates this by many years. It isn't clear who first came up with the idea, but this quote from George Gibson in 1889 shows it was long before 20th-century academics:

> [When] shares become publicly known in an open market, the value which they acquire may be regarded as the judgment of the best intelligence concerning them.[41]

Even Dow theorist Robert Rhea believed in the concept of informational efficiency, as the following quote from his 1932 book *The Dow Theory* shows:

> The Averages Discount Everything: The fluctuations of the daily closing prices of the Dow-Jones rail and industrial averages afford a composite index of all the hopes, disappointments, and knowledge of everyone who knows anything of financial matters, and for that reason the effects of coming events (excluding acts of God) are always properly anticipated in their movement. The averages quickly appraise such calamities as fires and earthquakes.[42]

Though the concept had been understood for a long time, it wasn't until the 20th century that academics started undertaking research on market efficiency and crunching some numbers. Bachelier kicked things off in 1900, but his work lay unacknowledged for decades—that is, until its rediscovery in the 1950s, which provided impetus to the growing academic interest in market efficiency. One leading academic at the time was Paul Samuelson, a brilliant economist from the Massachusetts Institute of Technology. The story of how Samuelson rediscovered Bachelier's turn-of-the-century thesis is an interesting one.

It starts with American mathematician Leonard 'Jimmie' Savage. To describe Savage as smart isn't paying him his full due. In his younger days he had compensated for Albert Einstein's deficiencies in mathematics by working as the great physicist's numbers man. Noted economist Milton Friedman described Savage as 'one of the people whom I have met whom I would label a genius'.[43]

In 1954 Savage was nosing around in the Yale Library when he came across a copy of Bachelier's thesis, reproduced in a 1914 French book. As Savage thumbed the pages between its dusty covers, he recognised the significance of Bachelier's work. He also realised there were a number of academics who would be more than interested in Bachelier's ground-breaking formulae. To spread the news of his exciting find he sent out a dozen or so postcards carrying the message (later paraphrased by Samuelson): 'Do any of you economist guys know about a 1914 French book on the theory of speculation by some French professor named Bachelier?'

When Samuelson received his postcard from Savage he went looking for the book in the MIT Library. This is where the story gets a bit confused. In the foreword to a 2006 book entitled *Louis Bachelier's Theory of Speculation*, Samuelson wrote that the library at MIT didn't possess Savage's 1914 reference but it did have something better—a copy of Bachelier's original thesis. Yet in an interview, in the documentary *The Midas Formula: Trillion Dollar Bet*, Samuelson said:

> In the early 1950s I was able to locate, by chance, this unknown book by a French graduate student in 1900 rotting in the library of the University of Paris. And when I opened it up it was as if a whole new world was laid out before me. In fact as I was reading it I arranged to get a translation in English because I wanted every precious pearl to be understood.

No reference to Jimmie Savage in this story. Specifics of how Samuelson actually came across Bachelier's thesis aside, we at least know that the rediscovery of Bachelier's calculations stimulated further interest in the subject of market pricing efficiency. The irony is that when Bachelier first presented his thesis to the Faculty of Sciences of the Academy of Paris on 29 March 1900 he was awarded the second-tier 'mention honorable', insufficient to win him an academic appointment at the university. It seems no-one then recognised what Bachelier's work offered—a mathematical formula that came remarkably close to describing how the market prices of financial securities behave in real life. Bachelier died in 1946, eight years before Savage's rediscovery of his work. He never had the chance to hear the accolades ultimately paid to him.

EUGENE FAMA

The term 'Efficient Market Hypothesis' is attributed to Chicago professor Eugene Fama. He studied, researched and further developed the efficiency concepts already proposed by others and published papers on them in the 1960s and 1970s. Fama's PhD thesis was published in the January 1965 issue of the *Journal of Business*. He concluded, as Bachelier had, that short-term stock price movements were random and therefore unpredictable. He proposed that the market price represented the best estimate of what a stock was worth at any point in time, and that it incorporated all available information about that stock. Any attempt by a lone investor to derive a more appropriate value was nothing more than an exercise in futility.

When Fama's work became public, it struck a chord. Here was a reason why many experienced investors found it impossible to consistently beat the market—something John Bogle, founder of the Vanguard Group, had come to realise years earlier. Bogle was a student at Princeton University back in 1949. Like many students he faced the problem of coming up with an idea for his university research paper. He decided to study the investment returns achieved by professional fund managers, and he found that after fees, and considered as a group, they failed to outperform the broad index. He figured that, since the index could be reproduced without undertaking any form of financial analysis, it would be far simpler to run a fund that aimed to match the index rather than beat it. It was these findings that ultimately led him to establish Vanguard's highly popular index funds.

If the efficient market theorists were correct, then the active fund managers weren't adding any value to the investment process. Of course the fund managers chose not to agree, particularly the successful ones. They'd respond: 'Don't throw averages at me. The results of my fund have been well above average. Just look at the league tables.'

But statistics are a wonderful thing. You don't have to shuffle them around for too long before finding numbers to suit your case. Consider the following. Gather a hundred people in a hall. Ask each to flip a coin one hundred times and record the result of each flip. Tell them the winner is the person who flips the most tails. I'm sure you'll appreciate that at the end of the exercise there won't be 100 flippers who have each flipped 50 heads and 50 tails. Some might have flipped 45 heads and 55 tails, some 45 tails and 55 heads. The laws of normal distribution apply. An outlier of 35 heads and 65 tails might be achieved, so winning the competition. I guess you can see where I'm heading with this one: luck can be obscured by vanity.

Fama and a colleague, Kenneth French, undertook a very interesting study looking at this whole issue of luck and performance. Their paper, 'Luck versus Skill in the Cross Section of Mutual Fund Returns', examined the investment returns delivered by actively managed US mutual funds between 1984 and 2006, focusing on funds invested primarily in US equities.[44]

Their first finding was one many earlier studies had also made — that, taken as a group, there was no evidence that active managers were capable of outperforming the index. And when management fees were included, returns were actually lower than the index delivered. Unfortunately, many people interpret statements like this as meaning that no fund manager is capable of outperforming the market. Clearly this fails to acknowledge that different skill levels can exist within a group. The smartest kid in the class doesn't want to be defined by the average class grade, just as the fund manager who achieves the highest investment return doesn't want to be told they're incapable of beating the market index. But is their outperformance of the market due to skill or luck?

To test this, Fama and French constructed a theoretical distribution of outcomes for a population of funds where chance alone determined the outcome. They ran this simulation 10 000 times and aggregated the results. Just like our hypothetical coin-flipping competition, there were winners and losers. If these results were presented in the real world, some of the fund managers would have been hailed as investing gurus, while some might have gone out of business. The most interesting finding of the study was the similarity between the simulated outcomes and the outcomes delivered by real-life fund managers. So similar were they that it places fund managers' claims of superior performance as being due to superior skill in extreme doubt. It doesn't prove that it's totally due to luck, but it certainly raises significant doubt that it's entirely due to skill.

So if luck can get a fund manager into the winner's circle, the moral of the story is that 'successful' managers need to make a lot of noise when they find themselves on top of the league tables, because it's unlikely they'll stay there for long.*

Interestingly, Fama has also gone on public record as saying that stock analysis isn't a total waste of time, but that very few investors are capable of gaining an edge from doing it. In the following quote he acknowledges that those with significant skill and an ability to think independently are likely to gain an edge:

> If there are many analysts who are fairly good at this sort of thing, however, and if they have substantial resources at their disposal, they help narrow discrepancies between actual prices and intrinsic values and cause actual prices, on the average, to adjust 'instantaneously' to changes in intrinsic values…Although the returns to these sophisticated analysts may be quite high, they establish a market in which fundamental analysis is a fairly useless procedure both for the average analyst and the average investor.[45]

Not everyone would agree with Fama that prices, on the average, 'adjust "instantaneously" to changes in intrinsic values'. Many would say that discrepancies between price and value can endure for longer periods.

MAKING SENSE OF THE EMH

How do we resolve some apparent contradictions that the EMH throws up? How, for example, do stock market crashes occur?

How can stock prices drop by 50 per cent in a matter of months only for everyone to later say it was because the stock market had previously been overpriced? Yet, on the other hand, why is the stock market efficient enough that most market professionals are incapable of beating it?

I like the way Warren Buffett reconciles this apparent contradiction. On referring to the efficient marketeers he said: 'Observing correctly that the market was frequently efficient, they went on to conclude incorrectly that it was always efficient. The difference between these propositions is night and day.'

---

*Other research has actually found this to be the case.

In other words, Buffett becomes more interested in the market when it's characterised by a significant degree of inefficient pricing, but he acknowledges that this is far from all the time. Fischer Black (of Black–Scholes option-pricing model fame) addressed the same issue in a paper titled 'Noise':

> All estimates of value are noisy, so we can never know how far away price is from value. However we might define an efficient market as one in which price is within a factor of 2 of value, i.e., the price is more than half of value and less than twice value. The factor of 2 is arbitrary, of course. Intuitively, though, it seems reasonable to me, in the light of sources of uncertainty about value and the strength of the forces tending to cause price to return to value. By definition, I think almost all markets are efficient almost all the time. 'Almost all' means at least 90%.[46]

The message I hear from the efficient marketeers sounds confused to me. There are those who see it as applying all the time, and there are those who say there are exceptions, times when it doesn't apply. Even Samuelson, a strong advocate of market efficiency, had this to say in his 1974 paper 'Challenge to Judgment':

> It is not ordered in heaven, or by the second law of thermodynamics, that a small group of intelligent and informed investors cannot systematically achieve higher mean portfolio gains with lower average variabilities. People differ in their heights, pulchritude, and acidity. Why not in their P.Q. or performance quotient?[47]

It seems the Buffetts of this world are capable of identifying inefficient stock pricing, which makes sense. For example, could not inefficient pricing occur during periods when markets are driven by extremes of emotion? When people are emotional, they fail to behave rationally. What's more, the process of socialisation leads people to react en masse, leading to widespread irrational behaviour and distortion of market prices. Efficiency should be limited to those times when investor behaviour is on a more rational plane. This helps explain Buffett's observation that markets display efficiency most of the time but not all the time. This is all that the patient investor requires: for the market to be inefficient some of the time, and to use those times to act. It also helps to explain why extended periods of inactivity are the hallmark of successful investors.

Chapter summary

- At most times the valuation of stocks by well-informed investors tends to protect those investors who either haven't formed or are incapable of rationally forming their own view on value.

- The concept of market efficiency has been considered for more than a century.

- Academics and financial market participants embraced Eugene Fama's Efficient Market Hypothesis as outlined in his PhD thesis, published in the January 1965 issue of the *Journal of Business*.

- The concept of market efficiency underpinned the expansion of index funds.

- Research undertaken by Fama and French suggests that luck could play a significant part in determining fund manager performance.

- While market efficiency might explain stock price movement most of the time, it's unlikely to explain stock prices when emotions are strong.

10

TRADER OR INVESTOR?

It's a common question, isn't it? Are you a trader or an investor? Do you try to profit by buying and selling on the short- to medium-term fluctuations in security prices, or do you own securities for the long haul, seeking returns from their capital appreciation and the income they deliver?

To draw an analogy, these two groups are a bit like Chevy drivers and Ford drivers. They pass each other on the highway believing the other guy drove out of the wrong dealership. In investing circles they call themselves 'technical analysts' and 'fundamental analysts'. Each tends to struggle with what's going through the other guy's mind.

Here's an example. A few years back I was sitting down to a dinner after delivering a presentation to a large group of technical analysts. During a lull in conversation a woman leaned across to ask me a question: 'What you told us earlier this evening about analysing stocks might be useful in deciding which are worth buying, but don't you still need technical analysis to determine the right time to buy them?' 'No', I said. 'I buy a stock when it's cheap.' She looked confused. It seemed I was speaking Russian and she was expecting Swahili. I left it at that and asked if she was enjoying her meal.

Here's another example. My business associate recently emailed me an article from a popular investment magazine titled 'Why Intrinsic Value is Rubbish'. He knew the title would catch my attention because it presented three reasons why the author felt the determination of an intrinsic value was a futile exercise. It's worth looking at his arguments, because they demonstrate how disparate views on this subject can be, and how passionately they can be held. The article was written by a trader. The responses, which are my own, are through the eyes of an investor.

Article point 1: If one hundred people calculate intrinsic value there will potentially be 100 different answers.

Correct: But it doesn't deny the process, just the capacity of many participants to undertake it. Nor is it necessary for the intrinsic value determination to be absolute for it to be useful. Different answers within an appropriate range can all be deemed useful.

Article point 2: If shares are trading for $65, and you want to sell for $75, there won't be any buyers.

Correct: So don't sell!

Article point 3: If your valuation is $55, and shares are trading for $65, no one will sell to you.

Correct: So don't buy!

There it was. That was the writer's total justification for intrinsic value being rubbish. The article finished by restating the well-worn justification for using charts: that they distil the opinions and emotions of all market participants. In judging this final statement I was reminded of Ben Graham, who said: 'There are two requirements for success in Wall Street. One you have to think correctly; and secondly you have to think independently.' If Graham is correct then surely your principal source of information shouldn't be a summary of the opinions and emotions of all market participants — unless you choose to do the opposite to what they are doing on the assumption that what they are doing is wrong. But even that doesn't deny the need to perform your own analysis. In its absence how would you know if doing the opposite is the correct thing to do? Being a contrarian does not mean always running against the crowd. It means questioning the actions of the majority, but only acting in a contrary manner if, after considering the facts, you believe it's the correct thing to do.

This article highlights how confusing it can be for newcomers in choosing an appropriate approach to the financial markets. By way of demonstration, consider the following: investors believe that the share price shouldn't be viewed as delivering information but rather as providing potential opportunity, yet traders believe that everything one needs to know about a stock is distilled in the share price!

Let's explore both views a bit further.

JESSE LIVERMORE VS WARREN BUFFETT

Investors pore over financial statements to ensure that the company they are researching has enough money in the bank to pay the bills and enough new business on the horizon to continue delivering a healthy dividend. They aren't totally buried in the past—judgements need to be made regarding the company's future business prospects—but they often rely on historical data to assist in divining the future. Traders who rely on technical analysis to guide their decision making reckon that's all a waste of time. They look for patterns in historical share price charts and study trade volume data. In other words, rather like investors, they use historical data to divine the future.

Which group is right? In an attempt to solve this conundrum let's pit a great trader against a great investor: Jesse Livermore against Warren Buffett.* I'll admit Livermore didn't rely on charts, but a trader he definitely was. Both were/are extremely intelligent men. Both devoted themselves to understanding the market—how it works, what moves it, how to beat it. Livermore was media shy but expressed his views in a book he wrote not long before he died. Buffett hasn't written a book but is far from media shy. Buffett has also outlined

---

*I make no apology for how often these two names appear in this book. Most traders would put Livermore on a pedestal, and most investors would put Buffett on a pedestal. Both brilliant. Livermore started trading at age 15, while Buffett bought his first stock at 11. Both made fortunes doing what they loved—Buffett was just better at hanging on to his.

his investment philosophy through his yearly chairman's letter to Berkshire Hathaway shareholders. So the views of both are on the public record. They operated in different eras — Buffett was 10 years old when Livermore died — and hence they never had the chance to discuss their views face to face. So let's create a hypothetical debate between them.

WHAT IS THE MARKET PRICE TELLING US?

Let's start with how each has interpreted market price. Both have stated that market price ultimately tracks value. Both have stated that sometimes market price reflects reality, sometimes not, but that over time a clear relationship between value and market price exists. No argument here between our combatants.

Would both suggest that factors other than value influence the market price? Yes, you'd get agreement here as well. Both would say the market price regularly deviates from value. The factors causing this are best described as influences on investors' *perceptions* of value. It's a distinction that both Livermore and Buffett have been able to make and capitalise on.

So far, so good. But from here Buffett and Livermore start to disagree. The main point of contention is how they apply their respective beliefs when interacting with the market. And it's a very interesting distinction. So here it is straight from the mouths of our combatants.

First Livermore: 'Markets are never wrong—opinions often are.'[48] Livermore is telling us that market prices are sacrosanct. The trader is trying to outsmart the market, but market prices are what they are and it's pointless disputing them. As he said: 'Just recognise that the movement is there and take advantage of it by steering your speculative ship along with the tide.'[49]

This runs afoul of a principle Buffett has held dear throughout his investment career, one he learned from his mentor, Ben Graham. Graham preached it through his 'Mr Market' allegory, which effectively says that the market doesn't provide you with information, but rather opportunity.

See the price movement, acknowledge it, but don't respect it or join in with it.

The following quote from Graham's bestseller, *The Intelligent Investor*, explains this reasoning:

> If you have formed a conclusion from the facts and if you know your judgment is sound, act on it—even though others may hesitate or differ. You are neither right nor wrong because the crowd disagrees with you. (You are right because your data and reasoning are right.)[50]

Buffett has often repeated in public this quote of Graham's. It is the creed of the value investor that the market price can be wrong, sometimes very wrong, which means the intelligent, Socratic investor is at times presented with the opportunity to profit from crazy prices. So just sit and wait until they're delivered to you.

So which is it? Should the market be considered as periodically wrong, as Buffett believes, or should it never be doubted, as Livermore believed? The environment is the same; it's just a different approach to interacting with it.

Livermore told us how he defined being right or wrong. For him it was black and white: 'The market will tell the speculator when he is wrong because he is losing money.'[51]

Buffett would disagree with this, not always but much of the time. He largely trusts his analysis and typically continues to call the market wrong even when prices are moving against him. There are times when he has stood defiant in the face of paper losses amounting to tens of billions of dollars. Buffett had this to say on the matter: 'Unless you can watch your stockholding decline by 50 per cent without becoming panic stricken, you should not be in the stock market.'

It would seem Livermore's and Buffett's views are irreconcilable. Given a falling stock price, Livermore would be quick on his feet—sell out, admit he's wrong. Buffett would usually stand firm, arguing that the market price has become 'more wrong'. He doesn't perceive them as real losses, just paper losses that will eventually correct themselves.

But, as disparate as their views seem to be, they *can* be reconciled. It's a sentence in chapter 12 of John Maynard Keynes' book *The General Theory of Employment, Interest and Money* that does so:

> If I may be allowed to appropriate the term speculation for the activity of forecasting the psychology of the market, and the term enterprise for the activity of forecasting the prospective yield of assets over their whole life ...

Clearly Livermore is acting as a speculator, betting on shifts in market sentiment and how it impacts market prices. Buffett is relying on the returns delivered by enterprise. The former can deliver trading profits or losses quickly; the latter typically delivers returns over a much longer period.

THE STOP LOSS ORDER

Another point of difference between Livermore and Buffett—and a source of confusion for those approaching the share market for the first time—is the stop loss order.

A stop loss order is a 'no exceptions' sell order established at a predetermined price in the event a purchased stock falls in price. It limits losses should the market move against you. It's preset and automatic so you can't fall prey to the paralysing emotion of hope in wishing a fallen share price back up.

The initial stop loss is typically set when you buy, commonly at 10 to 15 per cent below the purchase price. Many traders then employ a 'trailing stop loss', whereby the predetermined sale price is reset upwards as a stock increases in price. That way gains are locked in. Livermore believed strongly in the stop loss and set his limit at 10 per cent of his purchase price.*

Traders use stop loss orders because it fits in with their trading philosophy, which is based on short-term price movements. Since they are less likely

---

*This originated from his early days trading in Boston's bucket shops. Bucket shop trades operated purely on margin. A trader put up 10 per cent of the value of his trade. If the market price moved against him, the shop automatically wound up his position and took the money. Using the same reasoning Livermore advocated that stock traders should never meet a margin call. He saw the sale as a release from an incorrect decision.

to have a view on value, their aim is to limit losses. However, the stop loss makes less sense to investors. If they're confident in their research, they see a falling share price as manna from heaven—to them buying more stock at a lower price means an even better deal than the previous one.

But there's a third type of behaviour, and this one is dangerous. Many don't hold any conviction regarding a stock's value but still choose to buy more stock after it's fallen in price. They support their actions with comments like, 'Hey, if I buy more now it will lower my average buy-in price, then it will take less of a share price recovery for me to get out even.' Problem is, the stock market can't hear their hope. Livermore had very strong views about this process of 'averaging down': 'It is foolhardy to make a second trade, if your first trade shows you a loss. Never average losses. Let that thought be written indelibly on your mind.'[52]

So what should the budding market participant do? Sell or buy when a stock price falls? To answer this question you need first to be clear in your own mind whether you're a trader or an investor, because the stop loss is a trader's tool, not an investor's. Don't fall prey to the following logic: 'Sure I'm a value investor. I select stocks by studying the financials in my search for value, but if the price drops I'm out.'

If you're a trader then use a stop loss. But if you call yourself an investor and you use them, please save everyone the pain. You're not behaving as an investor would. An investor might choose to sell after a stock has fallen, but the decision would be based on a review of the facts, not because a stop loss has been triggered.

Buffett took many of his cues from Ben Graham, who was more a contemporary of Livermore than Buffett was. So how did Graham feel about Livermore's activity and how did Livermore feel about Graham's? This from Graham:

> We think that, regardless of preparation and method, success in trading is either accidental or impermanent or else due to a highly uncommon talent. Hence the vast majority of stock traders are inevitably doomed to failure.[53]

So Graham thought most traders were one step removed from gamblers. This from Livermore:

> From my viewpoint, the investors are the big gamblers. They make a bet, stay with it, and if it goes wrong, they lose it all. The speculator

might buy at the same time. But if he is an intelligent speculator, he will recognise—if he keeps records—the danger signal warning him all is not well. He will, by acting promptly, hold his losses to a minimum and await a more favorable opportunity to re-enter the market.[54]

He said, she said. Who do you believe?

Well, as they say in the classics, 'the proof of the pudding is in the eating'. Buffett's principles have allowed him to become the wealthiest man in the world. Livermore lost the lot (so much for 'holding his losses to a minimum'). A broken Livermore ended his life by placing a gun to his head at the age of 63; he'd made and lost a fortune several times over. And while it can never be known how much of Livermore's success was due to skill and how much to luck,* Graham was spot on in one respect: his description of success in trading as 'impermanent'. While Livermore wasn't completely broke when he died in 1940, he had long since lost most of the $100 million trading profit he'd made in the wake of the 1929 Crash.

'What to do?' asks the budding market participant. Am I to be a trader or an investor? Am I to be guided by Livermore or Buffett? Both with brilliant minds, both with a wealth of experience. The question remains, is there any way to reconcile these opposing views?

Fortunately there is. The first thing is to recognise that the two disciplines are built on similar premises. Both acknowledge that the market is driven by perceptions of value, and that these perceptions can become distorted at various times due to varying degrees of irrational behaviour. Investors and traders agree on this point; they differ principally in execution.

An investor will try to exclude behavioural issues from their analysis. They are the only sane person, watching the lunatics in the asylum, observing them but seeing no need to understand them. A trader also watches the lunatics in the asylum but wants to get amongst them, to understand them. What's running through the lunatics' minds holds the key to the short-term direction of the market. As long as the trader keeps their wits about them and stays quick on their feet, they can outsmart the lunatics. They're not interested that the slow-moving pendulum of value will eventually correct market prices.

---

*The same accusation has been thrown at Buffett.

They want to get on board the pendulum now and ride it profitably for a while.

It's as if the trader can understand the lunatics—appreciate them, empathise with them—but also shut them out, maintain a sane state and profit from the whole experience. The investor remains detached, remote and unsympathetic—allowing the lunatics to head off in any direction while confident in the knowledge they'll eventually come around to the value position, so correcting market prices and vindicating his position.

THROWING CHARLES DOW INTO THE MIX

I mentioned in chapter 7 that Charles Dow saw the stock market as having three forms of movement: long-term 'primary' movement (bull or bear), typically remaining in place for years; medium-term 'secondary' movement, typically running between 10 and 60 days; and short-term 'daily' movement, represented by random, erratic moves of no significance or informational value—market noise. It's interesting to consider how traders and investors operate within Dow's framework.

Dow would see some traders as performing an act of futility—trying to profit from the random and erratic daily movements of the market. There will be winners and losers but none of it due either to skill or a lack of it. Both Livermore and Buffett would agree that 'day trading', as it's called, is a waste of time. Livermore was a trader, but not a day trader. He was always looking for the bigger moves because he knew the little ones were unreadable.

Now to a consideration of the medium-term 'secondary' moves described by Dow, those occurring within a longer-term bull or bear market move. This is the space where Livermore was most active. While he wasn't a day trader, neither did he lock himself down to a long-term view on the market's direction. That is, he didn't like being tagged as a bull or a bear; these were expressions used by the press. He preferred to remain flexible, to move on either the buy or the sell side depending on the signals the market was delivering at any particular time.

Buffett would care very little for any of this discussion. Market direction and sentiment might be of interest to others but his interest lies in whether value is on offer. Trying to read shifts in sentiment doesn't tell him that. He simply sees the market price and his price; his senses remain immune to any other inputs.

So whether you choose to become an investor or a trader, the following applies:

- Success doesn't come easily, whichever approach is used.

- Both require discipline, training and experience.

- Both require control of one's own emotions.

- Neither approach will produce success all the time. It's like the house in a casino. The odds are set in a casino so that patrons can and do win, though the casino wins more often. Similarly, successful investors and traders don't aim to be right all the time but do aim to tip the odds of winning in their favour.

- Neither approach is applicable all the time. Experienced traders and investors alike describe extended periods when activity is futile.

- Both disciplines work best when the market is primed with emotion. Livermore had his biggest wins in the wake of the 1907 and 1929 crashes, while Buffett bought bargains in the wake of the 1973–74, 1987 and 2008 financial crises.

- Success using either approach typically involves a mix of skill and luck. It's not possible to know for sure how much each contributes to any outcome.

It's important to appreciate and understand the differences between the two skill sets associated with trading and investing. I've heard it said on several occasions that it makes sense to draw from both disciplines, and that increasingly investors/traders are working with a bag of tools derived from both. If you choose to do this then be careful, because bringing the wrong tools together can create a potentially dangerous mix (as we saw with the discussion of stop loss orders). Personally, I can't see any need to mix the two.

Chapter summary

- The at times contradictory approaches undertaken by traders and investors can confuse newcomers to the financial markets.

- Most traders and investors rely heavily on historical information when making decisions about the future.

- Traders and investors generally agree that stock prices tend to track the value of their underlying companies over time and that stock prices can diverge from value over the short to medium term.

- Investors attempt to identify mispricing and use it as their opportunity to buy or sell—they seek enterprise value. Traders act as speculators, attempting to identify market sentiment and to capitalise on the short- to medium-term movements of stocks or the market.

- Traders use stop loss orders and sell when a stock falls in price by a predetermined amount. Investors don't use stop loss orders. In fact, they're likely to buy in a falling market as long as their view on the investment merit of the stock remains intact.

- It's dangerous to buy more of a falling stock when your sole reason for doing so is a hope that the price will recover.

11

REALISTIC EXPECTATIONS OF RETURNS

I want now to switch the discussion to a very important topic—realistic expectations of investment returns. It's an important discussion, because for some reason many investors assume they're going to achieve outstanding returns simply because they're attempting to do so. It's a bit like that survey in Sweden that found that 90 per cent of drivers considered they had above-average driving skills. If it were true then it would definitely pay to get the other 10 per cent off the road quick smart!

The reality is investment returns are largely pedestrian. Even so, the wonders of compounding mean the patient investor can achieve a great return over time. If they're capable of achieving annual returns a few percentage points above average, then over time they'll achieve an outstanding result. So let's get a handle on what those realistic expectations should be.

In late 2009 I attended an investment expo. It was an interesting day but unfortunately the organisers let a spruiker up on stage. Maybe he'd curried favour with the event organisers—certainly, the large sales stand he'd hired at the expo to peddle his 'investment product' must have cost him a pretty penny.

He enthusiastically told us he knew how to make guaranteed profits from trading options and SPI futures contracts. The secret was locked up in his options trading software. And with pretty-coloured graphs projected on the auditorium wall he showed us how to make bucketloads of money by simply following the trading cues his software delivered. After winding up his presentation, he headed back to his sales stand. People followed him over and started swarming around the stand like bees around a honeypot. They stood three deep as attractive young saleswomen signed them up to year-long contracts.

I also went over to his sales stand, but purely out of interest. I listened to a spiel from one of the contract-bearing saleswomen and then left, shaking my head in disbelief. This was the claim: the trading software would deliver annual returns of 200 per cent, tripling your money every 12 months.

Several months later I was invited to deliver a series of lectures in capital cities down the east coast of Australia. The topic was asset allocation, and the theme of the day was to answer a hypothetical question: how best to invest $1 million? I was up on stage straight after lunch. And with my tongue very much in my cheek I started my presentation by telling the audience about the options trading software I'd seen earlier in the year:

> You guys have wasted your time listening to the earlier presentations today. You should have put me on this stage first thing this morning. I would have had the whole day's proceedings wrapped up by 10 o'clock this morning and then we could have all gone home. What to do with your $1 million is answered simply. Just invest using some options trading software I recently stumbled across. It triples your money every year—guaranteed, I was told. Which means in 10 short years your $1 million would be transformed into $59 billion and you'd be rubbing shoulders with the wealthiest people in the world. You might even be worth more than Warren Buffett and Bill Gates, because those two guys are pretty busy giving their money away at the moment. In 20 years you'd be worth $3500 trillion, enough to pay out the US national debt 240 times over. So ring the US President now. Tell him not to lose any more sleep worrying about that infernal debt problem. Tell him you've got it all worked out. Options trading? Sounds too risky to your ears? Okay then, rather than a million dollars just put in $10 of your money. I'm sure you all feel more comfortable about that. And in 20 years you'll be worth a more conservative $35 billion!

The audience got the point.

That day I also spoke of returns on property—that most Australians had unrealistic expectations regarding the long-term returns property delivers. This certainly wasn't the case in the US, given their relatively recent subprime meltdown. But Australian property prices had passed through the subprime crisis unscathed, and at the time of the presentation Australian house prices had experienced over two decades of capital growth at a rate that had significantly outstripped the national inflation rate. In fact, over the prior 24 years the real (inflation-adjusted) capital gain on property had averaged 3.6 per cent per year. That figure didn't raise an eyebrow in the auditorium. Three point six per cent; maybe some people thought the figure was too low. I knew it was correct, and I also knew it was outrageously high by long-term standards.

I went on to discuss my favourite property study, that of Piet Eichholtz from Maastricht University in the Netherlands. His study looked at property prices on Amsterdam's Herengracht, or 'Gentlemen's Canal'. He had access to over 300 years of meticulously kept sales records on the *same* houses; hence it provided a constant quality index virtually unheard of in any other real estate study. Eichholtz looked at property price movements between 1628 and 1973 and found that the annual geometric inflation-adjusted capital gain was a mere 0.2 per cent. Doesn't sound much but it sits within the realm of what one should realistically expect. A greater rate was unlikely because it would have meant the properties had become unaffordable — clearly something that can't happen in a functional marketplace.

Eichholtz found that property prices:

- were volatile (capital growth in sub-periods of the 345 years was quite irregular) and

- showed little *real* (inflation-adjusted) capital growth when viewed over the long term.

The study also showed there were prolonged periods when real property prices didn't go up at all. For example, if a single family had owned a Herengracht property during the 100-year period between the 1850s and the 1950s, not one inflation-adjusted dollar would have been made. The point my Australian audience was missing is that residential property is very much about affordability: no buyers, no sales. Affordability is ultimately linked to people's incomes, and hence to inflation. The relationship between house prices and affordability is also linked to mortgage rates. For example, the affordability of an interest-only $200 000 mortgage at a rate of 10 per cent is the same as that of a $400 000 mortgage at 5 per cent. Hence the tendency is for house prices to receive a boost when interest rates fall and to take a hit when interest rates rise. But, over the very long term, the influence of fluctuating interest rates on prices tends to be a zero-sum game.

The fact is that Australia had seen interest rates fall from 15.5 per cent to 6.5 per cent in the 24 years preceding my presentation. This meant it was possible for the inflation-adjusted price of a house to double without introducing any additional mortgage stress to debt-funded property owners. And that's exactly what had happened. Property prices had doubled in real terms over the preceding 24 years (hence the 3.6 per cent annual real growth). It was a powerful explanation as to why Aussie property prices had risen in real terms.

Some members of the audience were still having trouble digesting Eichholtz's long-term capital appreciation rate of 0.2 per cent. They felt more comfortable with the Aussie figure of 3.6 per cent. I explained it was absolutely ludicrous to expect property prices to continue to appreciate at 3.6 per cent real over the long term. And to demonstrate I plugged 3.6 per cent into the 345-year Herengracht example. At an annualised real increase of 3.6 per cent, a modern-day citizen of Amsterdam would need to pay nearly 200 000 times the real (inflation-adjusted) price for a Herengracht house that a citizen did back in the 1620s! This means that if a Herengracht house cost the equivalent of $500 000 (in today's money) back in 1628 then today it would cost $100 billion. Ridiculous expectations (3.6 per cent) require ridiculous answers. One audience member remained unconvinced: 'The figure you gave of 3.6 per cent was for 24 years', he said. 'That's long term in my book. I'm not going to be around in 345 years.' It seemed my blunt message was just too subtle for him. So I moved on.

I regularly hear of unrealistic expectations of share market returns: investors who expect consistent annual returns in the order of 20 to 30 per cent and are impatient to know when the share market will make them rich. As a friend of mine likes to say, 'Patience, Grasshopper.'

When compared with other asset classes, such as property, the share market has historically delivered exceptional returns. There are no rules about what those returns will be in the future, but if the past has been any guide then expect long-term returns more in the order of 10 per cent per annum (with dividends plus capital returns), and 7 per cent if you adjust those returns for inflation. Given the heady prices paid for stocks in 2015 returns are likely to be lower than this over the medium term.

Higher-than-average returns could be delivered if you develop market-beating skills—or are just plain lucky.

Chapter summary

- Annual investment returns from all asset classes are largely pedestrian when considered on a geometric average basis over a long period.

- The wonders of compounding mean the patient investor can achieve a good return given sufficient time.

- Realistic expectations of long-term capital gains on real estate (excluding rental returns) should be aligned with inflation.

- Real estate prices can and do underperform and outperform the inflation rate during sub-periods, and sometimes for decades.

- Realistic long-term stock market returns should sit in the medium to high single digits (inflation-adjusted capital gains plus dividends).

- Returns exceeding average returns might be due to skill, luck or a combination of both.

Part II

STOCK SCREENS AND VALUE METRICS

12

WHERE TO START: STOCK SCREEN OR TRIAD OF ANALYSIS?

In Part I we considered some very important broad issues, such as:

- Is it possible to time the market?

- Is economic forecasting effective?

- Do charts deliver useful information?

- Do computers improve our investing ability?

- Does it make more sense to trade or to invest?

- Is it possible to beat the market other than by luck?

It's important to sort these issues out early on, because they guide the way you interact with the stock market in much the same way that philosophy, religion and your moral compass guide the way you conduct your life.

I hope you're starting to develop your own broad (and rational) views on how to interact with the market. Now it's time for a major shift in direction. I'm going to take a side in the trading/investing debate: from now on I'll consider only the investment process, rather than the trading process (I believe that traders run a high risk of failing in their efforts). In doing so I'll take the same approach as I did in Part I; that is, I'll consider which approaches to investing appear to work and which don't—and the rationale behind my arguments on this score.

Let's first consider where we should *start* the investment process. There are two broad views: top down or bottom up. The top-down approach looks at three tiers: first the economy, then the business sector, then the individual company. The bottom-up approach begins with analysis at the individual company level. We'll now look at both methods, starting with the top-down approach.

STOCK ANALYSIS AT THE ECONOMY LEVEL

If you're of the top-down faith, the first step is making a call on where the economy is heading. Getting a handle on this is supposedly your key to committing investment funds at a favourable point in the economic cycle. If the outlook for the economy is good, then stocks are likely to benefit.

Given the damning conclusions I reached in chapters 3 and 4 regarding economists' abilities to forecast, you might think this discussion leads to a foregone conclusion—that I might simply state that starting your stock analysis with a view on the economy is a waste of time. And you'd be right.

But before I totally leave this subject I want to canvass the opinion of one of the greatest economists of the 20th century, John Maynard Keynes. Looking to Keynes for an opinion is doubly relevant because he was an extremely successful investor. Now you'd think that, being an economist, Keynes would be batting on the side of the top-down approach, but the following might surprise you.

Keynes managed the endowment of King's College at Cambridge University, with discretion over the management of part of the portfolio. The part he controlled beat the performance of the British common stock market index by an average of eight percentage points per year from 1921 to 1946.[55] It's a phenomenal result, which, if repeated today, would guarantee him status as one of the world's leading hedge fund managers.

Early on Keynes used a top-down approach, looking to time his investments in stocks, bonds and cash according to macroeconomic indicators. This produced lacklustre results, so he re-engineered his approach and, from the early 1930s onward, used a bottom-up approach. He selected individual stocks based on their business merit, buying when the market offered them at a discount to their intrinsic value. His views on the economy now took the back seat.

Keynes' year-by-year results show that he underperformed the UK equity index in only six of the 25 financial years he managed the fund—and four of those years were before he switched to a bottom-up approach. Before the switch he was actually lagging the index by a significant margin. So when he commenced his bottom-up stint he was starting with a handicap, yet he trounced the index when the whole period is considered.

STOCK ANALYSIS AT THE BUSINESS SECTOR LEVEL

Let's now move on to the second tier of top-down analysis—the business sector level.

Four hundred years ago, when brokers were congregating at the world's first organised stock market, in Amsterdam, the hottest sector wasn't biotech or internet stocks. It was trade between Europe and the East Indies in spices and soft commodities. Later, in the mid-19th century, it was transport—first canals then railroads. Later still, when the Dow Jones Industrial Index was created in the US in 1896, it included what were considered to be the 12 most important companies listed on the New York Stock Exchange, companies such as the American Cotton Oil Company, Distilling & Cattle Feeding Co. and the United States Leather Company—all now defunct.

Which all goes to show that sectors come ... and then they go. It's also why I prefer to seek out companies in sectors that are more likely to keep on keeping on. Food's a good start—as far as I can figure, people are going to keep eating the stuff for a fair time yet. But longevity is not in itself enough for a sector to be considered attractive; it also needs to be profitable. During the Roaring Twenties, leading up to the 1929 Crash, the fledgling airline and motorcar industries were viewed as the darling sectors of the age. Sure, both have prospered and grown into mature industries, but airline and motor stocks have proven to be anything but good investments over the years.

A similar but more recent example is the tech sector. While the public has taken to the internet like a duck to water, plenty of money has been lost on internet stocks. A strong sector doesn't automatically deliver great investments. Ben Graham acknowledged this fact in *The Intelligent*

Investor: 'Obvious prospects for physical growth in a business do not translate into obvious profits for investors.'

So how does that work? It seems counterintuitive. Why doesn't sector growth automatically translate into earnings growth for companies operating in that sector? Here's the answer.

Remember when plasma TVs cost $10 000? Now they cost 500 bucks. Mobile phones, electronic gear, computers—imagine the profits companies producing them would now be reaping if they'd been able to keep prices steady? The reality is, where competition between manufacturers is strong it's the consumer who benefits, not the business owners. Falling production costs are typically passed on as lower prices on the shop floor. Only a producer delivering something unique, something the competition can't replicate, is able to stand firm against the tide of price deflation.

So where does that leave us with the second tier—the business sector? As a screen for stock selection it has two uses:

We want to invest in business sectors that will be around for a long time yet. Rolls of Kodak photographic film, sold in little yellow boxes, were once all the go, but there's not much call for them now.

Appreciating the dynamics of a sector will assist you in judging how the company you're studying will prosper or falter as it performs in its competitive environment.

The take-home message? Keeping an eye on the business sector can be helpful, but never base your decision to buy a stock solely on the fact it's operating in a growth sector. You want the company you've selected to be both profitable and capable of maintaining that profitability, not to simply operate in a sector that's growing.

Which brings me to the third tier—analysis at the company level—where 'top-down' analysis ends, and 'bottom-up' analysis gets started.

FROM THE BOTTOM UP — STOCK ANALYSIS AT THE COMPANY LEVEL

May 2012 was the first time I was fortunate enough to hear Warren Buffett speak in person. I was in Omaha, Nebraska, attending the annual general meeting of Berkshire Hathaway, the company he heads. At the time Buffett was 81 years old and Charlie Munger, his able lieutenant, was 88. I figured I'd better get over there to see them because I didn't know how many AGMs they had left. Buffett and Munger were on stage for several hours fielding questions from shareholders. Some questions related to Berkshire, some were about life in general, and many covered general principles of investing. Much of it I had either read before or watched on cable, but when you're in their presence the words carry an impact no book or TV interview can deliver.

Buffett has an ability to distil complex issues into a couple of sentences — the sign of a good teacher. And something he said at that meeting seems particularly relevant to the current discussion. It related to what a prospective investor should aim to learn. He put it this way:

> Don't get too hung up on mathematics. Investing is not that complicated. It's all about valuing businesses. So understand which businesses you can value and which you can't. If I was running a business school I would teach only two subjects: how markets move and how to value businesses.

Expanding on Buffett's advice, you can develop an appreciation of how markets move from a thorough reading of financial history. How to value a business takes more work. Analysis at the company level attempts to answer two questions. Firstly, is the company going to go broke? And, secondly, are the returns it's likely to deliver worth telling your friends about? Both of these — risks and returns — are intimately linked with valuation. So it is at the company level that analysis really matters. It doesn't deny the need to understand the dynamics of the sector within which the company is operating, but these are so closely related that I consider them as one.

STOCK SCREENS

So if we commence our analysis at the company level, the question remains: how do we choose which companies to look at? There's a huge number of them out there and time doesn't allow us to research every one of them in depth. Is there a simple tool we can use to eliminate the subpar companies right from the start? Fortunately there is, and with computers the process is made even easier. I'll explain what I mean.

My business associate recently rang me with a request.

'Hey Mike, we have to get some figures together for our upcoming presentation on the principles of selecting stocks. Could you perform a simple screen to show how the stock selection process starts?'

'No worries', I said. 'But you realise there are over 2000 stocks listed on the ASX, so it could take me a while.'

'Don't use your own screen', he replied. 'Just run a proprietary screen through the computer. We're only using it as an example.'

These are the results my computer delivered:

Total number of companies listed on the Australian Securities Exchange: 2029

Of these 2029, how many have debt levels defined by a debt to equity ratio of <1 and an interest coverage ratio >3 times? *Answer:* 169

Of these 169, how many achieved a return on equity last year >15 per cent? *Answer:* 77

Of these 77, how many demonstrated positive earnings growth over the last four years? *Answer:* 44.

We have now quickly whittled our unmanageable total of 2029 companies down to a manageable 44 and in the process produced a list of companies to take a closer look at. It's important for me to mention that this screen isn't one I either use or necessarily advocate. I simply present it here as an example of how a screen operates. The reality is that there are many, many balance sheet, profitability and value metrics out there that can be incorporated into a screen, and while I can't possibly discuss all of them I do want to discuss some.

So let's take a close look at four popular metrics, namely:

1   price earnings ratio

2   earnings growth rate

3   price to book ratio

4   dividend yield.

My reason for selecting just these four will become clearer as you read on. Many investors place a lot of trust in them, so over the next four chapters let's see whether that trust is justified.

Chapter summary

- Top-down analysis is a three-tier stock selection process that considers firstly the state of the economy, then the business sector and finally the individual company.

- Economists have a poor record of predicting the future state of the economy. Hence the first stage of top-down analysis, the economy, is the least useful.

- The second tier, the business sector, is worth considering. However, when barriers to the entry of new participants are low, competition tends to be strong and profit margins low. So never base your decision to buy a stock solely on the fact it's operating in a growth sector.

- The most effective level of analysis is at the individual company level.

- A suitable combination of balance sheet and income statement based metrics provides a useful screen for eliminating subpar investment opportunities.

13

DON'T ACCEPT THE PE RATIO AT FACE VALUE

The word *ratio* conjures up images of high-school mathematics — the ratio of men to women, of mobile phones or motor vehicles per household, and so on. In finance, ratios are used extensively to get a feel for the risk, profitability and relative value of investments. For example, we might look at the price of an investment relative to its annual earnings or how much debt the company carries relative to its total assets. There are many, many different ratios used by analysts. I want to kick off with one of the most popular — the price earnings (PE) ratio. As a value indicator it's used more than any other. So is its popularity warranted? This chapter might hold some surprises for those who place a lot of faith in the PE.

The PE ratio is easy to calculate. Just divide the current share price by the most recently reported earnings per share (EPS). Investors commonly use it as a measure of relative value; that is, a stock with a low PE is considered cheap and a stock with a high PE is considered expensive. At best this relationship is a weak one. The reality is that there are plenty of low-PE stocks selling at excessively high prices, and some high-PE stocks that are bargains.

This whole relative value thing goes back to when the PE was first developed. It was adapted from a property valuation tool used centuries ago by England's landed gentry. Commercial property was valued by capitalising its annual rental stream — that is, by taking the property's annual rental and multiplying it by an appropriate PE to come up with the property's value. They didn't call it a 'PE' then. Instead it was referred to as 'number of years purchase', but really it meant the same thing. If a property had a number of years purchase of 10, it meant the property was valued at 10 times its annual rental stream.

Doing this is okay when an earnings stream is steady or growing at a relatively steady rate. But these are characteristics more typical of property than of stocks. It's an entirely different story when you apply the same logic to the stock market. That's because companies vary widely in terms of their risks, returns and rates of earnings growth, both between themselves and through time. And it's this inescapable reality that throws one very big spanner into the whole stock PE relative value story.

WHAT'S WRONG WITH THE PE?

Most investors are aware of one very obvious problem with the PE: the numerator (the current market price) is forever changing, but the denominator (the earnings per share) remains fixed between reporting periods. This means any price-sensitive information released since the last earnings report will be incorporated into the numerator but not the denominator. So a recently announced profit downgrade will likely see the share price drop and the conventionally calculated PE also drop. This has the potential to deliver a false signal that the stock is cheap even if it isn't. In an attempt to overcome this problem, the PE is often calculated using estimates of future earnings rather than those last reported. But this means dusting off the crystal ball, with all the inherent problems that introduces.

This criticism of the PE is commonly understood, so let's dig a bit deeper, because the PE has some further limitations that are less obvious. To demonstrate let's begin with a formula used by valuation theorists to justify a stock's price to book ratio.

$$\frac{P}{B} = \frac{ROE - g}{r - g}$$

where:

- P = current market share price
- ROE = return on equity (or return on book value)
- g = annual growth in earnings
- B = book value per share
- r = required rate of return (discount rate).

Since earnings per share (E) = (ROE) × (book value per share), dividing both sides of the above equation by ROE provides a platform for discussing the variables impacting the PE ratio.

$$\frac{P}{E} = \frac{ROE - g}{ROE(r - g)}$$

If you look at the right-hand side of the equation you'll see that the PE is influenced by perceptions of the stock's future ROE, growth in earnings per share (g) and the discount rate (r). The discount rate is in turn influenced by the inherent risk of the investment and prevailing interest rates. It's extremely unlikely two stocks will ever display the same mix of these parameters so, strictly speaking, the PEs of any two stocks shouldn't be used to compare their relative value. To explore this even further I've used the above formula to construct table 13.1 (overleaf).

To calculate a number for each cell of the table I've assumed a discount rate (r) of 10 per cent. Clearly there is no single discount rate applicable to all investments, but were I to generate additional tables, each with a different discount rate, there would be too many tables for a sensible discussion. Each of the PEs in the table represents the 'fair value' PE a stock should carry for each ROE (y-axis) and rate of earnings growth (x-axis) combination. For example, a stock with a perpetual earnings growth of 6 per cent and a perpetual ROE of 12 per cent should carry a PE of 12.50 to be judged fair value.

Table 13.1: fair PE for different return on equity and earnings growth

		Earnings growth								
		1%	2%	3%	4%	5%	6%	7%	8%	9%
Return on equity (ROE)	1%	0	–	–	–	–	–	–	–	–
	2%	5.56	0	–	–	–	–	–	–	–
	3%	7.41	4.17	0	–	–	–	–	–	–
	4%	8.33	6.52	3.57	0	–	–	–	–	–
	5%	8.89	7.50	5.71	3.33	0	–	–	–	–
	6%	9.26	8.33	7.14	5.56	3.33	0	–	–	–
	7%	9.52	8.93	8.16	7.14	5.71	3.57	0	–	–
	8%	9.72	9.38	8.93	8.33	7.50	6.25	4.17	0	–
	9%	9.88	9.72	9.52	9.26	8.89	8.33	7.41	5.56	0
	10%	10.0	10.0	10.0	10.0	10.0	10.0	10.0	10.0	10.0
	11%	10.10	10.23	10.39	10.61	10.91	11.36	12.12	13.64	18.18
	12%	10.19	10.42	10.71	11.11	11.67	12.50	13.89	16.67	25.00
	13%	10.26	10.58	10.99	11.54	12.31	13.46	15.38	19.23	30.77
	14%	10.32	10.71	11.22	11.90	12.86	14.29	16.67	21.43	35.71
	15%	10.37	10.83	11.43	12.22	13.33	15.00	17.78	23.33	40.00
	16%	10.42	10.94	11.61	12.50	13.75	15.63	18.75	25.00	43.75
	17%	10.46	11.03	11.76	12.75	14.12	16.18	19.61	26.47	47.06

USING THE PE TO SELECT STOCKS

Consider the relative value of two companies: company A has a PE of 9.72, while company B has a PE of 6.25. Both operate in the same industry. Because you've heard somewhere it's okay to use the PE as a basis of comparison when companies are operating in the same industry, you've decided company B, with the lower PE, is the one to buy. Strengthening your conviction is its higher anticipated rate of earnings growth (you've also heard that earnings growth is a good thing).

Well, you've just fallen into the 'PE trap'. Let's look more closely at the two companies. Refer to table 13.1 as we do.

- Company A is expected to deliver an ROE of 8 per cent and earnings growth of 1 per cent per year. The market has it on a PE of 9.72. That's a fair value.

- Company B is also expected to deliver an ROE of 8 per cent but higher earnings growth of 6 per cent. It's on a PE of 6.25. That's also a fair value.

The reality is that company B's lower PE doesn't represent unrecognised value at all. In fact the low PE the market has pinned on it is totally justified. The key to understanding this lies in the low anticipated ROE for both companies. The return of 8 per cent is lower than the 10 per cent you are demanding. If it were higher than 10 per cent, growth would be a good thing. But because it is lower it's a bad thing.

'How can growth in earnings be a bad thing?' you ask. It seems counterintuitive that growing earnings could ever be a bad thing, but the reason is that future earnings are being discounted at a greater rate than they're growing. So for every dollar management is retaining and reinvesting in the business, investors are receiving less than a dollar back (in today's value). In fact, in this example, in one year's time the reinvested dollar in company A (which earned 8 per cent and was discounted back to present value by 10 per cent) would be worth only 98.2 cents in today's money, and in two years it would be worth 96.4 cents. Once you understand this important nuance you'll make better investment decisions. More about this in the next chapter.

USING THE PE AS A SCREEN

In the previous chapter I talked about using metrics to construct a stock screen. So let's see how useful the PE is in this role.

Investors would typically screen for companies with low PEs, but this is a bit like fishing with a leaky net: a lot of good fish (that is, companies) will pass through the holes in the net. Similarly, you're going to haul in a lot of fish you wish had stayed in the ocean. The companies you will miss are those carrying a high PE that they are entitled to carry — those demonstrating high growth and an ROE well in excess of your required rate of return. But your net will haul in companies you don't want — those with low PEs that are justified or should be even lower.

BOB SHILLER AGAIN

Back in chapter 7, I described how US economist Bob Shiller uses an average PE (called the 'CAPE ratio') to gauge whether the market is cheap, expensive or fairly priced. This is not applied to individual stocks but rather to the entire S&P 500 index.

The long-term average for the 140-plus years that Shiller's composite PE ratio covers is 16.6. It peaked in 1901, 1929, 1966, late 1999/early 2000 and 2007 (and at the time of writing is again at pre-GFC levels). If you're a financial historian you'll recognise these past years as bull market peaks, so it looks like Shiller's PE is telling us something.

While his PE is not predictive, it does provide a relative feel for market value at any point in time. Factoring in the market's tendency for mean reversion, progressively lower than average PEs indicate an increasing chance the market will correct upwards, and progressively higher than average PEs indicate an increasing chance the market will correct downwards. Comparing his ratio at any time with the long-term average of 16.6 assists us in making that value judgement. It's an objective grounder that helps us resist the trap of getting caught up in excessive market optimism or pessimism.

Shiller's PE delivers information that's different from the information delivered by the PE of a single stock. A couple of examples will help explain.

Imagine you're trying to decide which of two people is the younger. You can't see or hear them; all you have is information regarding their height. You decide to select the shorter of the two since there's a relationship between age and height. Problem is, height doesn't define someone's age. You might be comparing a 13-year-old Michael Jordan with a 40-year-old Danny DeVito.

Consider a different situation. You're told the average height of a large group of US citizens, all of whom are the same age, is 160 cm. You're also told the average height of another large group, all of whom are the same age, is 180 cm. Which group represents the younger citizens? There is a very high chance it's the first group. Both of these examples use information about height to draw conclusions about age, but you would be much more confident about your second answer. When applied to a large group and expressed as an average, variations in the height data are simply ironed out.

Shiller's PE model is more like the second situation than the first. Just as heights vary among individuals, PEs vary among individual stocks. And we've already stated that these variations can, at any point in time, be due to differences in ROE, earnings growth rate and the appropriate discount rate for that company. But averages of large populations of PEs put a steamroller through these differences, which means the set of factors driving the average PE, while related to it, is not exactly the same as that driving the PEs of individual stocks. The factors influencing the large group are those that tend to influence all stocks, principally interest rates and investor sentiment. Shiller reckons the second one of these, investor sentiment, is an important factor—large swings in his composite PE can occur between periods when investors are overly optimistic (bull markets) or overly pessimistic (bear markets).

USING THE PE TO CONSTRUCT A PORTFOLIO

It has been suggested that the PE can be used as the sole metric to construct portfolios demonstrating high returns. This recommendation is based on the results of many studies that have calculated the returns that could have been achieved had an investor constructed a portfolio of low-PE stocks and held it for a long period. A large number of these studies split the study group of stocks into deciles—that is, into 10 groups based on the size of their PE. The conclusion often drawn was that the group of stocks in the lowest PE decile delivered a superior return to another decile group made up of higher PE stocks (often the highest PE decile). That's sort of interesting but what I really want is to compare things with the broad index. Two well-known investors, David Dreman and James O'Shaughnessy, have claimed the ability to construct market-beating portfolios relying simply on the PE.[56, 57]

Dreman describes a study in which he split 1500 companies into five equal groups ranked according to PE. He found that over the 27-year period from 1969 to 1996 the lowest PE group delivered a return of 19.0 per cent annually while the general market delivered 15.3 per cent. Dreman also found that the group containing the high-PE stocks underperformed the general market. O'Shaughnessy also came to the conclusion that portfolios constructed solely by selecting low-PE stocks delivered market-beating returns. Maybe both studies reflect the principle described in the epigraph to Ben Graham and David Dodd's book *Security Analysis*: 'Many shall be revived that now are fallen, and many fall that are now in honor.'

At first glance both Dreman's and O'Shaughnessy's empirical results appear to run counter to the seemingly logical discussion presented above—that the PE isn't a reliable measure of value. But it's important to realise that we're talking about portfolio returns, not individual stocks.

Hence we are dealing with averages again, not individual companies. Remember the average height of a basketball team can still be above six foot even if it carries a few Danny DeVitos. Dreman and O'Shaughnessy are advocating we buy a 'team' of stocks called the 'low-PE team'. This doesn't deny the logic of the above discussion regarding the limitations of the PE when applying it to individual stocks.

But the question remains: do Dreman's and O'Shaughnessy's methods work? Can you beat the market index simply by buying a portfolio of low-PE stocks? It's such a simple mechanical technique that anyone could be shown how to apply it in a matter of minutes. So you have to ask the question: why are so many investors wasting their time by not using it? In my mind there is doubt it does work. Of course it can't be ruled out that their findings were the result of chance but let's explore this more deeply.

Firstly, Dreman's data covered the 27-year period from December 1969 to December 1996. And, although Shiller calculates his PE differently, for much of Dreman's 27-year study Shiller's PE was well below its long-term average of 16.6. For seven years it was in single digits. Therefore the period of Dreman's study was atypical.

O'Shaughnessy's study period—from December 1951 to December 2003—was much longer than Dreman's. His hypothetical low-PE portfolio was rebalanced each year to hold the 50 stocks with the lowest PEs in any given year. The return premium achieved from holding the low-PE portfolio over the index was small—a geometric average of 13.77 per cent versus 13 per cent from holding the index. Such a small margin doesn't warrant bragging rights, particularly when you consider there was a period of 13 years when O'Shaughnessy's low-PE portfolio actually trailed the market average. And it wasn't until the 51-year mark (12 months before the study ended) that the low-PE portfolio made a final lunge to the finishing line, breasting the tape just ahead of the market portfolio. Put simply, his results weren't statistically significant.

It's easy to get excited when you read Dreman's and O'Shaughnessy's books. They suggest that success in the stock market can be achieved simply by constructing portfolios based on low-PE stocks. I guess that's why these two books were bestsellers. But if you decide to do this, you have a lot more faith in the metric than I do. The reality is, if you choose this investment technique, you should prepare yourself for the very real chance of less-than-stellar results.

Chapter summary

- The PE ratio is calculated by dividing the current share price by the most recently reported earnings per share (EPS).

- Investors commonly use the PE as a measure of relative value, judging a stock with a low PE to be cheap and a stock with a high PE to be expensive.

- A major drawback of the PE is that the numerator (the market price) is forever changing while the denominator (earnings per share) remains fixed between financial reporting periods.

- The PE is influenced by perceptions of a stock's future return on equity (ROE), growth in earnings and appropriate discount rate. The discount rate is in turn influenced by the inherent risk of the investment and the prevailing and anticipated interest rates.

- Using the PE to compare the relative value of two stocks has significant limitations.

- Using the PE as a value screen will mean some suitably priced companies will be ignored and some overpriced companies will be selected.

- The PE appears to be more useful when applied to groups of stocks rather than to individual stocks.

14

EARNINGS GROWTH ISN'T ALWAYS A GOOD THING

I now want to expand on the discussion introduced in the previous chapter regarding the desirability of earnings growth.

Earnings per share (EPS) is calculated by dividing a company's net profit after tax by the number of ordinary shares on issue. Investors often include a requirement for positive EPS growth in their stock screen. Chairpersons and CEOs love writing in the annual report that they've delivered EPS growth for the most recent financial year or for the past several years. They present this information in the form of bar graphs showing progressively higher bars for each successive year. Reported growth gives shareholders a warm, tingly feeling because their shares are earning more every year. The reality is sometimes it's all a bit of a con.

For starters, information regarding how much a company has earned, expressed either as total profit or as EPS, isn't telling us the whole story. Earnings need to be related to the amount of capital being used to achieve that profit. I really get frustrated when I see headlines like 'Customers of XYZ Bank Outraged after Record $1.2 Billion Profit'.

All the tongues start clicking and the fingers start pointing. 'The banks are making too much money', I hear people say. I say if XYZ

Bank has shareholders' equity of $8 billion then the profit figure is totally reasonable. But if it's returning $1.2 billion on shareholders' equity of $16 billion I'd be telling shareholders to find another place to invest their money, because the bank's 'record profit' is too low. Profits should always be related to a capital base when judging their appropriateness.

The problem is, buying stocks with growing EPS seems intuitively to be a sensible thing to do. But sometimes it can be the wrong thing to do, just as it can be wrong to select a stock solely because it has a low PE. For example, earnings will grow every year in a neglected bank account even if the bank is paying a meagre 1 per cent interest per year, but that doesn't mean you'd rejoice in the result.

Let's explore when EPS growth is a good thing and when it isn't. Table 13.1 (reproduced in table 14.1) will assist in the discussion. Remember we have assumed a required rate of return of 10 per cent.

Look at the top half of the table—that is, the top nine rows where the ROE is 9 per cent or less. Note two things. Firstly, as the ROE increases (moving down the table in any column) so too does the PE ratio. Secondly, as you move your eye from left to right within any row on the top half of the table, the PE falls as earnings growth increases. For many people this would seem to be counterintuitive. The price being placed on the same current earnings is becoming progressively lower as the rate of earnings growth increases. It's demonstrating that earnings growth can be a bad thing.

Let's take another tack in this discussion. All other things being equal, how does a company grow earnings? It does so in lots of ways. A gold-mining company could uncover a rich new seam of gold, or an oil and gas company could find a huge new oil reserve. A biotech company could discover a cure for the common cold, or a computer hardware company could revolutionise the microchip.

Table 14.1: fair PE for different return on equity and earnings growth

		Earnings growth							
	1%	2%	3%	4%	5%	6%	7%	8%	9%
1%	0	–	–	–	–	–	–	–	–
2%	5.56	0	–	–	–	–	–	–	–
3%	7.41	4.17	0	–	–	–	–	–	–
4%	8.33	6.52	3.57	0	–	–	–	–	–
5%	8.89	7.50	5.71	3.33	0	–	–	–	–
6%	9.26	8.33	7.14	5.56	3.33	0	–	–	–
7%	9.52	8.93	8.16	7.14	5.71	3.57	0	–	–
8%	9.72	9.38	8.93	8.33	7.50	6.25	4.17	0	–
9%	9.88	9.72	9.52	9.26	8.89	8.33	7.41	5.56	0
10%	10.0	10.0	10.0	10.0	10.0	10.0	10.0	10.0	10.0
11%	10.10	10.23	10.39	10.61	10.91	11.36	12.12	13.64	18.18
12%	10.19	10.42	10.71	11.11	11.67	12.50	13.89	16.67	25.00
13%	10.26	10.58	10.99	11.54	12.31	13.46	15.38	19.23	30.77
14%	10.32	10.71	11.22	11.90	12.86	14.29	16.67	21.43	35.71
15%	10.37	10.83	11.43	12.22	13.33	15.00	17.78	23.33	40.00
16%	10.42	10.94	11.61	12.50	13.75	15.63	18.75	25.00	43.75
17%	10.46	11.03	11.76	12.75	14.12	16.18	19.61	26.47	47.06

Left axis label: **Return on equity (ROE)**

It all sounds very exciting. But for most mature companies, earnings growth is typically delivered in a more pedestrian manner. These companies simply retain a proportion of each year's profit and reinvest it in more of the same business activities they've been undertaking for years.

Following this logic, the reason investors are prepared to invest a dollar is because they hope to see more than a dollar delivered back in the future. They should feel the same about the dollars the company is retaining and reinvesting in the business. After all, as shareholders they own the business, so the money being reinvested by management is theirs. Integral to this process is what management actually does with the money it retains; it's one of the factors that determines the rate of future earnings growth. For example, assuming all else remains constant, a company that is currently achieving an ROE of 5 per cent, and will continue to do so, needs to retain and reinvest every dollar of earnings to achieve a target of 5 per cent growth in earnings per share. Nothing will be left over to pay a dividend. Using a purely mathematical argument, if it were to pay out half the profit as a dividend it could achieve only a 2.5 per cent growth in earnings per share the following year. We can express the earnings growth rate with a simple equation:

Earnings growth = ROE × earnings retention rate

But think about it. If your aim as an investor is to achieve a minimum return of 10 per cent and management can achieve only 5 per cent on funds it invests on your behalf, you'd prefer they didn't. You'd prefer all profits be paid out as a dividend to provide you with the chance of obtaining a 10 per cent return in some other form of investment. This is why, in table 14.1, progressively lower PEs are awarded to companies delivering progressively higher earnings growth but at returns on equity lower than you demand (in this case 10 per cent). They are effectively destroying your wealth.

Refer back to the table and look at the row in the middle with all the 10s. This is where the ROE is 10 per cent, the rate you've chosen as your minimum required rate of return. At 10 per cent you don't care how much growth is being achieved—any level of earnings growth being generated from the reinvestment of retained earnings is just meeting your target. Therefore the price you place on these earnings (the 'P') keeps step with the increase in the earnings (the 'E'). So the PE ratio doesn't change with increased rates of earnings growth.

Finally, look at the bottom half of the table. Here the ROE is greater than your required rate of return. For any ROE, as earnings growth increases so too does the PE. But remember that in our perfect world every PE on the table represents fair value. As an investor you are indifferent between them if you have to pay that price to own them.

WHY MANAGEMENTS RETAIN PROFITS DESPITE DELIVERING A POOR ROE

You'd think boards and senior managers would understand the above financial logic even better than shareholders do—and probably they do. Yet the managements of many companies, with histories of delivering low ROE, still choose to retain significant proportions of annual profits. Why?

Consider a board meeting of a hypothetical company. It's bristling with managerial self-interest. One director kicks off the meeting by suggesting that since they're devoid of profitable new investment opportunities it would be best to pay out a larger dividend to shareholders this year. The others think that's a stupid idea. The directors have been granted copious volumes of options as part of their remuneration package, and their options become more valuable as the company's share price increases. By retaining earnings they have a better chance of the share price increasing in absolute terms.

They also know that investors like to see growth in earnings per share, something they also have a better chance of delivering if they retain earnings. After all, growing earnings per share looks good in the glossy graphs that adorn the first few pages of each year's annual report. If they pay out too much of the profit it lessens the chance that these 'desirable outcomes' will be achieved. Then the chairman settles the discussion: 'Hey team, I have to stand up in front of the shareholders at the AGM next year and tell them earnings are still growing. So I need as much of that money as we can hang on to. Reinvestment at any rate will help boost next year's earnings.' Then he turns to the director who first suggested that there were no suitable high-return investment opportunities and says: 'It seems you're not aware that the company's acquisitions team is looking at a couple of takeover targets at the moment. The returns they're offering aren't great but the CEO and I want this company to get bigger. So let's hang on to the cash. We might need it down the track if the acquisitions team come up with something.'

None of the above discussion is in the shareholders' best interests, but unfortunately dividend policy is not always based on maximising shareholder wealth. The concept of companies having a better chance of delivering earnings growth by reinvesting retained earnings has long been appreciated. This from more than one hundred years ago:

> Rich men whose income is in excess of their wants, can afford to forgo something in the way of yearly return for the sake of a strong prospect of appreciation in value. Such men naturally buy bank and trust-company stocks, whose general characteristic is a small return upon the money invested, but a strong likelihood of appreciation in value. This is owing to the general practice of well-regulated banks to distribute only about half their earnings in dividends and to credit the rest to surplus, thus insuring a steady rise in the book value of the stock.[58]

Considered purely in mathematical terms it makes sense that the reinvestment of retained profits results in a larger book value and enhanced earnings down the track. And this belief forms the bedrock of most valuation formulae, as I'll discuss later. But that's mathematics. The question remains: does this actually play out in real life? Surprisingly, there are studies that have shown that higher profit retention doesn't automatically lead to larger profits down the track. Let's take a look.

A study undertaken by Robert Arnott and Clifford Asness demonstrated a positive relationship between higher payout ratios and higher subsequent 10-year real earnings.[59] A later study by Ping Zhou and William Ruland came to a similar conclusion.[60]

These findings defy intuition. What's going on?

The researchers argue that dividend policy doesn't comply with our neat mathematical rules. In the real world, dividend policy is used as an instrument of wealth *distribution* (unfortunately not always to shareholders!); it is not always used as an instrument of wealth *creation*, as it should be. This subtlety escapes most investors. The reality is that dividend policy is influenced by many conflicting factors. I introduced a couple of these in the hypothetical board discussion above, but let's look at a couple more here.

Firstly, managements prefer not to reduce the annual dividend in any year of reduced profit. Their fear is that a lower dividend will send out a negative signal to the market about the company's future prospects. To keep the dividend steady they need to increase the payout ratio when the profit is down. This typically occurs at low points in the economic cycle, times when it might be better for management to retain profits for reinvestment. Even so, as the economy recovers, typically so do company profits. This presents a scenario where profit growth follows a high payout period, not low.

Secondly, managements can at times be accused of 'empire building' at the expense of the shareholders' best interests. Dividend policy is dictated by their focus on retaining earnings to accumulate a war chest of capital so they can acquire target companies. Ben Graham referred to this as 'personal aggrandisement'. Acquisition activity often reaches its peak when stock markets and assets are overpriced, which means management is retaining and reinvesting profits at the high point of the cycle, a time when it might be better to distribute them. Acquisitions are made at inflated prices, destroying shareholder wealth, so retained profits aren't converted into higher future earnings. Instead higher retention rates are followed by periods of lower profit.

As discussed, dividend policy can be further distorted when options are used as a form of management compensation. If management hold call options and/or their compensation is linked to an increase in the company's share price or earnings per share, there's a strong incentive for them to retain profits rather than pay them out as dividends. This might run counter to the best interests of other shareholders, particularly when the retained profits are invested at low rates of return.

Another factor influencing dividend policy is tax. In Australia the impost of double taxation on company earnings was removed in 1987 by the Hawke–Keating government. Since then, tax already paid by the company is added back to the dividends received by the shareholder and this 'grossed up' amount is taxed at the shareholder's marginal personal tax rate. This system of dividend imputation is fair but not enjoyed universally. Double taxation is one of the reasons lower dividend payout rates are seen in a number of countries around the world. This driver of profit retention is independent of future profit generation opportunities.

Chapter summary

- If profit is to have any real meaning, it should be related to the amount of capital employed to generate it.

- Earnings growth is undesirable when it's being delivered by the investment of capital at rates of return lower than an investor's required rate of return. Earnings growth is desirable when it's delivered by the investment of capital at a rate of return equal to or higher than an investor's required rate of return.

- A simplistic, formula-based determination of earnings growth is *earnings growth = ROE × earnings retention rate*. However, in real life the retention and reinvestment of earnings doesn't always deliver an increase in future earnings.

- Dividend policy is typically used as an instrument of wealth distribution rather than of wealth creation.

15

WHY DO PRICE TO BOOK RATIOS VARY?

A value metric that many investors use in their initial stock screen is the price to book or P/B ratio. It relates a company's current share price to the value of its net assets. The thinking is that the lower the ratio the better the value deal they get when buying a company's shares.

Book value, in the sense investors use the term, is what a company owns minus what it owes. It's the amount of capital shareholders have tied up in the company. Hence it's also referred to as shareholders' equity. Another way to think of it is: how much money would shareholders have to supply in order to reproduce the company?

Stock investors have long associated the value of a company's shares with the value of the net assets the company holds. In the 19th century the broad belief was that this association was one of equality; that is, the company's worth to the shareholders is the value of its hard assets less any debt. This view isn't widely held today—the potential for future earnings is what drives stock prices now. But book value is still an important consideration when it comes to valuation. For example, book value per share is used as an input to several valuation formulae, and it still provides a value anchor we shouldn't lose sight of when share prices are bid to crazy bull market heights.

That Warren Buffett likes this metric can be seen from the opening comments in his 1984 Chairman's letter to Berkshire shareholders:

> As we discussed last year, the gain in per-share intrinsic business value is the economic measurement that really counts. But calculations of intrinsic business value are subjective. In our case, book value serves as a useful, although somewhat understated proxy.

Buffett has continued to place significant importance on this metric, as was demonstrated in September 2011 when he announced, for just the second time under his stewardship, that Berkshire was prepared to buy back its own shares at a price directly related to its book value. He didn't specify a price at which Berkshire would buy back its shares; instead he announced the offer would remain open at any price up to a 10 per cent premium to book value.*

Clearly Buffett sees a strong link between the intrinsic value of Berkshire Hathaway and its book value. But, as Buffett points out, it's an association, not equality. Book value can either understate or overstate a business's economic value—that is, the value determined from an assessment of its earnings potential.

WHAT IS BOOK VALUE TELLING US?

Book value is listed in the company accounts in the Statement of Financial Position (balance sheet). Like the Income Statement, the Statement of Financial Position is constructed according to lots of accounting rules. This means, despite the best intentions of the accounting bodies, the rules deliver figures that can at times be removed from economic reality. If you want to explore some of the principal digressions, I've outlined them in appendix A. But rather than listing them here I'll demonstrate how this can occur using a real example.

Coca-Cola Amatil (CCL) is listed on the Australian Securities Exchange. It represents Coke's bottling interests in Australia, New Zealand, Papua New Guinea, Samoa, Fiji and Indonesia—a pretty strong and stable business, one would expect. Yet between 2004 and 2005 its book value plummeted by a staggering 54 per cent. The news would have worried shareholders terribly, until they realised what caused the drop.

---

*Buffett later lifted this to a 20 per cent premium.

The company's accounts were impacted by the adoption of Australian International Financial Reporting Standards (AIFRS). In 1999 CCL's management put a commercial value on its distribution licences and then reported this as an asset on the balance sheet, and it was indeed a very valuable asset. But the new AIFRS rules didn't allow the recognition of internally generated intangible assets, so in 2005 CCL was forced to remove this $1.9 billion asset from its balance sheet. This halved the reported shareholders' equity despite there being no change in the company's commercial value. Overnight the P/B ratio doubled, as did the ROE and gearing ratios. It was exactly the same company but now it had very different value and debt metrics.

As an investment it was no different from before, yet its changed metrics meant it now fell outside many stock screens that previously would have caught it.

RELATING BOOK VALUE PER SHARE TO MARKET PRICE

Let's take a closer look at the influences on the P/B ratio using the same formula we used to look at the PE ratio.

$$\frac{P}{B} = \frac{ROE - g}{r - g}$$

where:

- P = current market share price
- ROE = anticipated return on equity
- g = anticipated annual growth in earnings
- B = book value per share
- r = required rate of return (discount rate).

So the three underlying drivers of the P/B ratio are the anticipated ROE, the required rate of return and the anticipated earnings growth (g). Note the use of the word 'anticipated' in relation to the ROE and earnings growth. The market always values stocks in anticipation. Driving these expectations, and in the absence of a crystal ball, investors and analysts are very much influenced by the conditions experienced by the company at the time the judgement is being made, which means companies currently achieving high earnings growth and a high ROE tend to trade on a high P/B ratio. Investors need to judge whether these will be maintained, because if they aren't then the share price is likely to fall. That's why value investors go on so much about seeking out companies with an enduring competitive advantage.

Note that the above formula can also be adapted and used as a valuation formula. By multiplying both sides of the equation by the book value per share (B) we derive:

$$Value = B \times \frac{ROE - g}{r - g}$$

WHAT IS A LOW P/B RATIO TELLING US?

James O'Shaughnessy, whom I mentioned back in chapter 13, wrote that over the long term the market rewards stocks with low P/B ratios and punishes those with high ones.[61] But using the same argument I delivered regarding the PE ratio, it's risky to assume this will always be the case. There are plenty of reasons that stocks trade on low P/B ratios, and the formula above gives us an insight into what they might be. For example:

- A stock's ROE could be low.

- Its growth prospects could be low.

- The company could be in financial difficulty.

- The market could believe the book value is understated in the accounts.

Or finally:

- The share price could actually represent good value.

All of this means you can't base any decision regarding a stock purely on its P/B ratio. You can't escape the need to have a deeper understanding of the company itself and the business environment within which it operates. Then you can develop an appreciation of whether the P/B ratio the market has tagged it with is appropriate.

Chapter summary

- The price to book (P/B) ratio is a popular metric in stock screening.

- The P/B ratio relates market price to book value per share.

- In the 19th century the value of a company was typically equated to its book value.

- The book value listed in the company accounts doesn't always reflect economic reality, and the experienced analyst will make adjustments to account for this.

- The three underlying drivers of the P/B ratio are the anticipated return on equity, the required rate of return and the anticipated earnings growth.

- In the search for value, low-P/B stocks are sought, but low P/B should not be relied upon as the sole metric of stock selection.

- Companies with a low P/B are more attractive if they also have high and enduring ROE.

16

SELECTING STOCKS BY DIVIDEND YIELD

A stock's dividend yield is calculated by dividing the annual dividend it pays by the current market price; the answer is expressed as a percentage. Typically the dividend used in the calculation is that paid in the most recent year, but the anticipated dividend due in the coming year can also be used (referred to as the 'prospective dividend yield').

There's nothing new about investors choosing stocks based on their dividend yield. Note this near 300-year-old quote from 'Remarks on the Celebrated Calculations of the Value of South-Sea Stock' (1720, author unknown):

> The main principle, on which the whole science of stock-jobbing is built, viz. That the benefit of a dividend (considered as a motive to the buying or keeping of a stock) is always to be estimated according to the rate it bears to the price of the stock, because the purchaser is supposed to compare that rate with the profits he might make of money, if otherwise employed.[62]

And there's no doubt there are plenty of investors (me excluded) who still place a lot of weight on considering it. For example, several years ago I listened to a presentation given by a fellow who spoke for an hour about nothing else but his favourite metric — dividend yield. Seriously, he really did speak about nothing else for an hour. It was as if he had no other metric for selecting stocks.

So how important are dividends? After all, exempting returns of capital, it's the only money stock investors get paid. So let's explore it further.

DOGS OF THE DOW

Needless to say, you don't have to go far before finding an investment method based solely on choosing stocks with high dividend yields. One popular method is called 'Dogs of the Dow', or the 'Dow 10 Strategy'.

Dogs of the Dow is a simple mechanical system for selecting stocks that has (at times) provided superior returns to market indices. While its origins are disputed, its popularity grew following a description of the strategy in a 1991 book, *Beating the Dow*, by Michael O'Higgins and John Downes.

The strategy is simplicity itself. At the end of each calendar year select the 10 stocks from the Dow Jones Industrial Average (DJIA) demonstrating the highest dividend yield, then allocate 10 per cent of your investment capital to each. Hold these stocks for 12 months and repeat the process at the end of each successive year. At each annual review, sell those stocks that no longer meet the criterion and add those that do.

The concept underpinning Dogs of the Dow was proposed more than 70 years ago by Ben Graham. That is, solid companies can periodically fall out of favour due to a short-term change in investor sentiment or business conditions. This usually results in a depressed share price. Despite this, management will often maintain the dividend, reflecting their optimism of a return to favourable times. Maintaining the dividend, coupled with the lower share price, results in a high dividend yield. This provides the potential for investors to be rewarded both by way of a high dividend straight up and the possibility of a later rebound in the share price. This is very different from a search for value based on real earnings growth. It's based on growth relative to expectations.

Central to the success of the strategy is the capacity for the selected companies to recover from periods of adversity. Thus large-cap companies with strong balance sheets are best suited. To date this requirement has been met through the selection criterion for a company to be included in the DJIA. But applying the Dogs of the Dow strategy to indices that include smaller, highly geared companies could introduce some risks.

The question is: does it work? After all, there's a lot riding on just one metric—the dividend yield. The test of any strategy is how it performs against the relevant benchmark. O'Shaughnessy looked at the Dogs of the Dow in his book *What Works on Wall Street*. He found that, applied from 1928 to 2003, $10 000 would have grown to $57 662 527 (excluding taxes and commission costs). An investment in the S&P 500 would have seen $10 000 grow to just $10 366 726.

The difference is significant but there are three problems with accepting these findings at face value. Firstly, O'Shaughnessy's findings exclude taxes and commission costs, yet these are very real costs and need to be considered when comparing it to other investment strategies. Secondly, the Dogs of the Dow strategy was born out of a process called data mining—that is, extracting favourable patterns from historical data. There is no guarantee that past patterns can be confidently applied to the future. And thirdly, popularisation of clear and simple strategies can push up prices, so wiping out the benefit.

In regard to the third point, Dogs of the Dow has been a popular strategy for over 20 years. So has this popularity impacted its efficacy as an investment strategy? The Dogs of the Dow website (www.dogsofthedow.com) compares the returns achieved using this strategy against the benchmark returns delivered by the DJIA and S&P 500 indices. Results for the one-, three-, five-, 10- and 20-year periods ending 31 December 2011 are shown in table 16.1.

Table 16.1: comparing Dogs of the Dow returns against benchmark indices to 31 December 2011

Investment	1 year	3 year	5 year	10 year	20 year
Dogs of the Dow	16.3%	17.9%	3.4%	6.7%	10.8%
DJIA	8.4%	15.0%	4.4%	6.1%	10.8%
S&P 500	2.1%	14.5%	2.4%	4.9%	9.5%

On face value it looks sort of promising: it outperformed the S&P over all periods. But for the last 20 years of the comparison its performance was line ball with the Dow, not surprising since the Dow is the source of stocks for the strategy. Interestingly, research undertaken by Wharton professor Jeremy Siegel shows that the strategy works best during bear markets, and this proved to be the case following the 2008 Global Financial Crisis.

But the comparison looks quite different using the one-, three-, five- and 10-year periods ending 31 December 2014, as shown in table 16.2.

Table 16.2: comparing Dogs of the Dow returns against benchmark indices to 31 December 2014

Investment	1 year	3 year	5 year	10 year	Since 2000
Dogs of the Dow	10.8%	18.5%	18.5%	9.8%	8.3%
DJIA	10.0%	16.6%	14.5%	9.3%	6.7%
S&P 500	13.7%	20.7%	15.9%	9.5%	6.1%

In keeping with its application to large-cap stocks, the Dogs of the Dow strategy has been adapted for use in Australia by applying it to the S&P/ASX 50 index; appropriately it has been referred to as 'Dingoes Down Under'. However, the S&P/ASX 50 and the DJIA indices are constructed using different inclusion criteria, and this fact needs to be considered when applying it to Australian companies.

The DJIA comprises 30 large-cap stocks reflecting the spectrum of corporate activity in the US. Australia's ASX 50 simply represents the 50 largest listed companies in Australia by market capitalisation. It's dominated by several banks and miners and, unlike the DJIA, includes real estate investment trusts (REITs). Mining companies typically have low dividend payout ratios, often preferring to retain profits for exploration, capital expenditure and development activities, while REITs, which pay high distributions that have yet to be taxed, are arguably best excluded from the strategy altogether.

Before leaving the Dogs of the Dow, I want to make one more point.

Hopeful investors have been back-testing financial data for centuries in the search for simple investment and trading rules. Their efforts could be likened to the search for the pot of gold at the end of the rainbow. Interestingly, the search is not just a product of the computer age. Christoph Kurz, a 16th-century Antwerp commodities trader, wrote of his efforts to develop mechanical trading tools by back-testing data. He described his need to rise at four in the morning and:

> ... work as a man in the ocean with water, for our astrologers aforetime have written much, but little with reason; wherefore I trust not their doctrine, but seek mine own rules, and when I have them I search in the histories whether it hath fallen out right or wrong.[63]

Today's investors aren't exactly basking in financial rewards from centuries of back-testing data, are they?

RECEIVING NO DIVIDEND IS OKAY

Back in chapter 14, I mentioned that dividend policy is typically treated as an instrument of wealth distribution rather than of wealth creation. Someone who breaks this mould is Warren Buffett. To date his 50-year stewardship of Berkshire Hathaway has seen shareholders delivered just one dividend. Yet during this period Berkshire's share price has increased by a factor of several thousands. Compare this with Australian telecommunications company Telstra — its share price fell by 72 per cent between 1999 and 2012 despite paying a strong and consistently high dividend for the entire period.

Clearly there should be more to the sophisticated stock picker's armamentarium than simply chasing dividend yield. After all, total returns are delivered both by dividends and capital gains. So let's discuss some of the unappreciated issues surrounding dividend policy and its impact on wealth creation.

Firstly, back to Berkshire Hathaway. Since it hasn't delivered a dividend since 1967 (and that was only 10 cents), the uninitiated might argue that Berkshire is a non-income-producing investment. But to do so fails to recognise that the company has for many years been retaining and reinvesting all of its profits at generally high rates of return. Buffett has always felt the money was better in his hands than in those of the shareholders. Hence his now famous comment about that single dividend Berkshire paid back in 1967: 'I must have been in the bathroom when the dividend was declared.'

Despite Buffett's near five-decade stance on retaining and reinvesting all profits, he still had to field a question from a concerned shareholder at a recent Berkshire AGM. She wanted to know why, with over $30 billion in the bank and a share price of $120 000, Berkshire's directors still weren't prepared to pay a dividend. Buffett politely responded as if it was the first time he'd been asked the question. He explained that the share price was $120 000 *because* of years of profit retention and reinvestment. If she wanted a dividend then she was free to sell some of her stock.

So my response to the whole dividend question? As an investor, dividends are a convenient way to receive income if you rely on the money to fund living expenses. But the sophisticated stock picker should look beyond a selection process based solely on dividend yield. There are many factors to consider when assessing a stock, and the dividend it pays isn't at the top of the list.

SO WHICH METRICS SHOULD YOU USE?

Value-based metrics such as the PE and P/B ratio are popular, but advice on how useful they are is conflicting. For example, in 1992 Tweedy, Browne Company LLC, a well-known value investment firm, published a compilation of 44 research studies entitled 'What Has Worked in Investing'. The study found that what has worked is fairly simple: cheap stocks (measured by the P/B ratio, PE ratio or dividend yield) have reliably outperformed expensive ones. It also found that stocks that have underperformed (over prior three- and five-year periods) subsequently beat those that have lately performed well. Add these findings to the studies undertaken by Dreman and O'Shaughnessy, which I've already mentioned, and you might easily become a value metric disciple.

Yet my discussion over the past four chapters has highlighted the shortcomings of these metrics. So before I move on to Part III of the book I want to try to resolve the whole issue. As a start let's consider these words from Buffett's 1992 Chairman's letter to shareholders where he said of value investing that it connotes buying stocks:

> ... having attributes such as a low ratio of price to book value, a low price-earnings ratio, or a high dividend yield. Unfortunately, such characteristics, even if they appear in combination, are far from determinative as to whether an investor is indeed buying something for what it is worth ...

Buffett went on to add that:

> Correspondingly, opposite characteristics—a high ratio of price to book value, a high price-earnings ratio, and a low dividend yield—are in no way inconsistent with a 'value' purchase.

At first glance it would seem that Buffett's words contradict the findings of the Tweedy, Browne studies. Even more concerning is that both specifically name the same three metrics—price to book ratio, price earnings ratio and dividend yield. Might I add that it's no coincidence that the bulk of my discussion in this part of the book has been about these same three metrics. With these four chapters under your belt you should now be in a position to make sense of these seemingly disparate views. So let's do that.

I would suggest that the two views — of Buffett and of Tweedy, Browne — aren't contradictory at all, and that the criticism I've been delivering regarding these ratios fits with both views as well. The Tweedy, Browne studies are looking at these metrics in relation to the performance of entire portfolios, while Buffett is considering something quite different. He's saying that it's not enough to rely on these metrics when selecting an individual stock; there are bound to be exceptions to the rule.

Which returns us to the leaky fishing net analogy I made back in chapter 13. If you choose to use these metrics as part of a screening device, you're going to save a lot of time. Depending upon the demands of your screen, you're going to cut down the number of potential companies for in-depth analysis from thousands to dozens or even less. If the screen is linked to a computer program, then the time-saving will be significant.

But there's a trade-off. The screen will exclude some companies you might have otherwise chosen as investments. Your screen won't pick up stocks with high 'value' metrics. Hence Buffett's words: 'a high ratio of price to book value, a high price-earnings ratio, and a low dividend yield — are in no way inconsistent with a "value" purchase'.

Perhaps, then, it would be better not to refer to these as value metrics. And whether you choose to use a screen or not, it's important to remember that no screen is a substitute for in-depth stock analysis. Investors still need to go through the process of determining what a stock is worth and relating that to its current market price. So that's where we're heading in the next two parts of the book — how to go about valuing stocks.

But just before we get into it, I want to explain something. I've always found that things are best understood if you appreciate how they were derived. For example, as a student learning mathematics it wasn't enough for me to memorise a formula — I had to understand how the formula was developed using first principles. That's learning.

So in relation to the question 'Where did the concept of stock valuation come from?' let's take a journey back in time. What you're about to read may hold quite a few surprises.

Chapter summary

- The Dogs of the Dow strategy is a mechanical stock selection method whereby the 10 stocks with the highest dividend yields are bought and held for 12 months, after which they're either reselected or rejected using the same criterion.

- Wharton professor Jeremy Siegel found that Dogs of the Dow delivers its best returns during bear markets.

- Low or no dividend stocks can still provide sound investments, as long as the companies are profitable and retained profits are reinvested at high rates of return.

- Stock screens using popular value-based metrics are likely to exclude some sound and well-priced investments.

- Stock screens are not a substitute for in-depth stock analysis.

Part III
THE GENESIS OF STOCK VALUATION

17

IT ALL STARTED
IN EUROPE

The United States can lay claim to having the largest stock market in the world, but not the first. The Dutch laid the foundations for the first purpose-built stock exchange building the year before the first European even set foot on Mannahatta (as the locals, the Lenape, then called it), the small island that ultimately gave birth to the New York Stock Exchange. When explorer Henry Hudson dragged his skiff onto Mannahatta's shores in September 1609, Wall Street was an oak forest providing shelter to the Lenape. It would be another 180-odd years before the US had a stock market they could call their own. So we need to start our story in Europe, where the concept of general stock ownership and the valuation of shares began.

LEONARDO PISANO

People have been making judgements on what things are worth since one month's cave rental cost two woolly mammoth skins. But the focus of this book is stock markets. And while the Romans had developed a financial system of some sophistication by the 2nd century BC, it wasn't until the 17th century that publicly traded shares, as we recognise them today, were exposed to the question, 'What are they really worth?' In 1602, the Dutch provided the first publicly traded stock, of the Verenigde Oost-Indische Compagnie, or VOC for short, which we know better as the Dutch East India Company. But it was several centuries earlier that the valuation tool they turned to was conceived.

Our valuation story really starts in 1202, when the book *Liber Abaci* first adorned bookshelves. Written long before the printing press was conceived, for the next 300 years it was considered Europe's pre-eminent text on the subject of business-related mathematics, and the concepts it introduced shaped the valuation formulae we still use today. *Liber Abaci* was the work of an Italian, Leonardo Pisano, better known as Fibonacci.

Pisano spent much of his early life outside his native country. His father worked as a public official in a Bugian customs house on the Barbary Coast of North Africa; the customs house had been established by the city of Pisa to facilitate trade in the region. Pisano's father saw the importance of a solid grounding in the principles of mathematics; hence from a young age Leonardo was provided with mathematical instruction. In particular he was instructed in the 'Indian or Hindu Method', which used Arabic numerals.

It should be remembered that Europe had yet to adopt the Hindu number system, which is the system we use today. The Europe Pisano was born into was still using the abacus for performing calculations and the Roman number system to record the outcomes of these calculations. Pisano saw significant advantages in using the Hindu system, principally because it was less cumbersome than the Roman. Using the Hindu system it was possible to perform both the calculation and the recording. He explained that by combining the nine Indian figures (1, 2, 3, 4, 5, 6, 7, 8 and 9) with the sign 0, which the Arabs called zephyr, 'any number whatsoever is written'.[64]

Pisano wanted to see the widespread adoption of the Hindu system across Europe. When he left Bugia he travelled throughout the Mediterranean region, further developing his skills in trade and mathematics. In his own words, he learned from 'whoever was learned in it, from nearby Egypt, Syria, Greece, Sicily and Provence, and their various methods, to which locations of business I traveled considerably afterwards for much study'.[65] His scholarly and intellectual interactions saw him rise to become one of the pre-eminent and most creative mathematicians of his time.

Pisano wrote *Liber Abaci* soon after returning to Italy in around 1200. It contains the first written record of a tool that investment analysts still use today—discounted cash flow. Concepts of debt and the calculation of interest had been considered, taught and written about long before Pisano. What made his work revolutionary was that it introduced a practical method for calculating the financial impact of varying the timing of cash flows. Today we would call it calculating a 'present value'. The application of a discount rate to future cash flows is still central to the valuation of bonds and equities.

In chapter 12 of *Liber Abaci* Pisano poses a problem he calls 'On a Soldier Receiving Three Hundred Bezants for His Fief'. He asks us to consider the financial impact of changing the timing of payments a soldier receives from the king. One scenario sees the soldier receive his annual salary of 300 bezants in four three-monthly payments, each of 75 bezants. Under a second scenario the soldier receives a single annual payment of 300 bezants at the end of the period. Pisano provides us with the discount rate — a monthly interest rate of 2 per cent — and then shows us how to calculate the difference between the two present values.

Pisano's time coincided with the development of innovative long-term government debt instruments in northern Italy. Both Venice and Genoa began to issue loans, giving birth to the now common practice of government financing through national debt. Whether the present value formula sparked the development of the government debt market or the government's desire to borrow initiated the development of the formula isn't clear. Whichever was the case, Pisano's formula provided the tool for calculating bond values down to the last bezant.

Pisano had provided the business world with a tool for distilling variously timed cash flows into a single value — today's value. He could not have guessed back in 1202 that this was the tool that analysts would utilise centuries later when attempting to pin values on stocks.

JEAN TRENCHANT

Three and a half centuries after Pisano, French mathematician Jean Trenchant further advanced the mathematics of discounting. His 1558 book *L'Arithmétique* contained a practical table to facilitate the number crunching. His book also described perpetuities — the mathematics of infinite series. This was another valuation tool to be picked up by future stock analysts, as, for the purpose of valuation, companies are commonly considered to have an infinite life.

I've no doubt Pisano and Trenchant were justly proud of their achievements, but there is a very large elephant in the room when you start using these tools to value stocks. The formulae are mathematically sound, but formulae require accurate inputs in order to provide accurate outputs. Future cash flows can be defined for bonds and annuities, and both are financial instruments to which Pisano's and Trenchant's formulae can be usefully applied. But the accuracy is lost when calculating stock values. Stock analysts are left to plug in guesses (sorry, 'estimates'!) of what the future cash flows might be.

JOSEPH DE LA VEGA

The creation of the first publicly traded joint stock company, the Dutch East India Company (VOC), in 1602 launched a brand new sport: share trading. This meant an arena had to be built where traders could meet. Stock punters quickly discovered it wasn't much fun hanging around street corners during the cold Dutch winter. Work on the Amsterdam Exchange, the world's first purpose-built stock exchange, began in 1608 under the direction of architect and stonemason Hendrick de Keyser. Completed in 1611, it consisted of an open courtyard surrounded by a colonnaded archway to provide protection from the weather. And within this building a Sephardic Jew named Joseph de la Vega traded shares.

Fortunately for us, not only did de la Vega possess an intimate understanding of the Amsterdam Exchange, but he was also an accomplished writer. He left behind a priceless account of activity on the trading floor, *Confusion de Confusiones*, written in 1688. De la Vega's fascinating narrative reveals beliefs and experiences that were little different from those of modern-day analysts and investors. He judged that a driver of the stock price of the Dutch East India Company was whether 'the business of the Company is moving forward, whether its operations in Japan, Persia, China are proceeding favourably, whether many ships are sailing to the motherland, and whether they are richly laden, particularly with spices'. He also saw that 'opinion on the stock exchange itself' was important.[66]

Let's pause for a while to reflect on these two statements by de la Vega, and compare them to the writings of Keynes, two and a half centuries later. In his 1936 classic *The General Theory of Employment, Interest and Money*, Keynes describes returns on stocks as being driven by two factors in combination. They are 'enterprise', which relates to the prospects of the business, and 'speculation', which relates to the psychology of the market. With this in mind, let's read de la Vega's comments again (remembering that he wrote them almost 250 years before *The General Theory* was published). Just like Keynes, de la Vega describes as important 'the business of the company' (that is, enterprise) and the 'opinion on the stock exchange itself' (that is, the psychology of the market).

De la Vega also told us he used calculations to analyse stocks. He didn't outline his methodology, but he did make the following comment, which indicates he probably used estimates of future dividends as an input:

> The price of the shares is now 580, it seems to me that they will climb to a much higher price because of the good business of the Company, of the reputation of its goods, of the prospective dividends, and of the peace in Europe. Nevertheless I decide not to buy shares through fear that I might encounter a loss and might meet with embarrassment if my calculations should prove erroneous.[67]

That de la Vega placed significant weight on the dividends when valuing VOC stock was more pertinent then than it is now. The company had a policy of paying out nearly all earnings as dividends, something that is now the exception rather than the rule. And since 99 per cent of company profits were paid out, it meant that for 50 years dividends were treated as a proxy for earnings.[68] De la Vega wasn't the only investor of his day who saw the close link between dividends and the share price; during the first 70 years of VOC's operations its share price and dividends moved in lockstep.

De la Vega's comment that he gave consideration to 'the reputation of its goods' is interesting, as it evokes Buffett's contemporary advice to search out companies with an economic moat, among which might be those with a superior product or coveted brand or trademark. And de la Vega's fear that his 'calculations should prove erroneous' might have been allayed if he'd applied Graham's 'margin of safety' concept.* Pity Ben wasn't around to guide him.

---

*Employing a 'margin of safety' involves deriving a lower 'calculated value' to allow for inaccuracy in the inputs to its calculation, either by using conservative inputs or by reducing the product of the calculation. It asks that you buy your favoured stock only if the market price is at or below your adjusted value.

After discussing Pisano's discounted cash flow and de la Vega's dividend-based value calculations, it's interesting to reconsider the references to 20th-century financial economist John Burr Williams, who is sometimes hailed as the first to articulate the theory of discounted cash flow–based valuation, and is popularly credited with originating dividend-based valuation.

Wikipedia boldly states that Williams was one of the first to 'view stock prices as determined by intrinsic value', 'is recognised as a founder and developer of fundamental analysis...and was amongst the first to articulate the theory of discounted cash flow based valuation'.

Sorry, Wiki, but all three statements are wrong. Williams was born in 1900, centuries after those who should receive the credit for each of these ideas. It's unfortunate that such a popular source of information should dispense such myths, although, to be fair, Wikipedia is not alone in doing so.

SIR JOSIAH CHILD AND THE 17TH-CENTURY BUFFETT

The word 'intrinsic' comes from the Latin word *intrinsecus* meaning inwardly or inward. It isn't clear when it was first applied to stock valuation.

The fifth edition of Ben Graham's classic tome *Security Analysis* has this to say on the matter: 'We do not know when the term intrinsic value was first applied to investments, but it was mentioned in a pamphlet published in 1848, *Stocks, and Stock-jobbing in Wall Street* by William Armstrong.'

For the sanctity of Ben's memory it's fortunate these aren't actually his words (they were inserted in the fifth edition, which postdated his death), but whoever was responsible for them didn't dig deep enough. I don't know either when intrinsic value was first applied to investments, but I do know it was well before 1848. English aristocrat Sir Josiah Child, for example, referred to it in his 1681 book *A Treatise Concerning the East-India Trade*. He wrote:

> When we tell gentlemen, or others, they may buy stock, and come into the Company when they please: they presently reply, they know that, but then they must also pay 280l. for 100l. And when we say the intrinsick value is worth so much; which is as true as 2 and 2 makes 4, yet it is not so soon demonstrated to their apprehensions, notwithstanding it is no hard task to make out.

Interesting words from the 1st Baronet of Wanstead. Seems in 1681 most investors were just as uncertain as they are today regarding a stock's real worth. Having confidence in your own valuation is difficult particularly when it's not within a bull's roar of what everyone else thinks it should be. But the fact that Sir Josiah was both the English East India Company's governor and its largest shareholder might help explain his confidence in determining the company's 'intrinsick value'. A little bit of inside information always comes in handy in these matters.

Late in Sir Josiah's life a broadsheet published in London called the *Athenian Mercury* ran one of those 'Dear Abby' columns where readers write in for advice on a variety of matters. (In fact its editor, John Dunton, is credited with initiating the Dear Abby concept.) The 7 April 1691 edition carried a very interesting letter from a reader. At the time London's financial markets were in the grip of a bull market. The reader had holdings in the English East India Company and the Royal African Company, both of which were trading at prices much higher than he'd bought them for. In explaining his dilemma he stated he could 'now dispose of his interest at greater rates than he is assured they are really worth'. He even told the editor why someone might be stupid enough to buy his stock: 'the ignorant buyer be wholly guided by other men's actions'.

Today we call this bull market phenomenon the 'Greater Fool Theory'. Value is largely forgotten. Stocks are bought simply because they've been going up. And the expectation is they'll continue going up, so enabling the holder to pass them on later to another equally uninformed person at an even higher price. But this 17th-century reader seemed to break the mould. He appeared to be fairly savvy. He recognised share prices are subject to two powerful forces—value and emotion—and that an excessive amount of emotion was driving the prices he was observing. One might almost describe him as the 'Great-great-grandfather of Behavioural Finance'.

The letter went on to present his dilemma. He wasn't looking for investment advice; rather, he was asking a moral question. Given the circumstances, would it be wrong to sell the overvalued stock to another man? Now really! Try asking that question today. You'd be heavily sedated within minutes of the doctor's arrival, and certified within hours. The attitude held by today's investors is that it's perfectly ethical to achieve the best possible sale price without regard to the faceless buyer on the other side of the trade.

The newspaper replied with a quote from the Bible: 'Let no man go beyond, or defraud his Brother in any Matter, because the Lord is the Avenger of all such' (1 Thessalonians 4:6).

But is this 17th-century stock seller defrauding his brother? It assumes that his determination of value is the correct one. Consider also that 'the ignorant buyer' is not alone in his apparent ignorance. The stock price is set by the combined views of many market participants, meaning the market is ignorant. Is this not the principle upon which every value investor hopes to operate today? So for this 17th-century value investor we need to say: 'Bad luck, pal. You had the skills but you were born in the wrong century.' No investor today would consider this situation as a moral dilemma.

I wish I'd been able to talk to this 17th-century Warren Buffett, because this whole concept of what is a 'just price' is one that philosophers had grappled with long before his day. To mention just three: Greek philosopher Aristotle had reflected on the doctrine of just price three centuries before the birth of Christ; 13th-century Italian philosopher Thomas Aquinas addressed it in his best-known work, *Summa Theologica*; and in the 17th century English philosopher John Locke wrote of price morality in a four-page essay entitled 'Venditio'. Like Aristotle and Aquinas before him, Locke asks: what is the just price? Or, put another way, what is the price a moral person would charge another? Locke argued that the market price is the just price. So, according to Locke, our 17th-century Dear Abby writer shouldn't have been so worried.

Locke's justification was that if the shares were sold at a price below the market price they would likely be on-sold for profit by the next guy at the prevailing market price (today we refer to this as arbitrage). Under these circumstances the final owner of the shares would still have bought at the higher price. The first owner would simply have passed on his potential profit to an interim party.

THOMAS BASTON AND DANIEL DEFOE

The South Sea Bubble of 1720 preceded one of the most infamous stock market crashes in English history. And, as with every stock market bubble since, there were voices warning that it was all going to end in tears. Three of these voices belonged to Thomas Baston, Daniel Defoe (author of *Robinson Crusoe*) and Archibald Hutcheson. These three men didn't pin a date on the impending stock market crash. Rather, they acknowledged there is only so much air you can push into a balloon before it blows up in your face. The term 'intrinsick value' was used by each of them when expressing their concerns.

Baston released his book *Thoughts on Trade and a Publick Spirit* in 1716. In it he expressed his concern regarding the number of new share issues for companies without sound business stories: 'No sooner is any company erected ... but immediately 'tis divided into shares and then traded for in Exchange Alley, before 'tis known whether the project has any intrinsick value in it.'

At the height of the South Sea Bubble Defoe wrote a book titled *The Anatomy of Exchange-Alley: or, A System of Stock-Jobbing*. He was critical of activities in the coffee houses and streets around Exchange Alley, where London's stock speculators congregated to trade. He starts his book with all guns blazing, describing the market as characterised by rampant manipulation by stock-jobbers for their own personal gain. Interestingly, he makes specific reference to Sir Josiah Child (who by then was 20 years in his grave) as 'that original of Stock-Jobbing'. Defoe says: 'If Sir Josiah had a Mind to buy, the first thing he did was to Commission his Brokers to look sower, shake their heads, suggest bad News from India ...'

Defoe refers to 'Intrinsick Value' twice in his book, and in the first reference he uses the term as we use it today:

> That Six or Eight Men Shall Combine together, and by pretended Buying or Selling among themselves, raise or sink the Stock of the E. India Company, to what extravagant pitch of Price they will; so to wheedle others sometimes to Buy, sometimes to Sell, as their occasion require; and with so little regard to Intrinsick Value, or the circumstances of the Company ...

The vitriol runs through his book from the first page to the last. Makes you wonder whether Defoe might himself have lost a pay packet or two in the market.

ARCHIBALD HUTCHESON

Archibald Hutcheson was a member of parliament for 14 years, from 1713 to 1727, which means the South Sea Bubble burst exactly halfway through his political career. When one reads of this 18th-century financial fiasco Hutcheson's name pops up everywhere. As the bubble grew, he became increasingly vocal regarding the heady prices South Sea stock was fetching in Exchange Alley. His concerns were based on his own valuation of the stock. Indeed, his capacity to undertake an independent valuation and then back it with powerful conviction has prompted a modern-day author, Richard Dale, to dub Hutcheson 'the Father of Investment Analysis'. (Sincere apologies to Ben Graham from the Brits.)

Let's look at the tools Hutcheson had available for his valuation. Firstly, he used a method already being applied to valuing commercial property, the asset most commonly held by the moneyed gentry of his time. Steady rental streams meant property was relatively easy to value. As I've already mentioned, the income stream was capitalised by applying a multiple called 'number of years purchase'. It was from this that our popular P/E multiple was derived, and the technique is still used to value commercial properties today. Secondly, he had Pisano's discounting formula. It had long been used to value the other principal asset of the day, government bonds.

While Hutcheson had access to both of these valuation tools (PE and discounted cash flow), he knew valuing stocks presented a unique set of challenges.

The share price of the South Sea Company had risen dramatically amid the euphoria of the South Sea Bubble, and Hutcheson set out to demonstrate that it was trading at ridiculously inflated prices. The company had two sources of revenue, one real and one potential. The real source was a steady stream of interest paid on loans it had granted the British government. The company received its charter in 1711 and the associated *South Sea Act* provided for the conversion of over £9 million of British government debt into equity. The then holders of British sovereign debt gave up their debt certificates and were issued South Sea Company share certificates in their place. This meant the British government owed the £9 million to the South Sea Company. The government made interest payments into the South Sea coffers, which were then passed on to shareholders in the form of dividends. Hutcheson had no trouble valuing this cash flow. He valued it just as he would a bond—using the discounted cash flow formula.

But it was pinning a value on the second arm of the company's business activity that proved to be difficult. The company's charter also granted it a trading monopoly over a large area of South America. The Act authorised 'trading to the South Seas and other parts of America, and for the encouragement of fishing'.

At the time Hutcheson was making his 'intrinsick value' calculations, the South Sea Company had been in existence for nine years. It was obvious to him that this second arm of business activity, the South Sea trade, hadn't amounted to much at all, and he doubted it ever would. It was a pretty fair call since South America was largely controlled by the Spanish, and England and Spain had been at war for years. Philip V of Spain wasn't about to let bygones be bygones and open up Spain's lucrative trade routes to its sparring partner, so Hutcheson excluded this part of the company's activities from his valuation.

Hutcheson was well known for his warnings regarding the dangerous state of affairs in Exchange Alley, including the prediction that share prices were changing hands at such inflated prices a financial crash was inevitable. On 11 June 1720 he entered the House of Commons armed with his most recent calculations on the value of South Sea stock. On taking the floor he declared to the House that, based on his calculations, South Sea shares had an 'intrinsick value' of £200, against the current market price of £740. Hutcheson warned of what would happen when 'the present reigning madness should happen to cease'.[69]

Hutcheson's appeals for sanity were largely ignored and the share price of South Sea stock climbed even further. In July Hutcheson revised his calculations. Based on a recent third subscription of capital, he now valued it at around £300. The market price peaked that month at around £1000. The speculative frenzy had seen the share price increase eightfold since the start of the year.

If you were to speak charitably of the South Sea punters — those who were buying stock at nose-bleed prices — you might say they were just more optimistic about the company's trading opportunities in South America than Hutcheson, that they had the smell of Inca gold in their nostrils and believed the sky was the limit regarding future trading opportunities. But the reality is that few of them were giving any thought to these issues at all. All they saw was the rising share price, and the only trade they were thinking about was the one with the next mug punter who'd take the stock off their hands.

But economic reality always has a way of rearing its annoying head eventually, and by mid October South Sea's share price had collapsed by over 80 per cent from its July highs. Those who'd bought in at £1000 per share were crying poor. In the words of an anonymous pamphleteer of the day, their greed ensured they had become the 'hindmost':

> The additional rise of this stock above the true capital will be only imaginary; one added to one, by any rule of vulgar arithmetic, will never make three and a half, consequently, all the fictitious value must be a loss to some persons or other, first or last ... the only way to prevent it to oneself must be to sell out betimes, and so let the Devil take the hindmost.[70]

The craziness of the prices at which South Sea stock was trading is brought home when you consider that at its peak the total market capitalisation of the company was £400 million. That represented twice the value of all the land in England. As the events of 1720 were unfolding the Duchess of Marlborough wrote:

> Every mortal that has common sense or that knows anything of figures sees that 'tis not possible by all the arts and tricks upon earth to carry 400 000 000 of paper credit with 15 000 000 of specie. This makes me think that this project must burst in a while and fall to nothing.

Hutcheson wasn't drawn into the speculative madness as others were. Instead he behaved more like a battle-hardened analyst of the modern era. What he did was:

- perform his calculations without being influenced by the market price

- make a realistic assessment of where the business was heading

- apply a discount rate to derive a current value for the whole company

- divide this by the number of shares to establish an intrinsic value

- calculate the number of shares by applying a dilution factor for the potential exercise of outstanding options

- and (most importantly, and to borrow the words of Warren Buffett) prevent emotions from corroding his intellectual framework.[71]

So I ask: what's so modern about security analysis? I still hear people say it's an invention of the 20th century.

If you read Charles Mackay's classic book *Extraordinary Popular Delusions and the Madness of Crowds*, you might believe everyone in 1720 England had gone stark raving mad. But many were keeping their heads, and Hutcheson's calculations had an influence. Adam Anderson, the first historian of the South Sea Bubble, says the 'fair and candid calculations' of 'that ingenious gentleman Archibald Hutcheson' were having an influence in Exchange Alley and 'some began to have their eyes opened by [his] judicious calculations'.[72] Anderson would have known — he was working for the South Sea Company at the time.

It's important to stress, though, that Hutcheson wasn't a maverick defying the common belief of his time. Valuation metrics, familiar to us today, were regularly used in the 18th century. Another example is the use of dividend yield. Consider again these words, written nearly three hundred years ago by the author of 'Remarks on the Celebrated Calculations', which I presented in the previous chapter:

> The main principle, on which the whole science of stock-jobbing is built, viz. That the benefit of a dividend (considered as a motive to the buying or keeping of a stock) is always to be estimated according to the rate it bears to the price of the stock, because the purchaser is supposed to compare that rate with the profits he might make of money, if otherwise employed.[73]

A near-perfect explanation of why stock prices go up when interest rates go down.

I can't leave this discussion of Hutcheson without referring back to a point made in chapter 10. I was referring to an article written by a technical analyst who denied that determinations of underlying value serve any useful purpose. Instead he proposed that there was great benefit in the use of charts because 'the price chart summarizes the opinions and emotions of all market participants'. But after reading the story of the South Sea Bubble, can we really believe that Hutcheson would have been better informed had he based his judgement on 'the opinions and emotions of all market participants', the majority of whom were chasing the price of South Sea shares skyward with no consideration of value?

THOMAS MORTIMER

Born in 1730, Englishman Thomas Mortimer was, by the age of 20, writing on the subjects of economics, business and politics. In 1761 his popular investment book *Every Man His Own Broker* hit the bookshops. It remained in print for 46 years, running to its fourteenth and final edition in 1807. In Mortimer's day stockbrokers didn't have a monopoly on the buying and selling of shares. Any investor could wander down to where stocks were being traded, rub shoulders with the brokers and trade on their own account. Mortimer's book, as the title implies, was written as a self-help guide for those who wanted to get down to Exchange Alley and get amongst it.

The advice dispensed by Mortimer was, in part, a product of his own bitter experiences dealing with the professionals down at the exchange. In 1756 he made what proved to be a very poor investment. In order to save on brokerage he entered Jonathan's Coffee House in London and purchased scrip on his own account. As Mortimer describes it, he lost a 'genteel fortune'. His hostility towards stock-jobbers and their manipulative activities comes through in his writings.

In *Everyman His Own Broker* Mortimer offers his own views on stock valuation:

> Every original share of a trading company's stock must greatly increase in value, in proportion to the advantages arising from the commerce they are engaged in; and such is the nature of trade in general, that it either considerably increases, or falls into decline; and nothing can be greater proof of a company's trade being in a flourishing condition, than when their credit is remarkably good, and the original shares in their stock will sell at a considerable premium. This, for instance, has always been, and still is the case of EAST INDIA STOCK in particular, not to instance another. The present price of a share of £100 in the company's stock is £134. The reason of this advance on what cost the original proprietor only £100 is, that the company, by the profits they have made in trade, are enabled to pay £6 per annum interest or dividend for £100 share. But then it is uncertain how long they may continue to make so large an annual dividend, especially in time of war; for several circumstances may occur (though it is not likely they should) that may molest their trade in their settlements, and diminish their profits...[74]

Here Mortimer links the rationally determined share price to the sustainability of earnings and the size of the resultant dividends. He also highlights the importance of the company's credit (cash flow and gearing). Many of today's analysts would view these concepts as their modern-day intellectual property. Mortimer's words demonstrate how wrong that view is.

BEFORE CROSSING THE ATLANTIC

Before we leave Europe and cross to the United States, I want to recap the level of sophistication of both the financial analysis and financial securities already in use by the end of the 18th century. Let's use 1790 as our 'line in the sand'. This was the year the US opened its first exchange, the Philadelphia Stock Exchange. Before the US markets opened for business, the foundations underpinning modern-day financial markets were already well established in Europe. Not only had publicly traded stocks been around for nearly two centuries, but by 1790:

- options on shares had been available for a similarly long period. From the very beginning Europeans had used options to take leveraged speculative positions, for engineering different investment risk profiles and for hedging physical positions—all uses to which they are put today.

- contracts for difference (CFDs) had long been in use. Derivatives with similar properties (called *ducaton shares*) were being used by the Dutch in the 17th century. In England Sir John Barnard's *Act of 1734* specifically banned them or, as the legislation stated, prohibited 'the evil practice of making up differences for stocks'. Here, three centuries ago, the English had identified and legislated against the high risks associated with the use of CFDs and the financial grief their trade was causing. Today they've been reintroduced as some sort of innovative marvel.

- there had long been an appreciation of what drove financial markets, in terms of both fundamentals and human psychology. Our current understanding has advanced little.

- the principles of valuation underpinning modern financial analysis—namely the application of multiples to earnings, discounting prospective dividends, and an appreciation of buying companies with solid balance sheets, good management and favourable business prospects—were well understood and regularly described in the early financial literature.

Now let's move our story to the United States, which for more than a century has been home to many of the largest and most powerful financial institutions in the world.

Chapter summary

- In 1202 Leonardo Pisano provided the first written description of a method for calculating the present value of future cash flows by applying a discount rate to them.

- The principle of calculating the present value of future cash flows underlies today's most popular stock valuation formulae.

- While the formulae used for stock valuation are typically mathematically sound, the answers they deliver are compromised by our inability to determine accurate inputs.

- Contrary to popular belief, investors have been attempting to calculate the difference between a stock's market price and its underlying (intrinsic) value for centuries.

- The foundations underpinning modern-day financial markets were already well established in Europe centuries ago.

18

TIME TO CROSS
THE ATLANTIC

The bronze statue of George Washington on the steps of Wall Street's old Sub-Treasury Building marks the symbolic birthplace of a nation. It records the position where, on 30 April 1789, Washington stood on a balcony to be sworn in as the first President of the United States. Among the ten thousand witnessing the inauguration that day was a young lawyer named Alexander Hamilton. Hamilton had been Washington's trusted aide-de-camp in the war against the British, the war that had secured the new nation's independence five and a half years earlier.

Washington knew the nation he was about to lead required a strong financial system. To oversee its establishment he offered Robert Morris, financier of the war against the British, the job as the nation's first Secretary of the Treasury. Morris declined but recommended Hamilton be appointed instead. The young lawyer accepted and was appointed in September of 1789. He got the ball rolling quickly, creating a new central bank and issuing debt in the name of the United States government. The new bank scrip and government bonds required a secondary market for their trade. By March of 1792 a stock exchange had been organised at 22 Wall Street. Since there was no monopoly on stock trading, a rival group of brokers operated independently in the open air down the street. Five securities were traded—three forms of government bonds and the securities of the Bank of New York and the Bank of the United States.

Many historians record the symbolic birth of today's New York Stock Exchange as 17 May 1792. On that day, under a tree outside 68 Wall Street, 24 stockbrokers signed the Buttonwood Agreement. It established brokerage rates and conditions of trade between members of their self-selected group. Philadelphia might have been the first stock exchange in the US, but the Buttonwood Agreement marked the genesis of what was to become the largest and most powerful financial community the world has seen—Wall Street.

The US hadn't even celebrated its third birthday as a nation before it experienced its first financial panic. The Panic of 1792, like all the European panics before it and world panics since, was preceded by a period of rampant speculation. Everyone got pretty excited about having some new securities to trade, and a period of 'scriptomania' ensued. One fellow who got particularly carried away was Hamilton's first assistant secretary, William Duer. He ran up massive levels of debt to fund his speculation, but his propensity to borrow exceeded his skill as a speculator. Ultimately he owed money far and wide, and news of his bankruptcy created a flashpoint for the hysteria. The 1792 Panic had all the characteristics of those that followed—insider trading, embezzlement, rampant speculation, excessive leverage, market manipulation and, in the post-crash wash-up, debate among politicians and officials regarding the need for more regulation of financial markets.

The 19th century dawned in the wake of the crash. And by its end—that is, within a period of 100 years—the US had transformed itself from a largely agrarian nation into an industrial powerhouse.

INVESTORS OR COWBOYS?

The 19th century was a period of unbounded commercial growth in the US, and to feed this growth there developed an unquenchable thirst for new capital. Money initially flowed across the Atlantic from Europe, particularly from England. But by the mid 19th century the US stock market was starting to mature, and as the century progressed it was increasingly able to contribute to its own capital needs.

So what was the US stock market like during the mid to late 1800s? Historians and writers like to focus on the cowboy element. Since the Securities and Exchange Commission was yet to be created, it wasn't regulation that guided investor behaviour but rather the moral compass of each participant. Insider trading was rife, and an appointment to a company board or two meant there was no shortage of information to trade on. It's a period characterised by the 'robber barons'—stock manipulators such as Jacob Little, Daniel Drew, Jim Fisk and Jay Gould.

In describing this period, historians focus on the stories of insider trading and market manipulation, which means descriptions of how *legitimate* investors went about making investment decisions are difficult to find. Perhaps this is why Americans were perceived both then and for decades after as traders who looked on stocks as providing a quick buck rather than a long-term stream of dividend income. And maybe it's why Keynes held the same view when in 1936 he wrote, 'It is rare, one is told, for an American to invest, as many Englishmen still do, "for income"; and he will not readily purchase an investment except in the hope of capital appreciation.'[75]

But dig deep enough and you'll discover this view wasn't universal. Even in its infancy, Wall Street saw people behaving as true investors, calculating their own values for stocks and investing accordingly, rather than simply trading shifting stock prices. William Armstrong referred to 'intrinsic value' in his 1848 pamphlet 'Stocks, and Stock-jobbing in Wall Street'. He noted that, although intrinsic value is the principal determinant in setting the market prices of securities, it isn't the only factor involved.

CORNELIUS VANDERBILT

Investors in the 19th century paid a lot of attention to a stock's 'par value', being the minimum price at which new equity could be issued. Investors treated it as a base of value, in much the same way as the face value of a bond. Earnings yields and dividend yields were calculated using the fixed par value as the denominator, rather than the constantly changing market price as they are today.

This faith in par value was linked to investors' expectations that the price of any stock investment was matched by the value of its hard assets. The 19th-century financial analyst Henry Varnum Poor, founder of Standard & Poor's, wrote of stock issues where this didn't occur as follows: 'Such enormous additions to the capital of companies, without any increase in facilities … threaten more than anything else to destroy the value of railway property as well as to prove most oppressive to the public.'

Poor was stating that stocks are worth what their assets are worth. This view was so firmly held that stocks selling above book value per share (the net value of their assets as recorded on the balance sheet divided by the total number of shares) were referred to as 'watered down stock', and any suggested value above book value was referred to as 'water'. This view isn't held today. Value is now seen as coming from a company's earnings power, and a great business idea can see strong profits generated from a small asset base. Today we accept that stocks with good earnings prospects will trade at multiples of book value. This is perhaps one of the biggest conceptual shifts in stock valuation to have occurred since Poor's time.

But even then the idea that a stock's value and its book value were inseparably linked was being challenged. One of the challengers was the wealthy industrialist Cornelius Vanderbilt, who had built his wealth on the back of a steamship and rail empire second to none. In the years following the American Civil War, he'd gained controlling interests in several rail companies, one being the Hudson River Railroad. In 1867 he orchestrated a new issue of Hudson River stock. Shareholders were asked to stump up just $54 per share for a stock with a $100 par value. At the time this was an outrageous thing to do. Railroad regulator and executive Charles F. Adams Jr. described it as an 'astounding' act of 'financial legerdemain'.

In other words, Adams thought Vanderbilt was performing an act of trickery—of trying to make two equal one and a half. Vanderbilt didn't think intrinsic value should be measured in cold, hard assets. Despite having had a minimum of schooling he was a shrewd businessman. He'd built his wealth on an appreciation that cash flows and profits were the real drivers of value. Vanderbilt's critics felt that after the sub-par capital raising Hudson River's dividend must fall, but they were silenced when the company subsequently delivered a very healthy 8 per cent dividend on par.

JAY GOULD

An infamous business opponent of Vanderbilt was the cunning, ruthless and brilliant stock tactician Jay Gould. As already noted, Gould typified the manipulative activities of the 19th-century robber barons. When he died in 1892 he had amassed a fortune of $70 million. While historians like to emphasise his manipulative and speculative activities, there was a lot more to Gould than that. Charles Dow said of him: 'He endeavored to "foresee future conditions in a property" and to exercise patience in waiting for the desired results after a commitment has been made on the basis of the forecast of future value.'

This side of Gould's character is rarely written about. He is more commonly described as an inside trader and stock manipulator. But Dow's description of Gould sounds more characteristic of today's Warren Buffett, an investor capable of waiting patiently until a stock falls sufficiently in price to buy. So it seems the American value investor, while not prevalent, was around well before the dawn of the 20th century.

JAMES MEDBERY

US finance writer James Medbery died in 1873 while still in his mid thirties. His classic book, *Men and Mysteries of Wall Street*, had been published three years earlier. On reading it I found his writing to be characterised by a maturity you wouldn't expect in such a young person. Sections are pure Ben Graham.

Chapter 11 of his book carries the same message as chapter 8 of Graham's classic, *The Intelligent Investor*, a chapter Graham called 'The Investor and Market Fluctuations'. Predating Graham's book by nearly 80 years, Medbery observes that special and sensational crises can cause 'fluctuations below intrinsic value'. But perhaps the most interesting quote in Medbery's book foreshadows Buffett's well-worn quip, 'Be fearful when others are greedy and greedy when others are fearful'. Here it is:

> You will find confidence where the registry shows there should have been distrust, hesitation which ought to have been daring, doubts where faith would have been wealth. This weakness of humanity is the life of speculation.

Medbery also makes an interesting comment regarding the perennial bane of the investor's life — coming up with the most appropriate figures to plug into intrinsic value formulae. He states that what distinguishes successful from unsuccessful investors (in his day investors were called 'speculators') are the subjective inputs, in that successful investors possess insights others lack, and that blind reliance on systems and formulae doesn't deliver success. He writes:

> The reader ought to thoroughly understand, however, that there is no royal road to speculation. Given all the conditions of the problem, and profits could be ciphered out with the accuracy of a mathematical demonstration. But the unknown quantities are the stumbling-blocks of system mongers. Integrity and ability in directors, the earning capacity of the property of a corporation, the chances of the future as well as the past, are essential points to the final judgment...

Here, almost 150 years ago, Medbery was describing perfectly the dilemma facing today's stock analysts (as it no doubt will 150 years from now!). It's not about finding the best intrinsic value formula. It's not about black-box computing systems. It's not about the simple extrapolation of historical data. The most important inputs are insightful subjective judgements regarding a company's future business prospects.

In Medbery's day value investing was largely considered a pedestrian and unreliable way to make money. With an unregulated stock market, insider trading and market manipulation were seen as faster and more reliable. But Medbery leaves us in no doubt that the practice of calculating intrinsic values and comparing them to market prices did exist in 19th-century America. The question is: how many people invested this way?

A clue was offered by stockbroker-turned-investment-educator Richard Wyckoff. He describes activity in the Wall Street broking firm Price, McCormick & Co, where he worked in the late 19th century (you need to be aware that in his day 'statistics' was the term used for fundamental analysis):

> Few of these clients seemed to know much about the market... Everyone [the brokers] seemed to concentrate on handling the business. Little or no attention was paid to the statistical side – unearthing opportunities or trading in a scientific way. In fact this seemed to be the rule throughout the street. For everyone who considered the statistical side of securities, there were twenty trading on tips.

Cynics would argue that nothing has changed since Wyckoff's day.

UNITED STATES STEEL

The year 1901 saw the need for a corporate valuation the magnitude of which eclipsed any valuation before it. Sixty-five-year-old steel tycoon Andrew Carnegie had reached the end of his working career. In the decades following the American Civil War, Carnegie had built Carnegie Steel into the largest and most efficient steel producer in the US. At the turn of the 20th century the company, of which Carnegie owned half, was still in private hands.

The sale of Carnegie Steel was initiated by its 39-year-old President, Charles Schwab. Weeks before the sale, Schwab had been the guest speaker at a testimonial dinner in New York. He sensed that Carnegie was soon to retire, so that night, when he fell into conversation with New York's titan of corporate finance, J.P. Morgan, he was prepared for the direction the discussion was about to take. Morgan was keen for Carnegie to sell, and his plan was to combine the operations of Carnegie Steel with Federal Steel and nine other steel companies to create a publicly owned steel giant. The new company, United States Steel, would be listed on the Stock Exchange, with the House of Morgan controlling the $1.4 billion float. To put this into perspective, $1.4 billion represented four times the size of the US federal government budget of the day. Carnegie's take was $225 639 000, immediately gaining him the title of the wealthiest man in the world. So with all this moving and shaking you'd reckon some pretty sophisticated financial modelling would have gone into the valuation of both Carnegie Steel and the float price for US Steel. Not so. The following provides an insight into how the valuation was undertaken.

After Schwab's preliminary meetings with Morgan, he needed to broach the sale with Carnegie, and he sought advice from Carnegie's wife, Louise, regarding the best way to do it. Schwab felt comfortable talking to Louise so he visited her at the Carnegie home in New York. Twenty-two years her husband's junior, Louise was friendly with Schwab's own wife, Rana. Louise was keen for her husband to retire and was willing to offer advice to Schwab. Carnegie was a keen golfer so Louise suggested Schwab broach the subject of the sale over a round of golf.

At the completion of the quickly organised game (which Schwab ensured Carnegie won), Schwab raised the subject, asking Carnegie what price he'd be prepared to accept. Carnegie thought about it overnight and the next day presented Schwab with a single sheet of paper on which he'd scribbled a figure in pencil. The figure was $480 million, of which Carnegie was entitled to slightly less than half. Schwab took the piece of paper to Morgan, who agreed on the spot. There it was. The biggest corporate deal in history was valued without the benefit of a complex mathematical model, a corporate analyst or an advisory house.

It can only be speculated how Carnegie came up with his price; we have no insight into how he did. But given that he was an industrialist rather than a corporate financier it was unlikely to have been a sophisticated calculation. Whether Carnegie based his price on the cost of rebuilding his factories or on a multiple of the dollars his foundries and mills were spitting out, we'll never know. He was pitting his valuation skills against the great J.P. Morgan, the most savvy financier in the country. Morgan most likely based his calculation on projected earnings. Vanderbilt had stressed to Morgan years earlier that earnings were an important consideration in valuation, and, since Carnegie Steel was generating an annual profit of around $40 million, Carnegie sold out at a multiple of 12 times. We know Morgan was prepared to pay more; in fact, he later admitted to Carnegie he would have paid a $100 million more, which meant Morgan was looking at Carnegie Steel in terms of a 14.5 times multiple.

But perceptions of value are a moving feast. When US Steel first hit the stock market it opened at 38 and moved quickly to 55. Only two years later it was trading at 9. Subsequent to the float the US Bureau of Corporations issued its own valuation of US Steel, stating it was worth only half the $1.4 billion float price. Which all goes to show that valuation is a rubbery exercise at the best of times. Carnegie must have been amused by all of this price speculation subsequent to the sale. He took his $225 million in bonds, not shares. Carnegie had avoided the stock market all his life and wasn't about to throw his fortune into its unpredictable clutches. Carnegie spent the last 18 years of his life donating much of the sale proceeds to charity.

By now I hope you've developed a view on what the term 'intrinsic value' means—that it's an estimate at best rather than a figure that can be nailed precisely. Even so it's one of the most important principles underlying sound investment. Thomas Gibson put it this way in 1906 in his book *The Pitfalls of Speculation*: 'The great basic principle of speculation, the foundation upon which the entire structure rests, is the recognition of value.'[76]

CHARLES DOW

One man with great insight into the concepts of valuation and what ultimately drives share prices was Charles Dow, whose name has already been raised several times in this book.

In the 31 July 1902 edition of *The Wall Street Journal*, Dow responded to a reader who wrote asking, 'How can a man living at an interior city, where he sees quotations only once or twice a day, make money by trading in stocks?' Dow's reply warned of excessive trading and the handicap of brokers' commissions. He felt that in some ways the 'out-of-town trader' was advantaged by not being exposed to the rumours and sudden movements in prices that were the bane of the office trader. The following two quotes are drawn directly from the editorial:

> The out-of-towner wants to begin his campaign with a conviction that the stock which he buys is selling below its value.

> He must just sit on his stock, which is intrinsically below its value, until the other people observe that it is selling too low and begin to buy it or manipulate it.

Dow had fielded a similar question from another reader a year earlier: 'Is there any way by which an outsider who cannot watch fluctuations of the market hourly can trade in stocks with a fair chance of making money?' Dow's response was directed to both investors and traders. For the traders he stressed the importance of cutting losses and letting profits run, and for the investors he advised them to:

> ... buy stocks for investment; that is, to pay for them outright when they are selling below value and wait until they are up to value, getting the difference for profit. Value is determined by the margin of safety over dividends, the size and tendency of earnings: the soundness of the balance sheet and of operating methods, and general prospects for the future.[77]

These statements are remarkably similar to those made by Ben Graham decades later. Like Dow, Graham didn't believe that the out-of-towner was disadvantaged. Of the stock market Graham said: 'The farther away you get from it the more regular it appears—and the easier to profit by.'*[78]

For those of you who've read Graham's books *Security Analysis* and *The Intelligent Investor*, or those pithy one-liners by his 'out-of-towner' disciple Warren Buffett, Dow's editorials will have a familiar ring. The fact is that the seeds for much of what appears in *Security Analysis* were

---

*Legendary investor Sir John Templeton was once asked why he lived in Nassau, Bahamas. He replied, 'Because *The Wall Street Journal* arrives one day late.'

sown long before the release of its first edition in 1934, as the following should show.

VALUE INVESTING BEFORE BEN GRAHAM'S SECURITY ANALYSIS

Many believe that value investing had its birth in 1934, when *Security Analysis* was released. Here is a typical reference to the subject from a recent book: 'Graham, a value investor, invented the disciplines for analyzing stocks. Before Graham, Wall Street had no investing rules or principles.'[79] This statement fails to acknowledge the concepts and writings delivered by many great investors before Graham. To demonstrate, I'll let the following quotes do the talking. They describe investment principles often attributed to Graham yet delivered years before him.

Here's Henry Hall (1907) on Graham's requirement to seek a 'margin of safety' between the intrinsic value and market price before making an investment: 'So far as safety of capital is concerned, the ideal is most nearly attained by buying in times of great depression, or during a panic, when stocks are below their actual investment worth. The margin of safety on a purchase is then the largest.'[80]

And here's Charles Dow (1901) on the idea that the long-term determinant of prices is value: 'The tendency of prices over a considerable length of time will always be toward values.'[81]

Graham stressed that price and value were not the same thing. He personalised this phenomenon in the form of a hypothetical character called Mr Market, encouraging readers to take advantage of Mr Market's bipolar personality. So when Mr Market offered his business on the cheap he was there to be taken advantage of.

Here's Thomas Gibson (1910) on a similar theme: 'Prices frequently become divorced temporarily from values through manipulation, fighting for control or technical conditions, but the hiatus must sooner or later disappear and prices and values will be reconciled. It is when prices are lower or higher than values, present or prospective, that we have our greatest speculative opportunities.'[82]

And this from John Houghton (1694), more than two centuries before Gibson: '… if they have hopes of great Gain, they will not sell their *Share* for 10l. If they fear Loss they'll sell for less; and so *Actions* rise and fall according to hopes or fears...I find a great many understand not this affair, therefore I write this.'[83]

Graham was against buying on margin, but so were those before him, such as Moses Smith (1887): 'The position of a man who has paid for what he holds is impregnable. The bears may do their worst; but they cannot hurt him, if he will only keep cool, and laugh at their fictions.'[84]

Graham told us: 'To enjoy a reasonable chance for continued better than average results, the investor must follow policies which are not popular in Wall Street.'[85] In 1930 Fred Kelly said: '... your only chance to make money from Wall Street is to be somewhat unusual. Since the majority must be wrong, success can only come from doing the opposite from what the crowd is doing.'[86]

On the requirement for patience when investing, a common theme of Graham's, Joseph de la Vega (1688) said: 'Whoever wishes to win in this game must have patience and money.'[87]

Graham told us: 'The investor's chief problem—and even his worst enemy – is likely to be himself.' Richard Wyckoff (1930) said: 'Something in the very nature of most men seems to work against them.'[88] And William Worthington Fowler (1870) said: '... a man is befooled, bewitched and bedeviled by what he hears in the market'.[89]

Warren Buffett was enlightened when Graham taught him to value stocks by first looking at companies in their entirety. To again quote Henry Hall (1907): 'The purchase of a share of stock is an investment in the business, exactly as though the buyer were a partner in the enterprise.'[90]

Graham told us in *The Intelligent Investor*: 'You are neither right nor wrong because the crowd disagrees with you. You are right because your data and reasoning are right.' Philip L. Carret (1927) said: 'Seek facts diligently, advice never.'[91]

Graham described intrinsic value as a concept, not a specifically determinable number. Francis Wrigley Hirst (1911) said: 'The value is the real worth—a thing undefinable and impossible to ascertain.'[92]

In *Security Analysis* Graham said of intrinsic value that 'in general terms it is understood to be that value which is justified by the facts'. He also outlined the principles for inter-period and intercompany comparison.[93] Charles Dow (1902) said: 'The two requisites for analysis which shall be of any value are, first, the existence of such figures as will disclose the vital facts, and second, the existence of similar figures for previous years or for other companies with which fair comparison can be made.'[94]

Ben Graham was an investment great. He was an articulate teacher, and he had a superlative mind. The quotes given above, however, cover some of the most important principles he wrote of yet predate his teachings by decades or, in some cases, by centuries. This is in no way meant as a criticism or to be disrespectful. They merely remind us that many of the concepts found in *Security Analysis* had been embraced and taught by many great investors who came before him.

BUFFETT'S PITHY ONE-LINERS

Warren Buffett is well known for his ability to distil complex concepts of investing into simple and clear one-liners. Yet, like Graham, he was not the originator of most of these ideas. Here are some historical takes on several of his better-known quotes.

Buffett:'A truly great business must have an enduring "moat" that protects excellent returns on invested capital.'[95] Francis Wrigley Hirst (1911): 'A natural monopoly or a franchise conferred by public charter is the most stable basis for investment.'[96]

Buffett:'If we have a strength, it is in recognizing when we are operating well within our circle of competence and when we are approaching the perimeter.'[97] Charles Dow (1902): 'There is no getting away from the proposition that a man should not invest his money in something that he does not know about, and that when he does so, he is speculating, and moreover, speculation in a very dangerous fashion.'[98]

Buffett: 'In all cases an exceptional management is a vital factor.'[99] Francis Wrigley Hirst (1911): 'The most important consideration of all is management, and here the advantage of investment in a local concern with which the investor is well acquainted can readily be perceived.'[100]

Buffett, on investing successfully: 'What's needed is a sound intellectual framework for making decisions and the ability to keep emotions from corroding that framework.'[101] Henry Clews (1908): 'And yet self knowledge, with self control, may prevent these natural disqualifications from seriously interfering with success.'[102]

Buffett: 'Only buy something you'd be perfectly happy to hold if the market shut down for ten years.' Louis Guenther (1910): 'But as long as a stock has intrinsic merit behind it, returns good dividends and has borne a good reputation, it is immaterial from the investor's viewpoint whether it is listed or not.'[103]

Buffett: 'My favourite holding period is forever.' Matthew Hale Smith (1870): 'Men who buy long and hold what they buy, reap golden fortunes.'[104] And Francis Wrigley Hirst (1911): 'The essence of investment should be that it is for long periods.'[105]

Buffett: 'People who can't tolerate seeing their stocks fall by 50% shouldn't own stocks.' Thomas Mortimer (1801): 'The value of the funds, in this case, might sink near fifty per cent in a few days, owing to the vast concourse of sellers … and public tranquility being restored, the funds would recover their full value. If we have patience, some would say, and do not part with our property in the funds, the state of affairs may alter, and we shall not be losers.'[106]

Buffett, on selecting an appropriate discount rate: 'It is what can be produced by our second best investment idea. And then we aim to exceed it. In other words it's an opportunity cost.' The anonymous author of 'Remarks on the Celebrated Calculations' (1720), already quoted in chapters 16 and 17: 'The main principle, on which the whole science of stock-jobbing is built … is always to be estimated according to the rate [a dividend] bears to the price of the stock, because the purchaser is supposed to compare that rate with the profits he might make of money, if otherwise employed.'[107]

As with my comments about Graham, I'm not trying to be critical of Buffett. I have absolutely no right or any platform from which to do that anyway. Buffett has more runs on the board of investment success than any investor past or present, but he has placed on public record that none of his investment ideas are original. You often hear people say Buffett possesses a 'secret' that underlies his investment success. I feel that's unlikely, but I do believe he has an exceptional intellect, an intimate understanding of the financial markets, and the capacity to think and invest independently. Ultimately, he's taken the ideas of those who came before him and executed them brilliantly.

Chapter summary

- Even in its infancy Wall Street saw people acting as true investors by calculating their own values for stocks.

- Not all but most 19th-century investors believed that a stock's value was defined by the value of its hard assets. Today's investors typically look to earnings when valuing stocks, so companies earning high profits on low capital typically trade at significant multiples to their book value.

- Informed investors Charles Dow, Ben Graham and Warren Buffett have each held the view that it can be a disadvantage to be 'too close' to the stock market.

- Graham's classic 1934 book *Security Analysis* is a worthy bible for value investors, but the wisdom it contains cannot be attributed solely to him. Many of the principles it contains had been written about over preceding decades and centuries.

19

THE ADOPTION OF FINANCIAL REPORTING

Financier J.P. Morgan deserved his nickname 'Jupiter'. In the late 19th and early 20th century he was a godlike force presiding over the control and financing of large blocks of corporate America. Early in his career J.P. worked with his father, Junius. Both were financiers but they sat on opposite sides of the Atlantic—Junius in London and J.P. in New York. They acted as the conduit for the flow of money from English investors to capital-hungry American industrialists and railroad entrepreneurs. The US needed capital to tap its resources, produce its steel and build its factories, railroads, bridges and ships. But as America's wealth grew, so too did its capacity to fund its own expansion. At the start of J.P.'s career, London was the financial capital of the world; by its end New York wore the crown.

J.P. Morgan's career was at its zenith at the dawn of the 20th century. As already mentioned, it was he who orchestrated the first billion-dollar float, US Steel. Larger blocks of capital were needed to fund the creation of ever-larger companies, which meant this period saw a shift from private to public ownership of US enterprise. It was a new age—the age of share ownership by the common people.

This shift meant that manager and owner were no longer necessarily the same person. It created the need to establish effective lines of communication between those running the companies and those who owned them, namely the shareholders. But these lines of communication were slow to be established.

It wasn't the lack of a financial language that was preventing companies from reporting to their shareholders—the tools to facilitate this communication already existed. Double entry bookkeeping, the accounting method underlying today's financial reports, had been developed in Italy during the 15th century. No, the problem was attitudinal, one centred in America's boardrooms. Directors chose to behave more like owners of the business than employees of the shareholders. They welcomed shareholder capital but resented any form of accountability. The following statement made by the president of the American Sugar Refining Company, Henry O. Havemeyer, shows how management felt at the time:

> Let the buyer beware. That covers the whole business. You cannot wet-nurse people from the time they are born until the day they die. They have got to wade in and get stuck and that is the way men are educated and cultivated.[108]

J.P. Morgan's berating of a railroad president of the time shows Havemeyer wasn't the only director or president who thought like this. In reminding a company president that it was wrong to refer to the company's railroads as his own, Morgan bellowed: 'Your roads! Your roads belong to my clients!'

Around this time, however, the New York Stock Exchange became increasingly aware of the need to keep shareholders better informed. In 1895, only six years prior to the record-breaking US Steel float, it proposed what was then a radical idea—that companies distribute annual earnings reports to shareholders. But a proposal in the absence of legislation remained just a proposal. Compliance rates remained low, with companies offering many excuses for not publishing reports. A couple of the better ones of the day were that:

- in making their affairs known companies would 'lay their trade secrets before competitors'[109]

- stockholders should be wholly satisfied in receiving regular dividends and that financial disclosure would likely subject the directors to 'annoying inquisitions from tax gatherers'.[110]

The debate regarding the need for improved financial reporting gained momentum as the new century unfolded. Henry Clews, an influential broker at the time, was an early advocate of reform, and his calls were increasingly backed by some of the more ethically minded financiers.

But it takes massive shifts in public opinion for real reform to occur, and there's nothing like a full-blown financial crisis to heighten public opinion. There were two substantial crises around this time — the 1907 Panic and the 1929 Crash.

Government inquiries invariably follow crashes. When the public loses money you can be sure there will be a loud cry for the scalps of insider traders and morally corrupt brokers and bankers. In the wake of the 1907 Panic it was the Pujo Committee hearings of 1912. Louis D. Brandeis chronicled the investigation in his 1914 book *Other People's Money*. Brandeis saw the solution to financial excess as enhanced disclosure: 'Sunlight is said to be the best of disinfectants; electric light the most efficient policeman.'[111]

But it took yet another crash, two decades later, before Brandeis's sentiments would be embodied in law. The principal reforms coming out of the Pujo Committee hearings were the banking reforms associated with the establishment of the Federal Reserve. It wasn't until the aftermath of the 1929 Crash that financial reporting standards were substantially improved.

The period leading up to the 1929 Crash was an extremely interesting time. Like all boom times it was a period marked by excess, easy money and dubious moral behaviour. To gain an insight into that behaviour let's have a look at a couple of the principal corporate villains of the 1920s, Ivar Kreuger and Charles E. Mitchell.

THE MATCH KING

Ivar Kreuger emerged, over the course of the 1920s, as one of the most respected and profiled business moguls in the world. His friends included movie stars and presidents. His companies supplied nearly 70 per cent of the world's demand for matches. His empire included gold and mining interests, telecommunications and vast timber plantations. He owned real estate portfolios on both sides of the Atlantic. His companies provided loans to governments across Europe and South America. And where did he get much of the money for the corporate acquisitions and government loans? From the US equity markets. That's right. To Kreuger a dollar was a dollar no matter where it came from. Whether it came from bona fide business profits or the pockets of new investors, he looked upon every dollar as the same — his.

Clearly not everything in Kreuger's empire was as it appeared to the outside world—his wealth was in fact a mirage. Kreuger's house of cards had been built on the back of Wall Street's lax reporting standards. He'd tapped the equity markets for millions of dollars yet had provided little to no information about his companies' financial affairs. What Kreuger failed to produce in financial disclosure he more than made up for in charm and persuasion. He had the press, the public and the partners at stockbroker Lee, Higginson & Co. convinced he was the safest bet on Wall Street. In reality he was busy shuffling money from one subsidiary to another in a desperate attempt to keep his corporate raft from sinking. It was largely a Ponzi scheme.[*]

The Match King kept both his broker and his investors happy by confident reassurance and a succession of new capital raisings. His eventual demise came after the 1929 Crash. As Buffett likes to say, 'only when the tide goes out do you discover who's been swimming naked'. Kreuger committed suicide just before news of his scam became public. *The New York Times* had this to say five years after his suicide:

> From the record of falsehood and betrayal with which Kreuger besmirched the very pillars of finance in the leading countries of the world has come, particularly in the United States, the erection of new safeguards for investors. In our Securities Act are to be found preventives whose origin is to be traced definitely to the Kreuger experiences.[112]

So Kreuger was a big player. A government-generated report that preceded the *Securities Act of 1933* devoted more than 250 pages to him, and some historians have said his activities were a major contributor to the 1929 Crash. But it would be wrong to blame the Crash solely on Kreuger.

As an aside, it's interesting to compare Kreuger with Australian-born Tim Johnston, of Firepower fame. It seems that similar scams can be replayed to a different generation. In the early 2000s Johnston tried playing the same games Kreuger had 80 years earlier. Johnston claimed

---

[*]A Ponzi scheme is an investment scam named after fraudster Charles Ponzi. Rather than having any investment merit, it generates its money principally from new capital provided by new investors to the scheme. To attract new investors it pays existing investors handsomely, but when the flow of new capital dries up, as it invariably does, the scheme folds.

to have developed a pill that, when added to engine fuel, resulted in the dual benefits of reduction in fuel consumption and reduction in harmful emissions. He claimed to have multimillion-dollar contracts to sell his wonder pill around the world. None of it was true. The pill was less than useless and sales were close to nonexistent. Yet his persuasive charms had investors, politicians and government authorities around the world chasing him with investment dollars. Before his scam was exposed he'd duped them of more than $100 million.

But there's one thing that eluded Johnston: in the absence of scientific proof of the pill's efficacy or of audited financial statements proving his claimed sales revenues, he couldn't float Firepower on any stock exchange. Unlike 80 years earlier, when Kreuger was operating, the stock market's regulatory authorities had presented a strong barrier against unscrupulous behaviour.

POST-CRASH WALL STREET

When America was rocked by the 1929 Crash, stories started to emerge of the corporate excesses of the pre-Crash era. And while rising share prices had cloaked much of the morally questionable behaviour of the Roaring Twenties, the world was now a different place. Answers were demanded, scalps were sought—and solutions were needed. The time was ripe for legislative change.

The Committee on Banking and Currency was charged with delivering answers to those demanding to know what had happened in the 1929 Crash. But after 12 months it had come up with next to nothing and the hearings were due to be shelved. Even the incoming President, Franklin D. Roosevelt, a strong advocate for social and economic reform under the banner of the 'New Deal', had little interest in the committee continuing its investigations. That all changed in the early months of 1933.

In what were thought to be the dying days of the inquiry, a new Chief Counsel was appointed, Ferdinand Pecora. The press quickly picked up on the penetrating and aggressive courtroom style of the brilliant young Sicilian-born lawyer. His questions were probing, the disclosures more revealing. The inquiry quickly found its way onto the front pages of newspapers around the nation. Pecora single-handedly revived interest in the inquiry and as a result it was extended 14 months into Roosevelt's first term. Pecora exposed a culture of self-interest and moral corruption firmly embedded in the psyche of Wall Street's banking elite. The nation was shocked by the magnitude of the self-enriching deals, that the perpetrators denied any feelings of guilt and that the deals were all carried out behind a cloak of non-disclosure. Pecora's first scalp was Charles 'Sunshine Charley' Mitchell, the Chairman of National City Bank (now Citibank). Before Pecora exposed his activities, Mitchell had been one of the most respected bankers in the country.

Pecora uncovered City Bank's 'morale loans'. The bank's president, Gordon Rentschler, told the inquiry how the loans had worked. Like other investors who held stock on margin, many of City Bank's senior executives were exposed to mounting margin calls in the wake of the 1929 Crash. Indeed many faced financial ruin, so the bank's board offered each a financial lifeline. It authorised that large, unsecured, interest-free loans be advanced to the bank's top 100 executives. The board justified the loans as 'protecting such officers in the present emergency, and thereby sustaining the morale of the organization'. Hence the name 'morale loans'.

The loans were financed by shareholders, without their knowledge. Most of the executives were either unable to repay the loans or looked upon their repayment as optional. Only about 5 per cent were ever paid back. To avoid public disclosure the bad loans were shifted into an affiliate, the National City Company. Not surprisingly, this company never disclosed its annual income statements.

The National City Company was used to hide other dirty linen as well. The bank had suffered substantial losses on a Cuban sugar investment several years earlier, and Mitchell was responsible for both the failed deal and the subsequent cover-up. The $25 million financial hole was plugged with money from a public equity raising. Subscribers had no idea that half the $50 million they put up was being used to cover the loss; they assumed the money was being used for new investment. Pecora's revelations demonstrated to the nation that reporting standards required a major overhaul.

Pecora also painted a picture of City Bank as a high-pressure securities shop offloading second-rate stocks and bonds to unsuspecting investors. The man in the street, previously ignored by the broking industry, had been increasingly tapped for the speculative dollar during the course of the Roaring Twenties. And this was in no small part due to Mitchell. No stock was too overpriced and no bond was too risky for Sunshine Charley's boys to push onto innocent clients. His trained team of commission-driven brokers didn't feel the need to operate under the principle 'buyer be informed'; rather, they operated on *caveat emptor*—that is, 'buyer beware'.

Interestingly, just 18 months prior to the Pecora hearings one of City Bank's bond salesmen, Julian Sherrod, released a book that described the bank's high-pressure sales techniques. Unemployed and bankrupt, Sherrod wrote his book, *Scapegoats*, to generate sufficient dollars to put food on his family's table. In it he described the moral decay that infected Wall Street's financial institutions. While he was clearly describing the activities of City Bank and Mitchell, he never actually named them in his book.

SHIFTING EMPHASIS ON THE MEANS OF VALUATION

Julian Sherrod had also observed a shift in how company valuations were being presented in prospectuses. Values were no longer measured in terms of cold, hard assets but rather as multiples of potential earnings. A number of businessmen and investors (Cornelius Vanderbilt and J.P. Morgan among them) had adopted this method of valuation many years earlier. In 1910 Louis Guenther had described this change of emphasis when he wrote of departing from 'our more conservative methods of basing the capital on physical assets...Instead, the earnings possibilities of a corporation are capitalized'.[113] But even by the 1920s not everyone had come to accept this method of valuation. Sherrod was among them, as the following quote from *Scapegoats* shows:

> I have always had the feeling that the offering of 850 000 shares in Dodge Brothers Inc. Preference Stock (no par value) ushered in the Belshazzar era of finance. There is one thing about that deal which I have always admired. The Merchants just came right out and in the face of the circular stated in plain English that it was practically all what we call 'Water'. Here is the statement:
>
> 'The capital stock of the company (no par value) will be issued almost entirely against the established earnings power, which is not assigned a value in the balance sheet.'

Sherrod went on to say:

> That is one of the frankest and most honest statements I have ever seen in a circular. Then on the back of the circular is a balance sheet which shows you are buying nothing but goodwill and going concern value.*

After the Crash, but before he lost his job, Sherrod attended a conference organised for City Bank salesmen. He tells us that the Chairman, Charles Mitchell (the man Pecora grilled during the post-Crash hearings), addressed the sales team. He talked about the company's opaque affiliate, National City Company. Remember, this was the company that didn't report and had been used to hide the morale loans and Mitchell's failed Cuban sugar investment. Sherrod recalls Mitchell's words from his address at that sales conference:

> One reason the Security Company does not publish a statement is that earnings fluctuate widely and the Management feels that the stock should not zigzag with earnings.

Of course this was a ridiculous justification. The second reason he offered was much closer to the truth:

> Another reason is that 'We wash our dirty linen on the back porch rather than on the front porch'.[114]

Sherrod's book sold well, but it didn't produce anywhere near the impact the nation's newspapers later did. Their front pages carried the unfolding revelations of the Pecora-led commission 18 months after Sherrod's book was released. Pecora's findings were so damning that Mitchell resigned as chairman of City Bank within days of the ordeal. In a short time Pecora had exposed Mitchell for hiding huge financial losses from the bank's shareholders, paying himself and fellow directors undisclosed and overly generous bonuses, and failing to pay personal capital gains taxes. Remember that as the nation listened to these stories it was suffering its most crippling depression in decades. The public were screaming for change, and the politicians had to respond.

---

*It's interesting how perspectives on valuation have changed since then. Consider a company such as Coca-Cola. While the true value of Coca-Cola's goodwill would need to be tested in the market, I've heard present-day estimates of around $100 billion. Sherrod would have described this as 'water'. Buffett would today describe it as the price to acquire a valuable asset—a 'competitive moat'.

With public anger aroused by the Pecora-led inquiry, real reform could begin. Until then less than one-third of companies listed on US exchanges published quarterly reports, and a third of companies didn't publish any reports at all. The *Securities Act of 1933* laid out a bevy of financial disclosure requirements with the aim of making corporate activities more transparent. No longer could the directors of a listed company say to the shareholders, 'Just trust us.'

The disclosure requirements spelt out in the *Securities Act* were a big leap forward, but they didn't end the problem. Mandatory disclosure can never protect against fraud. And, as the relatively recent Enron, WorldCom and Madoff scandals remind us, there remains a risk in accepting financial accounts at face value.

Chapter summary

- The shift from private to public ownership of business enterprises over the course of the 19th and 20th centuries saw a growing need to establish effective lines of communication between those who ran companies and those who owned them.

- Directors and management were initially reluctant to provide financial reports, and legislation requiring them to do so did not exist.

- The excesses of the 1920s, as characterised by the Match King, Ivar Kreuger, and National City Bank Chairman, Charles Mitchell, were investigated by the Committee on Banking and Currency. The efforts of its star advocate, Ferdinand Pecora, exposed the dirty dealings of such men and created an atmosphere for legislative change.

- The primary purpose of the *Securities Act of 1933* was to ensure that investors received complete and accurate information to assist them in making investment decisions. Central to this was the provision of accurate financial statements.

20

THE MODERN ERA

As the 1920s progressed, the concept of basing a company's value on its projected earnings was gaining momentum. The long-established counterargument—that the balance sheet alone is sufficient to measure value—appealed to people's intuitive sense. There it was all laid out: what the business owned, what it owed. Take one from the other and that must be what it's worth. But increasingly analysts were questioning this idea. After all, if a kid could generate $50 a month selling homemade lemonade from a street stall, then surely that business had to be worth more than a trestle table, two pitchers and a lemon squeezer.

Ben Graham described the post–World War I period as being characterised by a shift to the 'New-Era Theory'.[115] It began with the release, in 1924, of Edgar Lawrence Smith's bestseller *Common Stocks as Long Term Investments*. The book contained a chart showing shifts in stock prices between 1837 and 1923. Smith had noticed that over the 86-year period values of listed companies had trended upwards, but not in a straight line. Smith overlaid two trend lines, each of which defined an ever-rising arc. He said the arcs were defined by a compounding function at the rate of 2.5 per cent per year; that is, on average, profits increased by 2.5 per cent every year. This increase in profits, he explained, was due to management retaining a proportion of earnings each year rather than paying out the lot as dividends, which meant the businesses were not only growing but doing so at an exponential rate. Smith was proposing that the stock market was a compounding machine:

> Over a period of years, the principal value of a well diversified holding of the common stocks of representative corporations, in essential industries, tends to increase in accordance with the operation of compound interest.

To date the analysts who'd been using earnings to calculate value were less concerned with future earnings. They'd been applying a multiple to recent (historical) earnings, believing that this way they were dealing with facts. The earnings they used had been seen, measured and recorded. Smith gave them a different focus. He said there was an important force driving stock prices — retained earnings — and this force was forever upward. He proposed that valuations be based on future not historical earnings. Since the economy was picking up steam around that time, earnings had been growing, which meant Smith's ideas really gained some traction. Adding fuel to the fire was the belief that his historical growth figure of 2.5 per cent was too conservative. Businesses were experiencing double-digit growth at that time. Many believed that ahead was an era of unlimited corporate growth and economic prosperity. The dawn of a New Era! No multiple seemed too large to apply to current earnings.

Smith didn't deny the existence of the market cycle, but he did propose there was little risk in buying stocks at very high prices. He argued that if prices subsequently fell it was only a matter of time before the compounding produced by retained earnings would see the stock price recover. His message was interpreted by the investing public to mean that price didn't matter. This caused share prices to rocket, and the rising prices only reinforced their belief that Smith must be correct — for a while anyway.

As a postscript to this story, Edgar Lawrence Smith has been given too much credit for coming up with the idea of the stock price growing due to the reinvestment of retained earnings. Maybe his book's popularity persuaded people of its originality. So many times history gets the facts wrong, and as the story is retold the myth is perpetuated. I can't tell you who first came up with the idea but George Garr Henry wrote the following words, 14 years before Smith's book was published:

> Rich men whose income is in excess of their wants can afford to forgo something in the way of yearly return for the sake of a strong prospect of

appreciation in value. Such men naturally buy bank and trust-company stocks, whose general characteristic is a small return upon the money invested, but a strong likelihood of appreciation in value. This is owing to the general practice of well-regulated banks to distribute only about half their earnings in dividends and to credit the rest to surplus, thus insuring a steady rise in the book value of the stock.[116]

Smith's theory didn't save investors from the bloodbath that followed the 1929 Crash. At its lowest post-Crash level the Dow Jones had collapsed by 89 per cent from its September 1929 peak, and it didn't recover its pre-Crash nominal value until 1954. It seems financial theories are great until subsequent events prove them to be wrong.

This whole issue of growth investing is periodically revisited, usually at times when the economy is buoyant. The concept of growth in earnings due to reinvestment of earnings is intuitively appealing. But the use of unrealistic growth projections re-emerges periodically, leading to periods of unrealistic valuations—and every time it happens, investors fall into the same old trap.

THE 1930s

The 1930s was a fertile period for investment theory. It saw the publication of Graham and Dodd's *Security Analysis*, John Burr Williams' *The Theory of Investment Value* and Keynes' *General Theory*. While Keynes' book is largely a work of economics, its eloquently written twelfth chapter, 'The State of Long-Term Expectation', is pure stock market.

The 1930s could well be remembered as the decade of the dividend. Robert Wise kicked it off. In an article he wrote for the 8 September 1930 issue of *Barron's* magazine, 'Investing for True Values', he defined a stock's value as follows: 'The proper price of any security, whether a stock or bond, is the sum of all future income payments discounted at the current rate of interest in order to arrive at the present value.'

Essentially it was a restatement of Pisano's 700-year-old concept of discounting future cash flows. Wise is barely remembered today, but Williams, who restated the same principle, is. Williams is credited with proposing that stocks can be valued by discounting their future dividends. Again the credit is undue but probably given because *The Theory of Investment Value*, in which he discussed the concept, was a bestseller. Interestingly, Williams never claimed the idea as his; other people made that mistake. He even acknowledged Wise's 1930 article in a footnote in chapter 5 of his book.

As far as stock analysis goes, there's no doubt the most significant work to come out of the 1930s was Graham and Dodd's *Security Analysis*, first published in 1934. Despite its dual authorship, *Security Analysis* is largely Graham's voice, based on his teachings at Columbia University. At Graham's request, Dodd sat in on his classes to take notes and subsequently assisted in compiling the manuscript. Graham had already been working as a Wall Street broker for 20 years and as a lecturer at Columbia University since 1928. He'd also established his credentials as a writer, having been published in *Forbes* magazine and *The Magazine of Wall Street*.

Security Analysis was released at a time when US authorities were tightening standards of financial reporting. Since Graham's style relied heavily on analysis of the balance sheet and profit and loss statement, *Security Analysis* was a book for its day.

FROM THE SIXTIES TO TODAY

Following the 1929 Crash investors turned their backs on the stock market. It wasn't until 1954, 25 years later, that the Dow Jones Industrial Index regained its September 1929 peak of 381 points. Twenty-five years was long enough for a new generation of investors to be present in the market, a generation ready to repeat the same mistakes their parents had. The 1960s delivered a rebirth of the 1920s growth stock phenomenon. The exuberant stock market of the sixties saw the development of the 'Nifty Fifty', which included market darlings Eastman Kodak, Xerox and Polaroid. In keeping with Edgar Lawrence Smith's concept of stocks as compounding machines, no multiple seemed too high to pay for these growth stocks. The Nifty Fifty was a group of buy-and-hold stocks promising the dream of future riches. Investors believed they could be bought at any price multiple for this dream to be delivered, so their prices were bid up to unrealistic levels certain to disappoint. And, just as in 1929, disappoint they did.

It reminds us that cycles repeat, and forever will continue to do so.

When it comes to valuation theory, some big names have cropped up in the decades from the early sixties to today: Edgar O. Edwards and Philip W. Bell (1961), Myron J. Gordon (1956, 1962), Ben Graham (again!

1976) and James Ohlson (1995). Their ideas sculpted Pisano's original discounting formula into the formulae familiar to and used by today's financial analysts. In Part IV we'll be taking a close look at them and asking the question: 'How do we "calculate" value?'

Chapter summary

- As the 1920s progressed the concept of using a company's earnings to calculate its stock value was gaining momentum.

- In 1924 Edgar Lawrence Smith proposed in his best-selling book *Common Stocks as Long Term Investments* that stock prices grew at an average compounding rate of 2.5 per cent per year.

- Smith's book popularised the idea that it was okay to pay high multiples of current earnings for companies offering the possibility of significant future growth.

- The concept of valuing stocks by discounting their potential future dividend stream was popularised by John Burr Williams in his 1938 book *The Theory of Investment Value*.

- During periods of stock euphoria, such as the late 1920s and the 1960s, investors became too optimistic regarding future earnings growth rates, leading to inflated stock prices.

Part IV
'CALCULATING' VALUE

21

INTRINSIC VALUE AND MARKET PRICE

In 2005 my wife and I decided to sell our family home. After more than 20 years living at the same address, we wanted to move into a smaller house. Trouble was, come auction day, there wasn't a buyer to be found. Sure, people turned up to gawk, but no-one actually put their hand in the air. Following the auction, excuses started flowing from the real estate agent: 'People don't want timber ceilings anymore. The staircase isn't grand enough. The garage is all wrong. The street's too narrow.' And so it went on. We left the house on the market and, after a seemingly endless stream of halfhearted post-auction tyre-kickers, we sold it three months later. The family who bought it had just moved into town, and after a prolonged period of haggling, down to the very last dollar, they eventually signed the contract.

The new owners put the house back on the market 18 months later. They were shifting town again. Another auction, same agent. But this time there were buyers at each other's throats, five of them in fact. I attended the auction and felt like screaming out: 'Hey guys, where were you 18 months ago when I was trying to sell the same house?' The house sold that day for nearly $1 million more than we sold it for. We had it 21 years, while the next owners had it 18 months and did nothing to it. Houses in the area hadn't risen much over that 18 months — except ours! Seems it was a one-house 'hot pocket' of real estate.

I never met the final owner, so I couldn't ask him directly why he paid so much for our old house, but in discussions with one of the neighbours I discovered the reason. Apparently he immediately fell in love with the house and was 'prepared to pay any price to own it'. So how much was our house really worth? What we sold it for or what the next owners sold it for? You tell me.

Price perversions crop up everywhere. What about Cabbage Patch Kids? They're the cute dolls you 'adopt', rather than buy. First created in 1976, by Christmas 1983 they were so popular shortages saw fights breaking out between handbag-wielding mothers in US department stores. Crowds in the hundreds and in some cases thousands descended on any store advertising it still had dolls in stock. One guy jumped onto a plane and crossed the Atlantic to buy a doll in the UK.

A radio station decided to play a prank. It announced that the manufacturer, Mattel, would make a delivery of dolls to a local football field via aeroplane. Buyers were asked to gather on the football field and hold their credit cards up in the air. Someone in the plane would use a telephoto lens to record their card details and an appropriate number of dolls would be dropped out of the aircraft. People actually turned up to the football field, credit cards ready. Worrying, isn't it, that these same people are actually allowed to vote!

So what prices have Cabbage Patch Kids fetched? Little Mildred, first delivered in May 1977, was 'readopted' 18 years later for $20 000. Others have changed address for twice that figure. You have to ask: 'Aren't there cheaper dolls out there that look just as cute?'

Emotion-driven price perversions affect stock prices as well. Stocks don't engender personal attachment like houses or dolls, but people do get emotional about money. And most people, when they look at stocks, don't see companies—they see dollar bills.

WHAT'S A STOCK REALLY WORTH?

I devoted chapter 9 to the views of a bunch of academics called the 'efficient market theorists'. Their theories run counter to the concept of emotion-driven price distortions. They'll tell you a stock's market price and its value are one and the same—that the market price is determined by the collective judgement of all investors active in that stock, that their buy and sell orders register their vote and the influence of this collective wisdom keeps stock prices aligned with their true value.

It's an attractive argument but it begs the question: is the collective judgement of market participants worth paying attention to? It could be if you believe an assumption underlying efficient market pricing, that investors are members of a rare breed of humans called *Homo economicus*—a sect of emotion-free, rational robotrons capable of making judgements as coldly and precisely as an IBM computer. Unfortunately that's where the whole price-equals-value argument starts to break down. The reality is that *Homo economicus* doesn't exist. He's like the Yeti or the Loch Ness Monster—talked about but never seen. The fact is people are capable of making very irrational decisions, particularly when taking their cue from hordes of others doing exactly the same.

Emotions and bias *do* affect judgement. Therefore emotions and bias *do* affect stock prices. Remember these are prices set by investors who, in their spare time, are probably out there buying Cabbage Patch Kids for their children. If you choose to run counter to the views of the efficient market theorists, and you believe that price and value do diverge, then you need to develop skills in valuing stocks, because without them you'll just run with the pack.

CALCULATING INTRINSIC VALUE

The term *intrinsic value* refers to an asset's underlying or real value, as distinct from its market price. More than anything it's a concept, but unfortunately it's a concept that gets terribly abused. For example, you often hear absolute statements being made like 'The intrinsic value of Acme Corporation is two dollars and three cents'. When I hear comments like this I have to ask, 'Where did the three cents come from?' The reality is it's not possible to pin a specific number on intrinsic value, so let's explore what intrinsic value really means, starting with some definitions.

The Chartered Financial Analysts Society defines intrinsic value as: 'The value that an investor considers on the basis of available facts, to be the true or real value that will become the market value when other investors reach the same conclusion.' This definition delivers an idea of what it is, but 'true or real' are just words. When investors think about intrinsic value they have a burning desire to quantify things. And this definition certainly doesn't tell us how that can be done.

Let's look at another definition, this time from Warren Buffett: 'It is the discounted value of the cash that can be taken out of a business.' Closer, but it still doesn't help that much. Again it's a conceptual, not a practical, definition. In fact it's so impractical that Buffett doesn't bother relying on it too much himself. In 2008 Buffett biographer Alice Schroeder stated in a presentation at the Darden School of Business that Buffett 'doesn't do any kind of discounted cash flow models or anything like that'.

This confirms a comment once made by Berkshire Hathaway's Vice-Chairman, and Buffett's long-time friend and business partner, Charlie Munger. At the 1996 Berkshire AGM he stated, 'Warren talks about these discounted cash flows. I've never seen him do one.' Buffett's immediate response at that meeting was, 'It's true. If a company's value doesn't just scream out at you, it's too close.'

Schroeder also made the following comment when describing the analysis Buffett used to back a decision early in his career to invest in Mid-Continent Tab Card Company: 'He relied totally on historical figures with no projections. I saw him do it over and over again.' No models, no projections and no discounted cash flow, just a determination of profit margins based on historical data.[117]

Schroeder and Munger are two people who, by any measure, should have the inside running on how Buffett values a business, particularly Munger. It's interesting then to read the notes to the financial statements in Berkshire's 2011 annual report, which outline how Berkshire calculates the fair value of its reporting units when judging the need for any impairment of goodwill:

> There are several methods of estimating a reporting unit's fair value, including market quotations, underlying asset and liability fair value determinations and other valuation techniques, such as discounted projected future net earnings or net cash flows and multiples of earnings. We primarily use discounted projected future earnings or cash flow methods.

Does the 'we' stated here include Buffett? Or is it a generic 'we' that refers only to Berkshire's accountants? And is this method applied only to the assets on Berkshire's balance sheet or is it a tool Buffett uses to size up potential stock investments and acquisition targets? It seems this apparent contradiction between how Buffett defines intrinsic value, how assets on Berkshire's balance sheet are valued and what Munger and Schroeder are on the record as saying about how Buffett values investments might not be a contradiction at all. Accounting standards define how assets are valued for the purpose of financial reporting, and regulatory frameworks stipulate that these standards are adhered to. And while Berkshire's accounts might value assets a certain way Buffett isn't required to dance to the same regulatory tune when undertaking his own valuations. He knows that most cash flow predictions deliver pretty rubbery figures.

So if formula-derived figures can't be relied upon, should we be using 'intrinsic value' to describe them? To the uninitiated the term conjures up images of precision. Ben Graham acknowledged the problem, referring to the values analysts calculate not as intrinsic values but as 'formula values'. Graham preferred to characterise intrinsic value as 'an elusive concept'—and there's no calculator I've ever seen that, after keying in the necessary figures, displays the answer 'elusive concept'.

I like US economist Paul Samuelson's description of intrinsic values. He referred to them as 'shadow prices' and as 'prices never seen on land or sea outside of economics libraries'. He acknowledged they couldn't be observed or calculated, yet insisted it is necessary to assume they exist.

It's worth reading the above comments again. Because the term 'intrinsic value' is thrown around so freely these days, it's easy to fall into the trap of believing it has a rock-solid identity. It doesn't. But, as Samuelson says, investors need something to work with. So how do we deal with all this uncertainty? Answer: calculate intrinsic values if you must, but allow a big margin for your calculation to be wrong. You cannot deny the near certainty that your calculations will be wrong, but your quest should be for your calculations to be 'less wrong' than the market's.

In Security Analysis Graham described intrinsic value as the 'value justified by the facts'. That's fine, but what did he mean by 'facts'? There's nothing factual about the future, and it's the future that intrinsic value is trying to get a handle on. So what is Graham suggesting? Let's look elsewhere for a clue.

Charles Dow referred to facts in an editorial in The Wall Street Journal on 22 March 1902. He saw the first requisite for analysis as 'the existence of such figures as will disclose the vital facts'. He felt there needed to be a number of years of facts for analysis to be valid; that is, he felt more confident about peering into the future if there was plenty to see in the rear-view mirror.

The essential use of intrinsic value is to compare it with the prevailing market price to see if the market is presenting opportunities to either buy or sell. Joseph de la Vega's writings show that Dutch investors were doing exactly the same thing more than 300 years ago. And Thomas Gibson wrote in 1910: 'Prices frequently become divorced temporarily from values ... It is when prices are lower or higher than values, present or prospective, that we have our greatest speculative opportunities.'[118]

The encouraging news is that even the world's most successful investors freely admit they're unable to nail precise figures on intrinsic value. Investing is never a process of certainty or precision. It's more like the game pitching pennies where players pitch a coin at a wall. To win, your coin doesn't have to actually make contact with the wall. You'll rarely be spot on—you just have to get your coin closer to the wall than the other players do. Similarly, investors attempt to derive intrinsic values that are closer to true value than the market price indicates. Plenty of times successful investors get it wrong; they just need to be less wrong and/or wrong on fewer occasions.

FROM CLICKS TO CHICKS

Despite the lessons of the 1920s and the 1960s, it happened again in the late 1990s, when the dot-com bubble corrupted the assumed financial wisdom and replaced it with collective stupidity. The stories of newly created corporate shells being floated on the stock markets of the world with no business plan beyond 'Let's rob these patsies blind, watch the share price fly, cash in our chips and get out of here as quickly as possible' make for fascinating reading.

The dot-com con was eerily similar to the South Sea Bubble of 1720. That era also saw pupil-popping prices paid for start-ups with mission statements that should have led with the words 'unfounded hope'. It's worth quickly revisiting the South Sea Bubble, because there was one Cockney corporate con man of the era who requires his own special place in history.

Picture early 18th-century London. With no formal stock exchange, share trading took place in the labyrinth of narrow streets bounded by Cornhill and Lombard streets called Exchange Alley. It was 1720 and England was witnessing a raging bull market, and as with every bull market since there was a wave of new offerings in start-up companies.

Some were legitimate businesses, many weren't. The crazy offerings were unaffectionately known as 'bubble companies'. But of all the bubble offerings of the time one stands above the rest. Its promoter saw an opportunity to make a quick buck and, without any idea of what line of business his new company might undertake, hurriedly cobbled together a prospectus describing it as 'A company for carrying on an undertaking of great advantage but nobody to know what it is'.[119]

Now we've all heard of the problems associated with a lack of corporate transparency, but this prospectus took things to a whole new level. The promoter's only saving grace was that he actually admitted to it!

The promoter of the bogus company collected £2000 in deposits from unwary investors in a single day and then did a runner—never to be seen again. And while you might see this story as amusing, if a little archaic, it carries a powerful message, particularly for those who believe that today's 'sophisticated investing public' would never be so gullible as to fall for such a trick. The reality is that the same thing happened only recently.

In 1999, near the peak of the dot-com bubble, a company called NetJ. com Corporation filed documents with the US Securities and Exchange Commission stating, 'The company is not currently engaged in any substantial activity and has no plans to engage in such activities in the foreseeable future'.

Sound familiar?

The $110 million capital raising was oversubscribed as profit-hungry investors dived in. NetJ's share price climbed 18-fold within months. But those who still held their NetJ shares in the wake of the dot-com bust lost their shirts. NetJ, not surprisingly, went belly up. What was NetJ's intrinsic value during the time it was trading? The same as the 1720 float described above—that is, zero. Simply using Graham's concept of 'the facts' would have told people that.

Now dial the clock forward to 2012, to a time when corporate profits were waning and investor sentiment was at a low ebb. In early 2012, I was attempting to value Collins Foods, a company that holds two principal businesses—a string of Sizzler restaurants and over 100 KFCs. Seemed like a safe bet. Selling buckets of fried chicken has been a proven business model since the Colonel first dropped a drumstick into his deep fryer back in 1930. The multiple franchise owner I was valuing had floated on the ASX several months earlier at $2.50 per share, but it was now trading at around $1.20. The share price had collapsed following an announcement that the company's next profit result was likely to be at the lower end of expectations. On that news, investors bolted for the doors. When the dust finally settled the stock was sitting on a grossed-up prospective dividend yield of 14 per cent at a conservative payout ratio of 50 per cent, and all this based on a business franchising model that had been operating successfully for 60 years. Compare the value reasoning here, where investors dumped a perfectly good stock just because of one announcement, to the dot-com craziness from 13 years earlier, when investors were willing to throw cash at a company with no intrinsic value at all!

To my mind the valuation pendulum had swung fully to the other side of the clock case. The behaviour of those who sold out their shares in Collins Foods on the basis of a reaffirmed profit forecast is well characterised by the following 300-year-old quote: 'They are all in haste to sell out, at more than half below the real Value, and will not wait with Patience and cool thoughts for the profitable Dividends.'[120]

There's that all-important word 'patience' again. So why the different views on value between the heady dot-com years and post-GFC 2012? The answer can be distilled into one simple word—sentiment. It's the second of the two important factors driving share prices.*

Before leaving this story there's one more important point I want to make. Despite the share price of Collins Foods being less than half its float price, despite its offering a grossed-up dividend yield of 14 per cent, its share price continued to languish for a year and at one point was as low as $1 per share. Why?

It's because investors will begin to accept a stock price as being correct even though the available information appears to contradict it. They put more faith in the market price than their own valuation. They convince themselves that the share price must be sitting at a low level for a reason,

---

*As noted earlier, in *The General Theory* Keynes described returns on stocks as being driven by two combined factors. They are 'enterprise', which relates to the prospects of the business, and 'speculation', which relates to the prevailing sentiment of the market.

one they've failed to identify. It's a bit like the farmer who opens the gate of a paddock to allow a flock of sheep to move out. They stand there blankly staring at the opening; since the other sheep aren't moving it's as if the opening doesn't exist. The problem is, if you behave this way opportunities will never be taken. Cheap stocks will never be bought. To profit from opportunity you need to have faith in your judgement and the conviction to act independently.

Here's why most people simply can't do that.

SOLOMON ASCH AND SPINNING WHEELS

In 1952 psychologist Solomon Asch conducted a now-famous study on how much we are influenced by other people's thinking. He coached groups of seven to nine participants to provide the wrong answer to a series of simple questions. Then a patsy was brought into the group, someone who wasn't privy to what was about to happen. Twelve simple questions were put to the group, to which the trained members unanimously provided incorrect answers. On one-third of occasions the unwitting ring-in also provided the incorrect answer, and this was in response to really simple questions with obvious answers like: 'Look at these two lines. Which is longer, A or B?'

If people can be influenced by the group to deliver incorrect answers to questions with obvious answers, then how would you expect them to perform in the uncertain world of financial markets, where answers to questions are far from obvious? The influence of groupthink on their conclusions is extremely powerful.

Psychologists Daniel Kahneman and Amos Tversky have undertaken studies along similar lines and have found that totally irrelevant information can influence the decision-making process. They performed a study where participants witnessed the spin of a wheel-of-fortune just prior to answering a question requiring a numerical answer. If the wheel showed a high number, they were more likely to give higher numbers when answering the unrelated question.

Kahneman describes another study where a group of visitors to the San Francisco Exploratorium were asked two questions:[121]

- Is the height of the tallest redwood more or less than 1200 feet?

- What is your best guess about the height of the tallest redwood?

A second group was asked:

- Is the height of the tallest redwood more or less than 180 feet?

- What is your best guess about the height of the tallest redwood?

Despite the second question being exactly the same for each group, the difference in mean estimates between the answers given by the two groups was staggering. For the first group it was 844 feet, while for the second it was 282 feet. People weren't even given the answer to the first question—it merely planted a suggestion. No wonder investors have trouble deriving their own independent value for a stock!

This behaviour carries the fancy title of the 'anchoring and adjustment heuristic', and it's rife in financial markets. When economists are asked for their views on the economic outlook, they base their judgement on present conditions. Analysts who value stocks are influenced by the current market price. The investors best able to win at this game are the ones who can jettison all this emotional baggage, but it's a difficult thing to do. We are fighting millennia of evolution that got our brain working the way it does.

WHAT IS MARKET PRICE?

Investors, in their search for opportunities, are constantly studying the relationship between price and value. I attempted to define 'intrinsic value' earlier in this chapter, so let's now explore what 'market price' is. Most investors don't think too much about it. After all, the market price is just the market price. You can't control it—it's just there, so simply accept it. And to an extent that's true. But it's fun to think about it anyway, and along the way we can gain a better understanding of what drives it.

First off, the market for any stock usually consists of multiple potential buyers and sellers. I say 'potential' because at any point in time most are simply observers. A single trade involves just two parties, the most optimistic buyer and the most pessimistic seller. And no matter what prices the other potential buyers and sellers are willing to act on, it's only the participants at the trading 'coal face' who are setting the price at that point. John Burr Williams described this as the *marginal* opinion.[122]

That means the market price is not equally influenced by the judgements of all those interested in buying or selling a stock. The market isn't a mechanism for processing the collective value judgements of all to produce a volume-weighted average price called the market price. Most value judgements don't impact the market price at all, and might never do so. What's more, the value judgement of many investors changes as the market price changes. The price/value relationship is a complex dynamic rather than a simplistic, unchanging comparison. For example, if someone believes a stock they own is worth $3.50 and intends to sell if it reaches $4.00, they might change their mind about selling if it does reach $4.00, believing it's now worth more.

WHAT DRIVES MARKET PRICE?

Investors have long stated that value is the long-term driver of a stock's market price. Typifying this belief is Ben Graham's oft-repeated comment that in the short term the market is a voting machine but in the long term it's a weighing machine. But it's a bit of a sticky point. If it's not possible to determine exactly what a stock is worth (its intrinsic value), then how do we know if the market price is approaching it? William Armstrong probably came close to the truth when he noted in 1848 that, although intrinsic value is the principal determinant in setting the market prices of securities, it's not the only factor involved.[123]

The influence other factors may have on market prices varies significantly from one period to the next. What then are these other factors? The principal one is sentiment, but what shapes sentiment? Perhaps the best answer I've seen is — everything! Which of course adds to the difficulty of calculating, modelling or predicting it. Market prices can even react in opposite ways to what is essentially the same news. In the wake of the 2008–09 GFC, the US Federal Reserve undertook a series of programs of quantitative easing. In an effort to support the US economy it initiated bond purchasing programs that pumped tens of billions of dollars of cash into the US economy every month. The stock market loved it and prices were generally bid up strongly. But in May 2013 rumours spread that the program was soon to be eased back, and the market went into a tailspin. As the months progressed and the rumours didn't crystallise, the market not only recovered but proceeded to hit new highs. In December the Fed finally confirmed it was commencing the tapering process. The market's reaction? This time it rallied. Figure that.

I hear people say that at the most fundamental level, stock prices are driven by forces of supply and demand. It's an idea commonly put forward by technical analysts. Indeed Richard Wyckoff, stock market educator and founder of *The Magazine of Wall Street*, whom many look upon as one of the pioneers of technical analysis, had this to say more than 80 years ago: 'I demonstrated the fact that the law of supply and demand controls the prices of stocks just as it does the prices of wheat, corn, labor and materials of all kinds.'[124] Wheat prices, as Wyckoff suggests, are subject to the forces of supply and demand. In fact, as I write this chapter the prices for the two largest US crops — corn and soybeans — have soared to all-time highs due to a drought-driven supply shortage, a case of plentiful dollars chasing limited supplies.

But stocks are different. The supply of stocks doesn't vary with drought, or much else for that matter. Excluding the exercise of options, new capital raisings and share buy-backs, the supply of stocks remains relatively fixed. The greater change is on the demand side. In bull markets, prices climb as enthusiastic speculators buy and sell stocks among themselves at ever-increasing prices. But as the enthusiasm dies so too do prices. There is little change in supply, but there is a substantial increase in greed-driven demand.

Of all the opinions and ideas I've read on what defines and drives the market price, I think Keynes came the closest to nailing it. In his Chairman's speech to the 1938 National Mutual Insurance Company annual meeting, he stated:

> [Markets] are governed by doubt rather than conviction, by fear more than forecast, by memories of last time and not by foreknowledge of next time. The level of stock prices does not mean that investors know, it means they do not know. Faced with the perplexities and uncertainties of the modern world, market values will fluctuate more widely than will seem reasonable in the light of after-events.

Clearly Keynes, were he alive today, would have little time for the efficient market theorists.

Chapter summary

- The Efficient Market Hypothesis (EMH) states that the market price represents the best assessment of a stock's underlying value since it is determined by the collective judgement of all investors active in that stock. But the EMH denies that extremes of collective emotion can result in markets mispricing stocks.

- The term 'intrinsic value' refers to an asset's underlying or real value, which might or might not equal its market price at any point in time.

- Intrinsic value has been defined as the discounted value of the cash that can be taken out of a business. It is best described as a concept and cannot be reliably calculated.

- Successful investors are those who act on calculated values that are 'less wrong' than the current market price.

- Both Charles Dow and Ben Graham believed that the most reliable calculations are made by using relevant information that can be reasonably substantiated, which they referred to as 'the facts'.

- General shifts in sentiment influence people's assessment of value.

- People's judgements can be powerfully influenced by other people's stated opinions, whether they are correct or not.

- It isn't simply value that drives market prices; rather it's perceptions of value, and perceptions of value are shaped by a multitude of factors.

22

EARNINGS AND
EARNINGS GROWTH

Okay, now that we've had a taste of what we're up against in calculating intrinsic value, it's time to look at how analysts actually go about the process. But let's not start with the actual formulae used for calculating value. They're fairly straightforward, and we'll take a look at them a couple of chapters down the track. Instead let's first look at the *inputs* to the formulae, because it's the quality of the inputs that distinguishes the capabilities of investors. No formula can deliver useful answers if the inputs are untenable.

Let's start with a basic intuitive concept regarding value: the price you pay for any investment should be based on what you expect it will return to you in the future. In the case of stocks, those future returns come in two forms—dividends and the difference between the purchase price and the sale price, should you ever sell.

The calculation of present value is undertaken by inserting estimates of these future cash flows into one of several formulae, most of which are variations of Pisano's 13th-century discounting formula. Pisano's formula required two inputs—future cash flows and an appropriate discount rate to apply to those flows. The discount rate converts the estimates of future dollars received into today's dollars. That's it. Two inputs—sounds easy. But as you're about to discover, it's not as straightforward as you'd think.

Let's start with the first of the two inputs—future cash flows. Unfortunately, the confusion starts immediately, because there is no consensus on what are the appropriate cash flows to use.

EARNINGS PER SHARE

To the uninitiated, a company's future profits seems the obvious place to start. Each shareholder is entitled to a part share of the company's profits based on how many shares they own. Sounds sensible, but it isn't the right way to go. That's because what a company reports as a profit is a different figure from what it makes. Reported profit is an accounting construct, a figure concocted according to a bevy of accounting rules. Hence 'net profit' is not synonymous with 'cold, hard cash'.

This means the figures in the accounts often need to be adjusted to better reflect economic reality. The steps to achieve this are well covered in other books, so it's not the aim of this one to comprehensively cover this area. But here are a couple of examples to illustrate the point.

There are two main areas where the Income Statement strays from reporting real cash flows. The first is how income and expenses are classified; the second is how they are timed—that is, in what period they are reported.

Firstly, classification. A simple example will suffice. During the 1980s Aussie entrepreneur Alan Bond built a listed company, Bond Corporation, using a minimum of equity and a mountain of debt. To soften the damage that the debt inflicted on the balance sheet, Bond Corp used the old trick of classifying expenses as assets. It's a neat trick that not only improves the appearance of the balance sheet but boosts the reported profit. A look at Bond Corp's 1989 accounts shows an asset of nearly $400 million classified as 'other assets'. A closer look shows that $280 million of these other assets related to advertising expenditure. Bondy's company owned a brewery, which produced Swan beer. He'd spent millions on an advertising campaign trying to capture market share from Foster's. Despite the TV attack, Swan Brewery lost further market share. So one could say, all else being equal, its goodwill was declining. But rather than expensing these as 'advertising costs', Bond Corp's accountants argued the advertising had enhanced an asset, the goodwill in the brand. The savvy analyst, on valuing Bond Corp, would spot the sleight of hand and correct the accounts accordingly. Assets down, expenses up.

Secondly, timing of income and expenses. Companies need, for example, to maintain the equipment they use (termed 'capital expenditure' or 'capex')—planes for Qantas, warehouse capability for Costco, port facilities for Toll Holdings. Failure to maintain equipment means a business is going backwards, but ironically failing to maintain its equipment means a company can overstate its earnings—at least for a short while.

The wearing out and associated devaluation of equipment already owned by a company is recognised in the accounts as the expense item 'depreciation'. Depreciation is calculated by allocating a proportion of the original purchase price of the equipment as a cost to each year it remains in service. But depreciation can understate the true cost of maintaining operational capability for a given year. For the investor the more relevant figure is the annual investment in capital equipment necessary to leave the company in the same productive shape at the end of the year as at the beginning. This requires an intimate appreciation of the operations and dynamics of the business. It also requires an informed judgement call, so the analyst is relying on judgement rather than the financial statements to determine the most appropriate cost for that year.

DIVIDENDS AS INPUTS

So there are classification and timing problems in using reported net profit as an input to valuation formulae. What's more, managements typically retain a healthy proportion of the profit each year before they distribute dividends to shareholders. What shareholders receive, then, rarely equals the net profit.

What investors do receive is dividends. In fact, apart from possible capital returns, dividends represent the only money they do receive during the time they hold the stock. So why not use dividends as a cash flow input to valuation formulae? It's an argument that's been put forward by many investors for a long, long time. The Dividend Discount Model (DDM) is a valuation formula based on this very principle. It asks the analyst to consider only future dividends when valuing a stock.

On face value the DDM seems like an appealing formula to use, but proponents of non-dividend formulae might mount the following counterargument. If management retains a proportion of profits, don't these retained earnings grow the value of the company? Therefore don't they drive capital gains for shareholders? And aren't capital gains realised by the shareholder when the shares are sold? Therefore don't retained earnings also have a value? The answer is 'yes' to all these questions, but retained earnings only have a value if management reinvests them profitably.

Proponents of the DDM can fire straight back, arguing that the DDM also takes retained earnings into consideration. To appreciate their line of argument you need to answer the following questions:

- How do you obtain a capital gain? *Answer:* you sell.

- Who will deliver the capital gain to you when you sell? *Answer:* the person who buys your shares.

- How will that person value the shares they purchase if they too are using the DDM? *Answer:* the present value of the dividend stream they expect to receive in the future.

Put another way, the capital gain you receive forms part of the new owner's dividend expectation. If management has invested the retained earnings during the term of your ownership, the company's capital base and/or its operational efficiency will have increased, enabling it to deliver larger dividends in the future. So it's possible to deliver a valuation by considering dividends alone.

Confused? Then it might be clearer if you ignore ownership changes altogether. Imagine that only one person ever holds the shares. To simplify the example even further, ignore capital raisings and capital returns. All that one person will ever receive is dividends. The underlying value of the shares won't change just because ownership does.

Sounds great, so what's the catch? Here are three biggies:

- Who knows what those future dividends are going to be? It's difficult enough predicting next year's dividend, let alone those well into the future.

- Money changes in value. In an inflationary environment future dollars will be worth less than today's dollars, which means each future dividend has to be discounted by an appropriate factor to bring it back to a present value (the appropriate factor is called the 'discount rate', but more about that soon). After all, it's present value you're attempting to calculate, not future value.

- The sheer logistics of the calculation are daunting. The DDM asks you to perform a separate calculation for every dividend yet to be received. Assuming an infinite company life, that's a lot of dividends to throw into the formula—clearly a mathematical nightmare.

John Burr Williams' name is often linked with the DDM, and, while it's wrong to give Williams full credit for the concept, he did discuss it extensively in his 1938 book *The Theory of Investment Value*. In 1939 Ben Graham was asked to review Williams' book for the *Journal of Political Economy*. He expressed concern that in order to apply Williams' method one needed to make some very large assumptions: 'One wonders whether there may not be too great a discrepancy between the necessarily hit-or-miss character of these assumptions and the highly refined mathematical treatment to which they are subjected.'[125]

What an eloquent way of saying 'garbage in, garbage out'.

Keynes had expressed similar sentiments regarding people's capacity to forecast future earnings yields just three years earlier in *The General Theory*:

> Our knowledge of the factors which govern the yield of an investment some years hence is usually very slight and often negligible. If we speak frankly, we have to admit that our basis of knowledge for estimating the yield ten years hence of a railway, a copper mine, a textile factory, the goodwill of a patent medicine, an Atlantic liner, a building in the City of London amounts to little and sometimes to nothing.[126]

So if plugging prospective dividends into the DDM is unlikely to deliver the results we're hoping for, let's move on.

GROWTH OF EARNINGS AND DIVIDENDS

Valuation formulae need to be practical and easy to use. It's cumbersome work deriving an estimate for every future cash flow that share ownership bestows, so simpler formulae have been developed. They ask for a current earnings or dividend figure and a growth rate to apply to that number. This neat simplification then accounts for all potential future cash flows.

But while this simplifies the calculation it doesn't solve the problem of having to deliver predictions. Now you are being asked to deliver a growth rate for those future earnings. The selection of appropriate earnings growth rates is not a recent frustration. Reports from the time of the South Sea

Bubble in 1720 show that it was frustrating analysts even then. As discussed in chapter 17, at the height of this 18th-century financial fiasco a number of analysts attempted to derive their own intrinsic values for South Sea shares. Their valuations varied widely despite the fact they were using essentially the same valuation methods. It was their different earnings growth estimates that caused the variations. That was 300 years ago, but it's still a problem today and will likely remain so 300 years from now.

So how do analysts go about selecting an appropriate rate of growth for a company's future earnings? Probably the wrong way. Too often they extrapolate recent past performance, and when I say recent past, I mean *recent* past — so stock prices can swing from one quarter's profit result to the next. The problem is that the recent past can provide a poor view of the future, particularly for companies operating in a dynamic and changing business sector.

The limitation of relying on recent past performance is further magnified if a company is currently enjoying a high level of earnings growth. That's because high growth rates typically taper, leading to lower economic values than an optimistic analyst might have anticipated.

Given that it's a difficult issue, I'd like to take a look at how three great investors have dealt with the earnings growth dilemma.

Ben Graham used to place a lot of importance on historical data, but not just on the recent past. He preferred to include at least 10 years of financial data, since he felt this better reflected a company's financial performance as it moved through the business cycle. He related this data to the needs of what he called the 'defensive investor' and the 'enterprising investor'. He said that companies suitable for the defensive investor should, over the last 10 years, have demonstrated an increase in earnings of at least one-third (33 per cent). In order to smooth out anomalous years, Graham insisted that the beginning and the end figures are the three-year average earnings figures of years one through three and years eight through ten respectively. For the enterprising investor (willing to take on more risk), Graham suggested the most recent annual earnings figure must be greater, by any percentage, than that of seven years ago.

That's all very interesting, but should one assume a similar rate of earnings growth for the next seven to ten years? A judgement needs to be made whether that's a safe thing to do. If the industry is stable and mature, and the company being valued has a sustainable position within its sector, then possibly so.

On now to Warren Buffett. Reviewing the prices Buffett has paid for investments over the years, I've come to the conclusion that he doesn't use high earnings growth rates in his valuations, no matter what the company's track record shows. This was confirmed to me in 2014 on one of my trips to Omaha. An analyst who'd worked alongside Buffett for several years addressed a group of 30 investors, of whom I was one. He put it succinctly: 'Buffett doesn't pay much for growth.'

What's more, Buffett appears to solve the problem of having to extrapolate earnings into the distant future by simply not doing it. Author Bob Miles told the 2014 'Genius of Buffett' class in Omaha that Buffett expects any investment to be paid back within seven years and that he assigns little value beyond ten.

This line of thinking appears to be equally embraced by other value investors. For example, Henry Singleton, the co-founder of Teledyne, Inc., one of America's most profitable conglomerates, simply never paid more than 12 times earnings for an acquisition. And given that the companies typically demonstrated explosive growth rates after he acquired them, one could say that at 12 times earnings he didn't pay up for growth either.*

LINKING EARNINGS GROWTH TO RETENTION OF EARNINGS

Earnings-based valuation formulae assume a direct link between the growth rate of earnings and the reinvestment of retained profits (that is, those profits not paid out to shareholders in the form of dividends). Here's how the thinking works.

Imagine a hypothetical company that has $200 million of shareholders' capital tied up in its operations (referred to as book value or shareholders' equity). Put another way, shareholders would need to stump up $200 million to reproduce the company. There are 10 million shares on issue; hence each share has a book value of $20. Let's assume the company

---

*There are many similarities between Singleton and Buffett, both in the way they have run their companies and in their approach to investing. Buffett has gone on the record expressing his respect for Singleton.

has earned a net profit of $20 million in the most recent year of operation — that's $2 of earnings for each share. The company's directors decide to retain half of this profit and to distribute the other half in the form of dividends. Here's the same information in mathematical form:

Shareholders' equity:	$200 million
Earnings:	$20 million
Retained earnings:	$10 million
New shareholders' equity:	$210 million

Because the company retains $10 million of earnings, rather than distributing the money to shareholders, the shareholders' stake in the business (shareholders' equity) has increased from $200 million to $210 million.

Question: If the company made $20 million this year, then how much do you expect it to make next year?

The simple answer is that next year's profit, just like any future profit, is unknown. It will be subject to a nearly endless list of variables — everything from shifts in demand for its products to changes in wage rates and currency fluctuations. But our simplistic valuation formulae don't allow for a large number of inputs. They ask for a few all-encompassing measures such as return on equity, earnings growth rate and discount rate. And for the simplest formulae these inputs are stated as single, unchanging numbers. So, aware of these limitations, let's calculate the earnings growth rate for our hypothetical company.

If it delivered a profit of $20 million using $200 million of shareholders' equity last year, that's a return of:

$20 million/$200 million = 10 per cent

And if the company can achieve the same rate of return in the coming year it will make:

$210 million × 10 per cent = $21 million

That's an extra $1 million or 5 per cent on the previous year.

If one assumes the company can repeat this performance year after year, then the anticipated earnings growth rate will remain at 5 per cent.

It's no coincidence that in this example the company retains half of its earnings each year and 5 per cent represents half of the company's return on equity (10 per cent). Put another way, the anticipated earnings growth rate equals the earnings retention rate times the company's return on equity.

Lovely and neat, isn't it? Earnings retained and reinvested. Result: a larger capital base. This produces more earnings. Result: earnings growth. And so the cycle continues like an efficient compounding machine, all of it being perfect input for valuation formulae.

This relationship has a name. It's called the 'clean surplus relation'. Stated mathematically:

$$B_t = B_{t-1} + E_t - D_t$$

where:

- B_t = book value at the end of the period
- B_{t-1} = book value at the beginning of the period
- E_t = earnings for the period
- D_t = dividends paid during the period.

In other words, the book value at the end of the period equals the beginning book value plus earnings minus dividends. The problem is, this neat equation rarely reflects real life. The two principal reasons for this are:

1 The adoption of generally accepted accounting principles means accounts aren't constructed in a manner that meets the needs of the clean surplus relationship. Put another way, reported earnings don't equate to real cash.

2 Retained earnings are rarely reinvested so efficiently.

More about point two. The formulae assume no leakage, no waste, when the retained earnings are reinvested. Again, this is a relationship that doesn't occur in real life. Let's take a look.

In November 1962 the *Bulletin of the Oxford University Institute of Economics & Statistics* published an article by Ian Little entitled 'Higgledy Piggledy Growth'. Little followed this up with a small book, first published in 1966, titled *Higgledy Piggledy Growth Again*. He set out to determine whether a company's past earnings growth tells us what its future earnings growth will be.

Little was particularly interested in the impact of retained earnings on earnings growth. He used the term 'plough back' to describe these retained and reinvested earnings. His findings weren't as neat as the valuation models suggest: 'Our tentative conclusion is that there is no relation between plough back and growth.'[127] And Little had this to say about extrapolating historical earnings growth rates into the future: 'Any unbiased reader of this chapter must come to the conclusion that there is no tendency for previous behaviour to be repeated in the future.'

While Little denied that past earnings growth could be extrapolated, he stopped short of suggesting that stock analysis was a waste of time. He spoke of the need to use 'extra factors' as input to the analytic process, leaving it up to the reader to determine what these extra factors might be. But his comment touches on an extremely important point, one that's been made by some investment greats: it's an appreciation of these extra factors that distinguishes great investors (I'll be exploring what these extra factors might be later in the book).

A diversion is needed here.

WHY COMPOUNDING IS FINITE

Let's look at why retained earnings don't automatically convert into mathematically determinable rates of earnings growth.

For those of you who haven't heard the story of how the Dutch acquired Manhattan Island from the Lenape, here it is. Seventeen years after Henry Hudson cemented his place in history as the first European to set foot on the island of Manhattan, the Dutch thought they'd buy the whole island. In 1626 Peter Minuit, in his capacity as governor-general of New Netherland (a Dutch colony covering parts of what would become New York, New Jersey, Pennsylvania, Maryland, Connecticut and Delaware), traded a bunch of trinkets worth 60 Dutch guilders with the Lenape. They thought the trinkets were a gift, while Minuit thought he'd just struck the greatest real estate deal of his life. Now, 1626 was long before US dollars were issued, but in 1846 historian John Romeyn Brodhead equated 60 Dutch guilders to about US$24. Whether you put faith in his calculations or not, the $24 price tag has stuck.

When people first hear this story they think the Lenape got the thin edge of the wedge, but like many stories this one has a twist. This is because the story of Minuit's cheap land purchase is more commonly used to demonstrate the power of compounding. If the Lenape had refused the trinkets and instead asked for, and invested, an equivalent amount of cash, then today their ancestors would be rich beyond their wildest dreams. That's because $24 placed in a bank account (presumably a Dutch one) back in 1626 would have compounded to over US$1 trillion by 2015, assuming an annual compounding rate of 6.5 per cent. Not one additional dollar had to be added to the initial seed capital in order to achieve this result. All the Lenape had to do was reinvest the interest each year and resist making a single withdrawal for nearly 400 years.

Of course none of this ever happened. Even armed with these figures it's unlikely anyone would choose to do it today. Firstly, who would you choose as the beneficiary of the final pot of gold – some as yet unborn distant relative? Why should you care if some great-great-great (etc.) descendant of yours finds themselves in the *Fortune* 500 Rich List in 2404? Secondly, do you really believe that the 15 or so interim generations of descendants would happily act as custodians of the money for the next four centuries without dipping their hands in the till? And, finally, even if you luck it with honest descendants, do you really believe that future governments would be able to keep their fiscally irresponsible hands off the money?

The fact is that all forms of wealth suffer leakage, both at a personal level (in the hands of investors) and at a corporate level (in the hands of the directors). Real money doesn't lend itself to being plugged into mathematical formulae. Gerald Loeb gave a great example of this in his 1935 classic *The Battle for Investment Survival*. He refers to a *Saturday Evening Post* story in January 1933 written by US financier Frank A. Vanderlip that said:

> If the rich Medici family in Italy just six hundred years ago had set aside at 5% compound interest an investment fund equal to $100 000, its 1933 value would be $517 100 000 000 000 000 (five hundred and seventeen quadrillions). The original sum could have been represented by a globe of gold about nine inches in diameter, and the final figure would be 46 million times the existing monetary gold stock of the world.

Why didn't it happen? Why didn't some 20th-century descendant of the Medici family own the world? There is one simple answer: real money, as opposed to hypothetical money, is dispersed.

Hetty Green, once the wealthiest woman in the world, provides another example. Just prior to her death in 1916, Hetty left her $100 million fortune to her two children, Ned and Sylvia. Neither Ned nor Sylvia had children of their own, which meant that upon their death the money was scattered far and wide. Hetty's money was compounded for less than two generations.

Consider also Cornelius Vanderbilt, the wealthiest American at the time of his death in 1877. He was the creator of the Vanderbilt dynasty, which burned brightly for several decades before being relegated to just an interesting story in history. Vanderbilt was a shrewd businessman and aware how fortunes could evaporate. So before he died in 1877 he put in place what he thought to be protection against this happening. He anointed his first son, William, as the sole perpetuator of the Vanderbilt empire. Cornelius had many children but it was William who received the bulk of his $100 million estate. The others each received token six-figure amounts—enough to keep them comfortable by the standards of the late 19th century. Even Vanderbilt's second wife had been asked to sign a prenuptial agreement in an effort to keep the fortune intact. But where is the Vanderbilt fortune now? Or for that matter the Astor, Carnegie and Rockefeller fortunes? Much of the money was returned to society in the form of charitable donations and, in the case of subsequent generations, hefty levels of government taxation. But it also seems subsequent generations didn't possess the business acumen, inclination or drive that these fortunes' originators did.

Okay, diversion over. Stories of the financial erosion of history's dynasties could fill a library. But what these examples highlight is that wealth is not some sterile figure you can simply plug into a compounding formula, and it's no different when valuing companies. After all, companies are run by people. The destinies of companies are determined by the same human frailties that govern the loss of family fortunes. There are massive leakages to corporate wealth—ill-timed and unprofitable entries into new markets, acquisitions undertaken to feed the CEO's ego rather than boost earnings per share, self-enriching managerial options schemes, heavy-taxing governments, sector-destroying shifts in technology...and the list goes on.

So what do we do? Do we simply ignore these realities and press on regardless? Do we continue to source figures from a company's financial accounts and plug them into simple compounding formulae? I think the answer is yes. Don't ignore the formulae, just handle them with care — appreciate their limitations, and use conservative inputs.

It's also a good idea to take your cue from Buffett: don't assume perpetuity. Work on having your investment repaid within a decade, then think of everything you receive beyond that as a bonus. And if you've chosen the right companies, it's going to be one very healthy bonus.

Chapter summary

- The value of investments should be based on expectations of what they will deliver in the future.

- Reported profit is an accounting construct and differs from real cash flows.

- There are two main areas where the Income Statement strays from reporting actual cash flows. They are: how income and expenses are classified, and the period in which they are reported.

- The Dividend Discount Model (DDM) uses only dividends as inputs in the valuation process since it can be argued that dividends are the only returns that stockholders actually receive.

- Value investors typically place a low value on earnings growth.

- A simplistic method for calculating earnings growth is to multiply the estimated future return on equity by an estimated earnings retention rate.

- Research undertaken by Ian Little found no relationship between earnings retention and earnings growth.

- Wealth disperses with time.

- A business should be valued with the investor's aim of being totally repaid within 10 years.

23

THE DISCOUNT RATE

Investors invest money today expecting more back in the future. But the important question remains: even if you can pin a number on what those future dollars might be, what are they actually worth today? Well, to work this out there are a couple of issues to address.

Firstly, there's the issue of inflation. In an inflationary environment, a dollar buys less in the future. Until the middle of the 20th century negative inflation (deflation) was as common an event as inflation; that is, there were periods when things got cheaper to buy. But in more recent decades it's been different. For the past 70 years, in fact, there's been a general expectation that prices will march forever upwards. This presents problems when placing a current value on future cash flows. Predicting future inflation rates can never be more than an educated guess. And, as with predictions of future earnings, it's a guess that's heavily influenced by the rate of inflation prevailing at the time the analyst is coming up with the estimate.

Secondly, there's the issue of the risk associated with the particular investment being valued. Investors are being asked to exchange something that is certain (cold, hard cash held today) for something that is far from certain (future cash flows based on the business prospects of the company).

The dollar-reducing effect of inflation and the potential dollar-reducing risk of investing in a substandard business are both embodied in a single figure called the 'discount rate'—the rate that is applied to estimated future cash flows to convert them into today's dollars. The higher the expected inflation, the higher the discount rate. The higher the anticipated company risk, the higher the discount rate.

Let's now consider how a discount rate is applied. A 5 per cent discount rate means that a dollar delivered in one year will be worth 5 per cent less than a dollar is today—that is, 95 cents. And a dollar delivered in two years will be worth 90.7 cents (95 cents less 5 per cent).

Okay, we've now covered Valuation 101. By now you've likely twigged to the magnitude of the problems we're facing. For starters, we don't know what future levels of inflation (or deflation) will be. And we have no way of quantifying risk since we don't know how the business will perform in the future. We want to apply this indefinable discount rate to indefinable future cash flows. And, just to add complexity to uncertainty, there can never be a single discount rate appropriate for all companies or for any single company over time.

But again let's relegate these problems to the back seat. In our efforts to feed the needs of the real world, let's press on. We'll start by looking at a couple of people who thought long and hard about the problem and eventually came up with their version of a mathematical solution.

THE CAPITAL ASSET PRICING MODEL

The story of the Capital Asset Pricing Model (CAPM) begins with a 25-year-old graduate student at the University of Chicago called Harry Markowitz. In 1952 Markowitz released a research paper entitled 'Portfolio Selection', in which he argued that investors should view investment risk in terms of their entire portfolio, rather than the individual stocks within that portfolio. And that was fair enough. It was a long-held belief that it was risky to 'put all your eggs in one basket' by investing in only one stock.*

---

*People have recognised for centuries that financial securities carrying higher risk needed to be rewarded by higher rates of return. For example, on page two of *Every Man His Own Broker* (1801) Thomas Mortimer states: 'Higher interest may indeed be obtained, but then the security is not so good.'

But it was how Markowitz went on to define risk that was novel: he related stock price movement to a statistical term called 'covariance', which could describe how the prices of two stocks move in relation to each other. If their prices or returns move together, they have a 'positive covariance'. For example, if the iron ore price increases, this is great news for all companies that mine iron ore. Other things being equal, the stock prices of all companies that mine iron ore should rise. They are described as having high positive covariance. The same news should also be positive for companies supporting the mining industry, such as producers of explosives and mining equipment. They would be said to have a positive covariance with the iron ore producers, although the covariance might be lower than that between the iron ore producers themselves.

On the other side of the coin, two stocks are said to have a 'negative covariance' when their share prices move in opposite directions following the release of certain news; this may apply, for example, to oil stocks and airline stocks. If the price of oil goes up, the news will be positive for oil stocks and negative for airline stocks (heavy fuel users). Markowitz incorporated these concepts into a model defining the trade-off between risk and reward. Ultimately his concept became widely accepted, and for his work he was awarded the Nobel Memorial Prize in Economic Sciences in 1990.

Markowitz believed the optimal balance between risk and reward was to be found in a diversified portfolio, but not just any diversified portfolio. He developed a formula for defining the optimal mix of assets within a portfolio, and when his formula was traced out as a graph it presented as a curved line referred to as the 'efficient frontier'. Build a portfolio that sits anywhere on this line and you have the optimal balance between risk and reward. So 'Modern Portfolio Theory' was born.

Others worked to develop Markowitz's ideas. His initial formula was difficult for people to get their heads around and cumbersome to use. It was also time consuming to calculate and, considering the limitations of computing power at the time, expensive to calculate. Enter a brilliant young economist called William Sharpe. Sharpe whipped Markowitz's theory into the simplified working formula we now refer to as the Capital Asset Pricing Model (CAPM).

Sharpe's 1964 breakthrough was to take Markowitz's concept of equating risk with stock price movement and to simplify how it was measured.

To do this he compared each stock's price movement not to other single stocks but to those of a well-diversified portfolio. And what more appropriate example of a diversified portfolio could there be than the entire stock market?

Sharpe's revision of Markowitz's formula meant it was now simple to use, and it provided a practical way for analysts to pin an actual number on risk. Armed with this number, investors felt they were now able to price derivatives, determine the intrinsic values of stocks, and construct better performing and less risky portfolios.

The CAPM can be stated as follows:

Required return on a particular stock (discount rate) = Current expected risk-free rate + β (equity risk premium)

There are three inputs to the CAPM formula:

- current expected risk-free rate
- equity risk premium
- beta (β).

These three inputs can be thought of as three layers of return and risk. The first layer is the return you would expect from a 'risk-free' investment. The second layer is the extra return (the return above the risk-free rate) you would expect from holding a broad-based portfolio of stocks. And the third layer is the extra risk associated with holding just one stock, the stock you're calculating the discount rate for. Let's discuss each.

The risk-free rate

The risk-free rate is the interest rate attached to sovereign debt (money that a government has borrowed). Take it that the risk-free rate relates to the bonds of fiscally responsible governments. (The fact is that governments occasionally blow themselves up by borrowing too much — the Spanish, Greek and Italian stock analysts, for example, were hard pushed to come up with a figure for their risk-free rate during the 2010–13 Euro debt crisis.) But in the case of the US the thinking is that you can lend to Uncle Sam and there's a good chance you'll get your money back. In choosing between the interest rates on short-dated Treasury bills ('T-bills') and long-term government bonds, many argue it's more appropriate to use the 10-year bond rate since it better represents long-term return expectations. And that's more in line with the returns delivered by stocks, since they're also long-term investments.

But are bonds actually a 'risk-free' investment? Sure, they provide a near guaranteed return if you hold them to maturity. But remember Markowitz's own definition of risk: he equated risk with price volatility, and the market prices of 10-year bonds can demonstrate extreme volatility over the short term.

I still remember the first day I walked into the Bankers Trust dealing room in Melbourne in 1987. My role on BT's dealing desk was to trade bank bills, and the typical maturity of these debt instruments was 90 days. Unless interest rates changed significantly, the value at which they traded didn't change much. Sure, their price varied over the 90-odd days they were on issue, but not significantly. They were always soon to mature. And when they did, bank bill investors would simply roll over their investment at the new rate. Nothing much gained, nothing much lost. Fairly capital stable, little stress, little excitement.

But it was a whole different story up the other end of the dealing room, where the bond traders were sitting. I soon realised that those boys got a lot more excited when interest rates moved. At first I was confused — my impression was that bonds were boring instruments. Buy a 10-year, put it in the bottom drawer, and collect the interest payments every six months until it expires sometime in the distant future. Why were these guys getting so excited?

The penny dropped when I eventually learned how to price a bond. I discovered that because interest payments are fixed (that is, the interest payment or coupon doesn't change when interest rates do), a move in interest rates necessarily impacts the price investors are prepared to pay for the bond. And the period to maturity is like a lever on price — the longer the bond, the bigger the price move. I realised these guys up the other end of the trading room were playing with highly volatile instruments. If bond traders made a wrong move they could lose their shirt. So, relating this back to the CAPM, which equates risk to price volatility, how can long-term bonds be presented as a risk-free investment under its definition?

It seems to me that CAPM applies a different definition of risk to stocks than it does to bonds in order to facilitate a convenient solution to a difficult problem. To derive a discount rate in the CAPM, Markowitz, Sharpe and their disciples were defining the 'risk-free' nature of bonds as 'non-default'. Yet the 'risk' of holding stocks was being defined differently — not as the risk of default but rather as the volatility of price and return.

Before I leave this part of our discussion of the CAPM, I just want to give an example of Warren Buffett's perception of its usefulness, or should I say lack of usefulness. The CAPM suggests that lower interest rates deliver lower discount rates, and these should lead to higher stock valuations when plugged into valuation formulae. It's intuitively appealing because in a low interest rate environment investors chase the yields of stocks down, and hence their market prices increase. It's not surprising then that the following paragraph, from Robert Hagstrom's book *The Warren Buffett Portfolio*, caught my attention:

> Buffett tells us that, in a low interest rate environment, he adjusts the discount rate upward. When bond yields dipped below 7 percent, Buffett adjusted his discount rate up to 10 percent. If interest rates work themselves higher over time, he has successfully matched his discount rate to the long-term rate. If they do not, he has increased his margin of safety by three additional points.[128]

By using a higher discount rate when interest rates are historically low, Buffett is allowing for the increased chance that interest rates could rise and that stock prices could fall. It's a reminder that we should be thinking in terms of 'mean reversion'. Just because interest rates are abnormally high or low at the time of the valuation doesn't mean they'll always remain that way.

The equity risk premium

On to the second input: the equity risk premium. The CAPM says that stocks are a riskier bet than government bonds, so a premium needs to be added to the 'risk-free rate' delivered by bonds to reflect this. Intuitively you'd think this premium would be easy to calculate. After all, stocks and bonds have been traded for centuries, and reliable records of stock prices, stock indices and their relationship to bond rates have existed for more than a century. Just compare the difference between the historical returns on holding stocks versus bonds, right? Unfortunately, there are a few problems with what would seem to be a good idea. Let's list them:

- What period do you choose for the comparison? Because the premium has varied through time—a lot.

- What broad-based equity index do you use for the comparison?

- What government debt instrument(s) do you use for the comparison?

- What country do you look at? Because the premium has varied from one country to the next—a lot.

- Are historical comparisons even relevant? After all, it's the future that matters in investing, not the past.

Got the idea? It just isn't possible to nail a single figure on the equity risk premium.

Beta

Beta is the third and final input to our CAPM-determined discount rate, and it requires a bit of explanation.

Beta compares the risk of holding a single stock (the one we're ultimately trying to derive the discount rate for) to that of holding a broad-based portfolio of stocks. It measures the sensitivity of a single stock's returns to those of the broad-based portfolio. A beta of one means the returns from holding the single stock vary the same as for the broad-based portfolio. A beta greater than one means the single stock returns vary to a greater degree; less than one and it's more stable. A beta of zero means there's no relationship between the returns of the two. So the use of beta is supposed to be the factor that adjusts the equity risk premium (which has been calculated for the broad-based portfolio of stocks) into a risk premium specific to the single stock you're attempting to value.

Are there any problems with this approach? Absolutely. Beta is a statistical measure, and the stock market doesn't dance to statistics.

Markowitz would have been better served if he'd taken note of the earlier writings of US economist Frank Knight and British economist John Maynard Keynes.

In 1921 Knight released a groundbreaking book titled *Risk, Uncertainty, and Profit*. He argued that financial markets are characterised by ambiguity—that is, future uncertainty. Risk in financial markets is unquantifiable because a set of future outcomes cannot be defined, nor could probabilities be assigned to them were it possible.

Let's demonstrate what Knight is saying through an example. You have a pair of dice, and you throw one of them across the table. What's the chance a five will come up? Easy: one in six. How do you know this? Because, as Knight has said, you can define the set of possible outcomes (1, 2, 3, 4, 5 or 6) and you can apply probabilities to each outcome (equal probabilities, or one in six for each outcome). Without these two prerequisites you can't define outcomes statistically. But, as Knight also states, neither is definable in the stock market. Possible outcomes? Near limitless. Assignment of probabilities to each outcome? Who knows!

Keynes added to the argument in his 1921 book *A Treatise on Probability*. He stated that probability cannot be measured purely from observed frequency. If you flip a coin many times it's unlikely to demonstrate a pure 50:50 outcome. It's more likely that the outcome will be something approximating that ratio. Yet anybody, if asked, would say the expected outcome of a coin toss is 50:50 heads or tails. Indeed I can guarantee that any book on statistics will state that the odds are 50:50. Keynes justified the discrepancy between outcome and theory by stating that probabilities are based on expectations, not on actual outcomes.

Having taken this on board, now consider the probability of a stock market crash occurring next week, next month or next year. No idea? Join the queue. We're incapable of placing probabilities on stock market outcomes. Keynes summarised this concept succinctly in *The General Theory*: 'It can easily be shown that the assumption of arithmetically equal probabilities based on a state of ignorance leads to absurdities.'

What then of actuaries working for insurance companies? Don't they apply probabilities to unknown future outcomes? Do their actions deny what Knight and Keynes are saying? After all, when you set off for a journey in your car isn't the future ambiguous, uncertain, unpredictable? You can't predict whether you're about to have a car crash. To use Keynes' words, isn't this outcome preceded by 'a state of ignorance'? Yet somehow insurance companies are able to calculate the odds that accidents will occur and then use these to price insurance policies.

But there is one sizeable difference between motor accidents and the stock market. There are over one billion cars on the road. Car accidents are governed by the law of high numbers. There are plenty of statistics to splice, dice and dissect. And while the insurance companies can't use past observations to predict the future with absolute accuracy, they'll come close enough to enable them to turn a profit on the insurance policies they write. Compare that with the financial markets, which experience a decent fender-bender only every decade or two.

Put it all together and you'll find that beta is not a proxy for risk, as many academics wish us to believe.

Short-term price volatility is a risk only to short-term traders. To investors, price fluctuations don't present a risk but rather an opportunity. Just ask any hardcore investor how they feel about a stock market crash: they love it, seeing it as an opportunity to buy cheap stocks. Yet this is a time when volatility, the academic's proxy for risk, goes through the roof. The academic's position is that a stock that has fallen significantly in price has a high beta.

But to an investor the same stock, under the same circumstances, might represent great value and therefore less risk. The investor's argument intuitively makes more sense.

The dictionary defines volatility as 'a liability to change rapidly and unpredictably'. I would say that sums up what stock markets do most of the time. Markowitz equated risk to price fluctuation. Now I don't know whether Markowitz read *The Intelligent Investor*, but Graham held a very different view on the matter, stating that stocks 'should not be termed "risky" merely because of the element of price fluctuation'.[129]

To my mind Graham was right. What's more, he delivered this conclusion after several decades of experience operating in Wall Street. He had a razor-sharp mind and a penetrating sense of logic. In contrast, Markowitz, when he first came up with his concept of risk, was a young university student with no financial market experience. In his attempt to find an interesting topic for a thesis, he chose to quantify the unquantifiable. His equations were ultimately presented to a finance profession that wanted to believe in them. It was a convenient attempt to resolve an inconvenient problem.

As an additional consideration, volatility is representative of both upward and downward price movements, but financial market risk is unidirectional — it is the risk of losing money. As New York University's Peter Carr said of price volatility, 'It is only a good measure of risk if you feel that being rich then being poor is the same as being poor then rich.'

As noted, fluctuating share prices, to the seasoned investor, represent opportunity not risk. This was the premise behind Graham's classic tale of Mr Market and has been the bedrock of Buffett's stock purchases for Berkshire Hathaway for decades.

A case in point is the movement of the Chicago Board Options Exchange Volatility Index (VIX) during the GFC. Based on the implied volatility of 30-day options on the S&P 500, it reached its highest recorded levels at the very time the US stock market was offering its best buying opportunities for years. It's a perverse investor who thinks buying sound assets at cheap prices is associated with higher levels of risk.

Because volatility is a short-term concept it's understandable traders would interpret volatility as being at least partly representative of risk. But, unlike traders, investors give themselves the luxury of time, and with time the relevance of volatility diminishes.

There is no single measure of risk or single discount rate that is applicable to a single company through time. Changing debt levels, new competitors, shifts in technology and alterations in economic conditions mean these measures are an ever-changing thing. In response to this concern, Nobel laureate Robert Merton set about developing a dynamic version of the CAPM dubbed 'the intertemporal capital asset pricing model'. While Merton has a great mind, his model did not prevail over the insurmountable.

History has virtually forgotten Cambridge academic A.D. Roy. Like Markowitz, he published an article on portfolio theory — interestingly in 1952, the same year Markowitz published his. Despite being conceptually similar, it is Markowitz, not Roy, who has been credited as the father of Modern Portfolio Theory. It is interesting then to hear Roy's comments after reviewing Markowitz's 1959 book, effectively a publication of his 1952 thesis:

> While Dr. Markowitz warns that past experience is unlikely to be a very good guide to future performance, he gives us no clear indication of how either we, or our investment advisers, can provide ourselves with sufficiently precise or generally agreed expectations to merit their processing in an elaborate way...

> Mr. Markowitz presses for a precision in the specification of both motives and of expectations which it seems unlikely that any existing investor can reasonably be expected to possess or to express coherently.[130]

So let's summarise where we're at with the CAPM, our academic attempt to determine a useful discount rate. Remember that:

> The required return on a particular stock = Current expected risk-free rate + β (equity risk premium)

It states that the discount rate applicable to the stock varies with the risk-free rate (government bond rate). To borrow the CAPM's own terminology, it assumes a positive covariance between stocks and bonds. I'd suggest that this relationship is not so direct. The reality is that the covariance can be positive or negative, high or low, depending upon the mood investors and central bankers are in at any point in time. The next variable, beta, is a hypothetical figure that does a poor job of describing reality. And the 'constant'—the equity risk premium—is not a constant at all.

BARR ROSENBERG'S BARRA

Berkeley graduate Barr Rosenberg was interested in risk, and particularly in how it could be modelled and measured, so naturally his attention turned to the CAPM. Common sense told him, as it told most people, that the risk of holding a stock is influenced by many more factors than variations in its market price. What about the type of industry it operates in, its capital structure, the diversification of its customer base, the quality of management and the threat of competition—just to name a few. Based on his academic insights, in 1973 Rosenberg formed the consulting organisation Barr Rosenberg and Associates; the name was subsequently shortened to BARRA.

BARRA developed computer programs that, among other things, attempted to predict a stock's beta using numerous inputs. The investment industry felt Rosenberg was on to something, and his list of clients grew. Rosenberg left BARRA in 1985 to start a portfolio management business, but in 2011 he was found guilty of securities fraud and consented to a lifetime securities industry bar. The Securities and Exchange Commission disclosure stated he had concealed 'a significant error in the computer code of the quantitative investment model that he developed and provided to the firm's entities for use in managing client assets'. More specifically, the error disabled one of its key components for managing risk.

Given the difficulty in deriving an appropriate discount rate let's now investigate how variations in the discount rate impact our valuation.

SENSITIVITY OF THE DISCOUNT RATE

You might be thinking I'm exploring this whole discount rate issue a bit too thoroughly. After all, does it really matter whether you use a discount rate of 5 per cent or 6 per cent when calculating a stock's value? The answer is yes, it does matter. What appears to be a small shift in the discount rate can have a significant impact on the valuation. To demonstrate, I'd like to introduce you to the Gordon Growth Model, named after financial economist Myron J. Gordon. I'll be discussing it at length in the next chapter, but at this stage I'll use it simply as a useful platform for discussion. The Gordon Growth Model is a simple valuation formula that requires just three inputs:

$$(V_0) = \frac{D^1}{r - g}$$

where:

- V_0 = stock value

- D^1 = estimate of next year's dividend

- r = discount rate

- g = growth rate of dividends.

Using this simple formula let's test the impact on the valuation of a change in the discount rate. To do this we'll first keep the dividend and dividend growth rate constant. Assume the company being valued will pay a dividend of 10 cents next year and that the dividend will grow at a rate of 4 per cent every year after that. If a 10 per cent discount rate is used, the formula value will be:

$$(V_0) = \frac{0.10}{0.10 - 0.04} = \$1.67$$

However, if a discount rate of 8 per cent is chosen, the formula value is $2.50. Changing the discount rate from 10 per cent to 8 per cent has resulted in a 50 per cent increase in the valuation. Let's see what happens when we start playing around with the other inputs as well.

First set of assumptions:

- Next year's dividend: 10 cents

- Discount rate: 10%

- Dividend growth rate: 2%

- Formula value: $1.25

Second set of assumptions:

- Next year's dividend: 11 cents

- Discount rate: 8%

- Dividend growth rate: 4%

- Formula value: $2.75

So with what we thought were small adjustments to our inputs we see a 120 per cent lift in our valuation.

MORE PRACTICAL MEASURES OF RETURN AND RISK

Okay, so I've punched a lot of holes in the CAPM, but we still need a figure for the discount rate to plug into our formulae. To me it makes sense to ignore the insurmountable problems listed above and simplify our approach to choosing an appropriate discount rate. And to make it official let's also make a name change. Let's now refer to the discount rate as the 'required rate of return' or 'RRR'. This is the minimum rate of return we demand our investment to deliver. We set the rate by considering our alternatives — the returns being delivered by other investments.

It's also the way the two kings of common sense, Warren Buffett and Charlie Munger, have resolved the issue. I was at the 2014 Berkshire Hathaway AGM, along with 39 000 other people, when Buffett addressed the issue. He described the process of selecting a discount rate as 'what can be produced by our second best investment idea. And then we aim to exceed it. In other words it's an opportunity cost'. Munger added: 'Cost of capital is defined in a very silly way in business schools.' While not specifically stating it, Munger was clearly referring to the CAPM and the weighted average cost of capital.

In assessing investment risk I prefer not to think about beta, the CAPM and other theoretical concepts. I'd rather focus on real-life risks. And the first risk, since we're talking about money, is the risk of losing it — either some of it (receiving either a substandard or negative return) or all of it (if the company you've invested in goes bust).

There are three ways you'll end up receiving a substandard return:

- by paying too much when you buy
- by selling at a low price
- by receiving a low dividend stream during the time you own the stock that isn't sufficiently compensated for by capital gain.

So this type of risk can be distilled down to price, price again and income. To minimise this risk, buy cheaply, sell at a premium, and buy companies that are not only financially sound but produce lots of cash.

You might have noticed the discussion has now become a bit circular. We started by attempting to quantify risk so we could value the stock; that is, risk was an input to stock valuation. But we've now turned things around to say price is integral to the determination of risk!

Let's now consider the risk of the company going broke. There's no need to think like a statistician here — just think like a banker.

You've got capital at risk, so don't hand it over to Shonky Brothers Ltd. As I've previously said, I don't want this book to turn into a tome on financial analysis, so I won't delve deeply into techniques of determining creditworthiness. Just remember that as a stock holder you're standing at the end of a pretty long queue. For example, if the company goes down, you're behind the bankers. So, in theory, your assessment of creditworthiness should be more thorough than theirs. The main issues in judging a company's creditworthiness are:

- too much debt. As Ben Graham used to say, 'A company should own at least twice what it owes.'[131]

- strong cash flow. Don't accept what the Income Statement in the annual report is telling you—get to know your way around the Cash Flow Statement.

- the viability of the company's business model.

That's all I'm going to say here, but if you want to explore the subject of debt and risk further then I refer you to appendix B. Let's turn instead to another concept of risk—one that also doesn't rely on abstract mathematical theories.

THE RISK OF BEING HUMAN

Financial markets haven't been around long enough to influence the way humans think; in evolutionary terms we've barely left the African savanna. Our behaviour is driven by the same instincts of survival found in every other species on this planet. In the face of unacceptable danger we choose to run. Accordingly, when financial markets collapse our natural instinct is also to run—that is, to sell. We reinforce one another's natural instincts, meaning we buy and sell with a pack mentality. So when investors are doing dumb things, like selling when stock prices are down, many others tend to do exactly the same. The problem is this isn't exactly market-beating behaviour.

Financial markets are bedevilled by the counterintuitive. For example, risk in financial markets is actually at its lowest when everyone believes it's high. The time of greatest risk is when few perceive it. Ironically it's a time usually characterised by a sense of unbounded, blind optimism—something that has preceded every stock market crash since equity markets began. Here's a quote from Joseph de la Vega's *Confusion de Confusiones* describing the mood immediately before Holland's wealth-destroying stock market crash in 1688:

> ... on the Exchange, a goodly supply of money and abundant credit were available; there were splendid prospects for exports; a vigorous spirit of enterprise; brilliant military forces under famous leaders were [protecting

the country]; there was favourable news, incomparable knowledge of business, a swelling population, a strong fleet, advantageous alliances. Therefore not the slightest concern, not the least apprehension reigned, not the smallest cloud, not the most fleeting shadow was to be seen.[132]

So familiar was finance writer Henry Hall with the optimism felt by investors just prior to a stock market crash that he described the buoyant mood prior to the 1907 Panic as being of 'the old, old way'.[133]

Blind optimism followed by stock market crashes is still how events pan out today, and most likely always will. The question often asked is: why does the mood change so quickly? What's the trigger that causes investors' enthusiasm to be switched off and panic to be switched on?

Applying logic to answer this question seems to be a waste of time, but applying logic is exactly what every inevitable post-crash inquiry attempts to do. The reasons start rolling in: monetary policy was too tight, monetary policy was too loose. In 1907 it was an earthquake. In 1987 it was a storm in the UK. No, it was programmed trading in the US. No, it was changes in tax policy. Market manipulation, leverage, you name it—everything has at some stage copped the blame. Interestingly the common culprit, unrealistic and unbridled pre-crash optimism, barely rates a mention. Yet it should. Howard Marks nailed it when he said: 'I'm convinced that it's usually more correct to attribute a bust to the excesses of the preceding boom than to the specific event that sets off the correction.'[134] This is not dissimilar to a comment made by Graham in *The Intelligent Investor* as to a principal cause of the Great Depression: 'The extreme depth of the depression of the early 1930's was accounted for in good part, this writer believes, by the insane height of the preceding stock boom.'[135]

When six major investigations failed to come up with a credible reason for the 23 per cent collapse in the Dow Jones Index on 19 October 1987, it was Bob Shiller who offered the best explanation. In surveying investors as to why they sold that day, the common response he found was that they were reacting to the crash itself. In other words, they sold because everyone else was.

Here then we have the reality. Markets can climb due to a wave of contagious, unbridled enthusiasm. And they can collapse due to a wave of contagious, unbridled fear. This is something no formula can quantify.

Since risk is at its greatest when most market commentators are telling us conditions are great, and at its least when they are telling us not to invest a dime, I don't take my cue from commentators. I take my cue from the actions of grey-haired and wealthy investors who've been through a stock market cycle or five. This is one of my favourite quotes, taken from Henry Clews' *Fifty Years in Wall Street*, first published in 1908:

> If young men had only the patience to watch the speculative signs of the times, as manifested in the periodical egress of these old prophetic speculators from their shells of security, they would make more money at these intervals than by following up the slippery 'tips' of the professional 'pointers' of the Stock Exchange...I say to the young speculators, therefore, watch the ominous visits to the Street of these old men. They are as certain to be seen on the eve of a panic as spiders creeping stealthily and noiselessly from their cobwebs just before rain.[136]

FURTHER INPUTS — THE CO-STARS

So now we've covered the two main inputs to valuation formulae—the same two inputs demanded by Pisano's eight-centuries-old discounted cash flow formula: cash flow and discount rate. But many valuation formulae ask for inputs other than these. This might seem strange, since the formulae are supposed to be working out the same thing—until you realise these other inputs are simply a different way of expressing the same information. So before we move on to looking at the formulae there are just two more inputs I want to discuss—book value and return on equity.

Book value

I defined book value back in chapter 15 but it's worth a quick refresher before we move on to the next chapter.

Book value is taken from the Balance Sheet in the company's financial accounts (also referred to as the Statement of Financial Position). It's calculated by subtracting what a company owes (total liabilities) from what it owns (total assets). It's also referred to as net assets or shareholders' equity.

In theory, book value indicates how much shareholders would receive if the company were to be wound up on the date the accounts were constructed—what's left over after everything is sold up and all debts paid off. I say 'in theory' because financial statements are accounting constructs and therefore they often differ from economic reality.

Book value is commonly expressed on a per share basis. This is calculated by dividing the total book value of the company by the total number of shares on issue.

Return on equity

Return on equity (ROE) measures the rate of return the company delivers on the book value or shareholders' equity. For example, if the book value per share is one dollar and the company returns a profit after tax of 15 cents on every share, the return on equity is 15 per cent. It measures the return shareholders are receiving on the money they've tied up in the company, and it assists them in judging whether their return expectations are being met.

Many formulae ask for book value and return on equity as inputs. Does using them enhance our ability to value stocks? No, it doesn't. Remember the trouble we had in determining what future cash flows will be? Remember our concerns about extrapolating historical figures into the future? Remember the questions we raised about using net profit after tax as an input to our valuation formulae? Using return on equity and book value resolves none of these concerns because:

Net profit after tax = Return on equity × book value

So let's now move on to the formulae themselves.

....

Chapter summary

- To bring future cash flows back to current dollar values, they need to be adjusted using a discount rate.

- The Capital Asset Pricing Model (CAPM) is a mathematical method that has been developed for deriving discount rates. It can be summarised as: current expected risk-free rate + β multiplied by (equity risk premium).

- Government bonds (sovereign debt) of fiscally prudent countries have low default risk but do demonstrate significant price volatility. The price volatility of bonds increases as the term to maturity increases, all other things being equal.

- The equity risk premium varies both with the study period and the country being considered.

- Beta is a statistical measure, and the stock market doesn't dance to the tune of statistics. Beta isn't a proxy for investment risk, as some academics wish us to believe.

- Risk is often high when many market participants perceive it to be low, such as just before a stock market crash.

- Beta increases both during a stock market crash and in its aftermath, yet this is often the time when value investors perceive the market as having its lowest level of risk.

- Volatility is representative of both upward and downward price movement, but financial risk should be described by loss, which is asymmetric.

- Warren Buffett doesn't believe that the CAPM is based on sound principles. He judges the cost of capital to be the opportunity cost of capital—in other words, the return he could have achieved by employing his second best investment idea.

- The discount rate can also be described as the required rate of return (RRR).

- Valuations are sensitive to the discount rate applied.

- A significant risk in financial markets is behavioural risk.

24

THE FORMULAE

As I run my eyes across the bookshelves covering the far wall of my study, something quickly becomes obvious: the books I own on stock valuation are the thickest books on the shelves. Their size clearly reflects the extended message their authors felt compelled to tell, which is surprising considering how Ben Graham felt about the valuation process. Graham was an insightful investor, and he loved mathematics. If anyone was capable of writing a great book on valuation it was him. Yet his two most popular books, *Security Analysis* and *The Intelligent Investor*, devote few words to the actual process of calculating intrinsic value. In 1958 he had this to say:

> In 44 years of Wall Street experience and study, I have never seen dependable calculations made about common stock values, or related policies, that went beyond simple arithmetic or the most elementary algebra. Whenever calculus is brought in, or higher algebra, you could take it as a warning signal that the operator was trying to substitute theory for experience, and usually also to give speculation the deceptive guise of investment.

There's no doubt that formulae are necessary, but let's take Graham's advice and keep things simple.

With this in mind, let's restate a valuation truth: what you pay for a stock today should be based on your expectation of what it will return in the future. That return will come (hopefully) in the form of capital gains and dividends. That's it in a nutshell. Such a simple concept begs the question: why are there so many formulae? As you're about to discover, there aren't—there just appears to be. The reality is that most are the same formula dressed up in different clothing.

THE POPULAR FORMULAE

The most popular earnings-based valuation formulae are:

- the Dividend Discount Model
- the Gordon Growth Model
- Multistage Dividend Discount models
- Free Cash Flow to the Firm and Free Cash Flow to Equity
- Residual Income Valuation.

They might have fancy names but they're all just algebraic manipulations of what Pisano presented in *Liber Abaci* eight centuries ago, which means they're all built from the same DNA (which is kind of amusing, since I've heard analysts condemn one formula while supporting another). Running from top to bottom on the list above, let's explore them.

The Dividend Discount Model

The Dividend Discount Model (DDM) is used to calculate the present value of all future dividends a stock is expected to deliver. It's basically just the discounted cash flow formula with dividends plugged in as the cash flow. Stated mathematically:

$$\text{Present value} = \frac{\text{Dividend}^1}{(1+r)^1} + \frac{\text{Dividend}^2}{(1+r)^2} + \cdots + \frac{\text{Dividend}^n}{(1+r)^n}$$

where:

- r = the discount rate
- n = the time (usually expressed by the year) when the dividend is paid.

As you can see from the formula, it asks for an estimate of every future dividend, and that makes calculation rather cumbersome. The Gordon Growth Model simplifies the process.

The Gordon Growth Model

I feel sorry for US economist Myron Gordon, whose name is linked to a formula he discussed in a 1956 paper and later in his 1962 book *The Investment, Financing, and Valuation of the Corporation*. Gordon was a smart guy, and his book is a good one. But the formula bearing his name has some obvious limitations, hence the Gordon Growth Model is a valuation formula people love to criticise. The irony is, Gordon criticised it as well. After presenting it in his book he used it as a conceptual punching bag. Just like today's critics, he felt it was too simplistic.

But the model isn't really his. It's a restatement of Swiss mathematician Jacob Bernoulli's formula for determining the present value of the sum of an infinite series of numbers growing at a constant rate. Despite presenting it three centuries before Gordon he somehow missed out on the naming rights.

The Gordon Growth Model is merely a simple form of the DDM. The simplification is delivered by making one very large assumption — that future dividends will forever grow at a constant rate. This assumption overcomes one of the major drawbacks of the full form of the DDM — that is, coming up with an estimate for every dividend between now and eternity. So the Gordon Growth Model transforms the cumbersome DDM into something that's simple, neat and clean. But, alas, it's no better at divining the correct answer than the formula from which it's derived.

The Gordon Growth Model requires just three inputs to calculate a stock's value: next year's dividend (D^1), a single discount rate (r) and a single dividend growth rate (g). Here it is:

$$\text{Present value } (V_0) = \frac{D^1}{r - g}$$

Let's see, in mathematical notation, how the Gordon Growth Model is derived. First let's restate the basic DDM:

$$\text{Present value} = \frac{\text{Dividend}^1}{(1+r)^1} + \frac{\text{Dividend}^2}{(1+r)^2} + \cdots + \frac{\text{Dividend}^n}{(1+r)^n}$$

where:

- r = the discount rate
- n = the time (usually expressed by the year) when the dividend is paid.

We start with the current dividend (D^0). Next year's dividend (D^1) is expected to have grown by rate (g), and all subsequent dividends are expected to grow at the same rate since g is assumed to be constant. That is:

$$\text{Present value } (V_0) = \frac{D^1}{(1+r)^1} + \frac{D^1(1+g)^1}{(1+r)^2} + \cdots + \frac{D^1(1+g)^\infty}{(1+r)^\infty}$$

$$V_0 = \frac{D^0(1+g)^1}{(1+r)^1} + \frac{D^0(1+g)^2}{(1+r)^2} + \cdots + \frac{D^0(1+g)^\infty}{(1+r)^\infty}$$

Each successive term is increasing by the factor:

$$\frac{(1+g)}{(1+r)}$$

Note the growth rate (g) of the dividend has to be smaller than the discount rate (r). If not, we're saying this stock will eventually become so valuable it will take over the world. To make mathematical sense, g must be less than r, so we're adding ever-diminishing increments of real (discount rate adjusted) value. It then has a finite and determinable present value. It's like moving forward with ever-decreasing steps. That limits how far you eventually move forward, even if you take an infinite number of steps. Alternatively, with ever-increasing infinite steps, your destination would be boundless.

The infinite series above can be mathematically simplified to:

$$\text{Present value } (V_0) = \frac{D^1}{r - g}$$

... which is the Gordon Growth Model. It states that the value of a stock equals next year's dividend divided by the discount rate minus the growth rate of its dividend. As already noted, it's pretty easy to punch holes in this one and there's no shortage of people who enjoy doing exactly that. That Gordon himself didn't see it as a realistic valuation model is demonstrated by his own words:

> The assumptions that a corporation *will* earn a return on investment of r and retain a fraction of income b in every future period are clearly untenable in building a theory the purpose of which is to deal with an uncertain world. An investor cannot know r and b.[137]

Despite its limitations many analysts still like to use the Gordon Growth Model. I believe that many do so because it's a convenient way to solve an inconvenient problem. One popular use is in calculating what's referred to as the 'terminal value'. Analysts estimate the size of dividends for the next several years, apply a discount rate to bring them back to a present value, and use the Gordon Growth Model to calculate the present value of all the dividends beyond the near-term estimates (the terminal value).

Multistage Dividend Discount models

Companies don't experience singular rates of earnings growth as the Gordon Growth Model asks us to believe. For example, companies might show rapid rates of growth early in their corporate life and slower rates as their business matures.

Multistage Dividend Discount models acknowledge this, allowing the analyst to dial in different rates of earnings growth for different future periods. While this delivers greater flexibility for the analyst to apply their judgement, it still requires those judgements to be based on sound assumptions for the output of their formula to be useful.

Free Cash Flow to the Firm and Free Cash Flow to Equity

Many analysts prefer to use real cash flows as input to their value calculations rather than dividends or reported profits. They feel that cash flows are less open to manipulation, distortion or interpretative influences. These influences have already been discussed at length.

Valuation models based on free cash flow source the information from the Cash Flow Statement, which reports the actual dollars flowing into and out of a business. For this reason they're viewed as a 'purer' representation of the financial performance of the company. I'm not going to go through the methodology here—seek it out if you wish. But it still means plugging figures into discounting formulae. And, yes, I'll say it again, the figures still represent future estimates.

Residual Income Valuation

The Income Statement reports net profit after the cost of debt (interest expense) has been deducted. In this sense it is a report to shareholders, because what they receive is measured after the interest bill has been paid. But presenting information this way can disguise an unsavoury truth: a profit can be reported even when wealth is being destroyed, that is, when the return being delivered to shareholders is less than their required rate of return.

Residual Income Valuation (RIV) acknowledges that businesses are funded by two principal sources of capital—the shareholders' own money (shareholders' equity) and debt. It considers both, not just the debt, as a cost. It charges equity at the shareholders' required rate of return. With this being recognised as an additional cost, if a positive return is still achieved it is referred to as 'residual income'. RIV expresses intrinsic value as the sum of two components:

- the current book value, and

- the present value of future residual income (whether positive or negative).

Some propose that recognising the book value as a distinct component of the calculation ensures valuations aren't way out of the ballpark, that book value acts like a value anchor, keeping an analyst's calculations within sight of economic reality. I disagree with this logic. You can gain an equal level of reassurance by using one of the other formulae and then simply comparing your answer to the actual book value.

Some hail RIV as a breakthrough, but to me the enthusiasm is unfounded. Just like other formulae, it requires a discount rate and estimates of earnings growth. Get them wrong and it spits out some very wrong valuations, which isn't surprising given it shares a common heritage with the other formulae.

For those of you who are mathematically inclined, here's the proof that the Dividend Discount Model and RIV share identical DNA: Starting with the Dividend Discount Model:

$$(V_0) = \frac{D^1}{(1+r)^1} + \frac{D^2}{(1+r)^2} + \cdots\cdots + \frac{D^\infty}{(1+r)^\infty}$$

If we assume, as proponents of these formulae like to do, that book value increases by the amount of retained earnings, then it's a given that:

$$D_t = E_t - (B_t - B_{t-1})$$

where:

- D_t = expected dividend for period t
- E_t = expected EPS for period t
- B_t = expected book value per share for period t.

Moving the symbols around:

$$D_t = E_t + B_{t-1} - B_t$$

Now substitute this dividend equivalent into the Dividend Discount Model:

$$(V_0) = \frac{E_1 + B_0 - B_1}{(1+r)} + \frac{E_2 + B_1 - B_2}{(1+r)^2} + \cdots \frac{E^\infty + B^{\infty-1} - B^\infty}{(1+r)^\infty}$$

The next line of algebra isolates out the anchor (the book value):

$$(V_0) = B_0 \frac{E_1 - rB_0}{(1+r)} + \frac{E_2 - rB_1}{(1+r)^2} + \cdots$$

$$(V_0) = B_0 + \sum_{t=1}^{\infty} + \frac{E_t - r\,B_{t-1}}{(1+r)^t}$$

where:

- B = book value
- E_t = expected EPS for period t
- R = required rate of return or discount rate.

Voila! A pass of the magician's wand and one has become the other. Residual Income Valuation is simply the Dividend Discount Model in different clothes.

BEN GRAHAM'S FORMULA

I mentioned at the start of this chapter that Ben Graham saw no point in using complex mathematical formulae in calculating stock values. In an effort to introduce his own form of simplicity to the process, he outlined an intrinsic value formula in the 1962 edition of *Security Analysis*:

$$V = EPS \times (8.5 + 2g)$$

where:

- V = intrinsic value
- EPS = trailing 12-month earnings per share
- 8.5 = PE for a non-growth company
- g = reasonably expected earnings growth rate.

Graham's formula is saying that a non-growth company should carry a PE of 8.5. For companies demonstrating earnings growth, progressively higher PEs would apply as increasing levels of earnings growth are anticipated.

In 1974 Graham refined the formula to allow for changes in long-term interest rates. It was his acknowledgement that as interest rates change typically so too does the discount rate. His refined formula was:

$$V = \frac{EPS \times (8.5 + 2g) \times 4.4}{Y}$$

where:

- 4.4 = the average yield of high-grade corporate bonds in 1962, when Graham first proposed the model

- Y = the yield on high-grade corporate bonds at the point in time the formula is being used.

Note that Graham did appreciate the limitation of his formula, namely that it relies on assumptions not dissimilar to those of the Gordon Growth Model.

'BUFFETTOLOGY'

In 2001 Warren Buffett's former daughter-in-law, Mary Buffett, released a valuation workbook entitled *The Buffettology Workbook*. Presented as an insight into the way Warren Buffett values stocks, it's nothing more than an algebraic variant of other formulae.

To me the process of coming up with 'new' valuation formulae seems to be a bit like putting brussels sprouts through a food blender and then adding your own form of food colouring. When it's dished out on the plate it might look different, but the inescapable truth is that it's still brussels sprouts.

DEALING WITH UNCERTAINTY — THE MARGIN OF SAFETY

The following is part of an interview from the US Public Broadcasting Service (PBS) that was broadcast on 26 November 2012, involving interviewer Charlie Rose and investor Warren Buffett:

Rose: How is it that you know value so well?

Buffett: I only get into situations where I know the value. There's thousands of companies whose values I don't know. But I know the ones that I know and incidentally you don't pinpoint things. If somebody walks in this door now and they weigh between 300 and 350 pounds I don't need to say they weigh 327 to say they're fat. If they're in that zone I'm fine with it. But I also know there's all kinds of companies that I can't figure out so I do know, I usually know, when I'm dealing with companies that I understand and accounting is a language and it's a language I like.

In this interview Buffett is simply restating concepts delivered in chapter 20 of Graham's *The Intelligent Investor*. His comments are an acknowledgement that intrinsic values cannot be calculated with pinpoint accuracy. With all the knowledge in the world one can only hope to come close to calculating a stock's real worth—realistically some of the time and hopefully most of the time. So how do you deal with this uncertainty? If intrinsic value cannot be calculated accurately, then what value do you assign to it?

The answer lies in being conservative and employing a technique that investors have been using for a long, long time called the 'margin of safety'. As defined earlier it asks that you adjust your value calculation to a lesser value, so allowing for this inaccuracy. This can be achieved either by using conservative inputs to the formula you're using or by reducing the product of your calculation. And it asks that you buy your favoured stock only if the market price is at or below your adjusted value.

Graham's name is so closely linked to the margin of safety concept that it's common to hear people say that he came up with it. But, as I've already noted, both Charles Dow (1901) and Henry Hall (1907) used exactly this term long before Graham wrote *Security Analysis*, and they used it in the same financial context.

But we can push back even further than Dow and Hall, because the concept of applying a margin of safety to stock valuations has actually been around for centuries. In Richard Dale's 2004 book *The First Crash*, a study of the South Sea Bubble, he tells us that in 1720:

> Whatever valuation method was used, the problem for those trying to assess the value of stocks was, of course, the uncertainty relating to the prospective flow of dividends. To take account of this risk or uncertainty, it was customary to deduct, say, three years' purchase from the valuation or (which amounted to the same thing) to adopt an above market discount rate in arriving at a present value.

Here, two centuries before Graham, investors were clearly building a margin of safety into their value calculations.

IT'S NOT THE MATHS THAT DELIVERS THE ANSWERS

So the question remains: if it's not the choice of formula that delivers the edge in investing, what does? The answer is that it's what *goes into* the formula. And this is what we're going to explore in Part V of this book. As Ian Little told us back in 1962, it's the 'extra factors' that determine success in the analytic process.[138]

And to show how important they are, I'll start this fifth and final part with a true story.

....

Chapter summary

- The popular earnings-based stock valuation formulae are all simply variations of the discounted cash flow formula.

- Since intrinsic values cannot be calculated with accuracy, formula values should be adjusted by a margin of safety.

- The most important factor is not the formula used, but the quality of the inputs going into the formula.

Part V
BEATING THE STOCK MARKET

25

THE DURANT-DORT CARRIAGE COMPANY

On a September evening in 1886, 24-year-old William Crapo 'Billy' Durant was walking down the street in Flint, Michigan, and bumped into his friend Johnny Alger outside the local hardware store. Alger noticed that Durant was eyeing off his two-wheeled horse-drawn road cart, so he offered Durant a ride. That suited Durant since he was on foot and was in a hurry to get to a meeting.

Durant was impressed with the ride and construction of the cart, so he inquired where it had been made. That led him to a town called Coldwater and a meeting with the owner of the Coldwater Road Cart Company. The owner was willing to sell his entire operation, and Durant was keen to buy. They shook hands on the deal, and ownership of the company changed hands for the sum of $1500. Durant figured he needed an additional $500 to move the business to Flint and get it set up.

Durant had a keen nose for business and was an excellent salesman. After seven years under Durant's ownership the now-named Flint Road Cart Company was capitalised at $150 000. The 75-fold growth in value was generated principally from retained profits. An analyst valuing the company would have been impressed by its strong cash flow, its dynamic management and its explosive earnings growth. If the Flint Road Cart Company had been listed on the stock exchange it would have carried a very healthy price earnings multiple.

In the 1890s the company expanded its business model to produce a range of more sophisticated and substantial carriages. The business of constructing horse-drawn carriages and buggies was booming, and Flint was home to three large carriage-makers. By the turn of the century the big three were producing a combined annual volume of more than 100 000 horse-drawn vehicles and Durant's recently renamed Durant-Dort Carriage Company was the biggest producer of the three. To an analyst this company had become a gem, a 'blue chip'. It was the market leader in its sector, it had a high return on equity, it had low debt, and it was operating in a well-established and stable business sector. Horses had been domesticated and used as the principal means of land transport for more than 5000 years. Five thousand years! How more stable or certain could the future for this business be? Production of a solid earnings stream potentially stretching into eternity!

In 1901 Durant's right-hand man, Alexander Hardy, tossed in the towel. He'd had enough of the unrelenting, gruelling pressure of work at the Durant-Dort Carriage Company. He resigned and went for an extended trip to Europe with his wife. There he noticed a new form of vehicle appearing on European roads — one that didn't depend upon a horse for its locomotion. Hardy returned to Flint in late 1901 and reported his findings to Durant-Dort's directors. He told them that horseless carriages were the future form of personal transportation, that they should get out of the buggy business altogether. They didn't listen.

In 1917 the Durant-Dort Carriage Company ceased business and closed its doors. Demand for its horse-drawn carriages had well and truly been supplanted by demand for the automobile. So much, then, for our hypothetical analyst's optimistic valuations of the company several years earlier.

But this story does have a bright side. Billy Durant had more foresight than Durant-Dort's directors. At a fairly early stage he branched off on his own into automobile production. He took over the unprofitable Buick Motor Company, turned it around and used it as the platform to form General Motors in 1906. Previously Durant had seen automobiles as a fad, nothing more than an unreliable, noisy novelty. But in a similar fashion to that first ride with his friend Johnny Alger in the two-wheeled horse-drawn road cart nearly two decades earlier, it was Durant's first ride in a Buick that sold him on the idea of buying the company. In September 1904 Flint resident Dr Herbert Hills had taken Durant for a ride in his Buick. Not long after that Durant took control of the Buick Motor Company. His business acumen and ability to sell product worked its magic, and the floundering company became a profit-making enterprise.

So what's the take-home message in this story? There are two.

Firstly, in 1904 the analyst searching for value by reviewing historical financials would have come to the totally wrong conclusion about both businesses. The Durant-Dort Carriage Company was thriving but soon to flounder, while Buick was floundering but soon to thrive. 'Of course', I hear you say. 'It's obvious. It was the pivotal point when the automobile was about to take over from the horse-drawn buggy as the principal means of personal transport.' That's true, but it wasn't obvious at the time. New technology always goes hand in hand with uncertainty. Few would have possessed either the vision or the faith in their judgement to make that call. At the time most people looked on the automobile as a novelty, at best a rich man's toy. Most didn't consider it a threat to the principal source of personal transport—the horse.

The Durant-Dort Carriage Company was, in its heyday, returning an attractively high return on equity (ROE) and a high rate of earnings growth. These two metrics together are like steroids for a company's share price. But remember, it's difficult to know what the future holds for a company. It's one thing to base valuations on historical information, but the most important question is: where is the business heading in the future?

Secondly, when Alexander Hardy returned to Flint in 1901 and advised the directors of the Durant-Dort Carriage Company that the automobile was likely to replace the horse and buggy, they didn't act. But Billy Durant did see the future benefits of horseless transport and bought the ailing Buick Motor Company. This was the same man who'd built the tiny Coldwater Road Cart Company into the largest carriage company in Flint. Repeating his earlier success, Durant turned Buick around and used it as the seed to build the mighty General Motors.

So this story demonstrates both that extrapolation of past company performance is a dangerous thing (particularly when it's under technological threat) and that one of the most important 'extra factors' you need to identify in your search for quality companies is quality management.

Now that might sound like an introduction to the next chapter of this book—a chapter about how to identify sound management—but I've chosen not to explore the issue in detail. The reason is that the principal focus of this book is to challenge investment beliefs and techniques, not to describe those techniques in depth. What's more, some great books on identifying quality management have already been written. A couple that come to mind are *The Warren Buffett CEO*, by Robert P. Miles, and *The Investment Checklist* (specifically chapters 7, 8 and 9), by Michael Shearn.

In reality your assessment of the management of the companies you research is an ongoing task. It relies on continually reading about and viewing their results, achievements, and corporate and personal behaviour. Ask whether they combine high ethical standards with talent and success. Look for a correlation between what they claim to do and what they actually deliver. Their moral compass and talent are important and are largely unrecognised by many analysts.

Chapter summary

- Stock valuation is about future performance, not past performance.

- While analysts rely heavily on historical financial data, doing so isn't without its risks, particularly when technological change threatens the business they're valuing.

- The capability of management is a very important factor to consider when assessing business quality and value.

26
SEARCHING FOR NUMERIC CONSTANTS

It is possible that the previous chapter has dampened your confidence in using past financials as a guide to the future. But it's important to realise that this is just one story, and it was about an industry on the verge of extinction. The fact is, analysts commonly study past financials in their search for inputs to their valuation formulae. They do this because, as 18th-century politician Patrick Henry said, 'I know of no way of judging the future but by the past.'

So, rather than rejecting the use of historical financials, let's ask another question: *when* can they be relied upon? Back in chapter 22, I mentioned Ian Little's study on the link between past and future corporate results, in which he concluded: 'Any unbiased reader of this chapter must come to the conclusion that there is no tendency for previous behaviour to be repeated in the future.'

But does Little's conclusion apply to all types of businesses or just some? For example, are the past results of an established consumer staples company, with entrenched brand loyalty and a dominant position in its sector, more likely to be repeated than those of a tech company that is perpetually threatened by competitors developing better ways of doing the same thing? Let's explore this a bit further.

EXTRAPOLATING EARNINGS GROWTH — THE 1929 BULL MARKET

The year 1929 is etched in the mind of every stock market historian. The October 1929 Crash heralded the start of the worst bear market in US history. As already noted, by July 1932 the Dow was down a staggering 89 per cent from its September 1929 high. The crash triggered the worst depression in American history, sent thousands of banks to the wall, and bankrupted countless investors and businesses.

As with most 'overcooked' markets, it's often asked why more investors didn't realise the 1929 Crash was coming. Problem was, like all bull markets, it wasn't obvious to them at the time. And, contrary to popular belief, not all stocks appeared to be overvalued to investors of the day.

Tables 26.1 and 26.2 show seven popular stocks both at the time of the Crash and in 1962. With the exception of General Electric their PEs weren't at stratospheric levels prior to the 1929 Crash. (Full acknowledgement for the information they include goes to Robert Sobel, who presented them in his book *The Great Bull Market: Wall Street in the 1920s*.[139])

Table 26.1: prices and earnings of selected issues in 1929

Stock	1929 high	1929 earnings	PE multiple
American Can	184½	$8.02	22.97
Eastman Kodak	264¾	$9.57	27.66
General Electric	403	$8.97	44.92
Goodrich	105¾	$4.87	21.71
International Harvester	142	$7.11	19.97
Standard Oil (N.J.)	83	$4.75	17.47
United States Steel	198¾	$21.19	9.38

Table 26.2: prices and earnings of the same companies in 1962

Stock	1962 high	1962 earnings	PE multiple
American Can	47½	$2.81	16.9
Eastman Kodak	55¼	$1.73	31.94
General Electric	78½	$2.97	26.43
Goodrich	72½	$2.87	25.26
International Harvester	31⅝	$2.13	14.85
Standard Oil (N.J.)	76⅝	$4.74	16.17
United States Steel	57½	$3.30	17.42

It's interesting to note the staggering drop in the share prices of these companies from 1929 to 1962. The reason for this is the marked difference between what investors in 1929 expected regarding future earnings growth and what actually happened. Those investors who'd extrapolated the earnings growth rates that industrial stocks were delivering prior to the 1929 Crash would have been disappointed with their 1929 purchases for decades.

So, if extrapolation didn't work here, how does one select an appropriate earnings growth rate? Like the many examples given throughout this book, on every subject from the performance of the economy to the capital appreciation of real estate to share market returns, think 'mean reversion'. In exuberant times, dial down the market's expectations of growth, and in depressed times dial them up. I know it's appealing to search exclusively for companies with the potential to deliver explosive growth, but the chances are you won't find them. Investing is about playing the odds, not buying winning lottery tickets. And the most likely odds are that companies, when considered as a group, will perform more in line with the long-term performance of the economy. You'll deliver more realistic valuations if you think earnings growth in the realm of low single digits.

I've previously described how a couple of great investors have dealt with the growth question. Ben Graham recommended that defensive investors seek companies that have demonstrated earnings growth over the previous 10 years of at least 33 per cent. That's an average geometric rate of just below 3 per cent per year. Graham proposed this for inclusion in a stock screen, but it also provides for the development of realistic assumptions. And, as I mentioned in chapter 22, I was told by a fund manager who worked with Warren Buffett for several years that 'Buffett doesn't pay much for growth'.

Now I know that plenty of people can present real-life examples of companies that have delivered much higher earnings growth rates than I've mentioned here. But no company can do it forever, and of course these spurts of high growth are quoted after the event. To have gambled on them before they were delivered is an entirely different game, a high-stakes game. I'd liken it to spending your time chasing pots of gold at the end of rainbows. While you're off chasing them, you'll miss the more obvious opportunities that present themselves back at home from selecting undervalued companies you've identified using lower growth assumptions. If you approach things this way, any future surprises regarding rates of earnings growth actually delivered will more likely be pleasant ones. Again, we're working the odds in our favour. Edward Sherwood Mead and Julius Grodinsky, in their 1939 book *The Ebb and Flow of Investment Values*, made the powerful point that it's the natural course of events for corporate growth to slow. So paying a high price for a high rate of current growth means you're playing a game where the odds are stacked against you.

EXTRAPOLATING RETURN ON EQUITY

Closely tied to the concept of earnings growth is that of return on equity. Not surprising when you consider that:

Earnings = ROE × book value

Also not surprising when you consider that companies capable of maintaining a high ROE are more likely to demonstrate high rates of earnings growth.

Therefore I'll try not to repeat the discussion we've already had. But since many valuation formulae ask specifically for ROE as an input, I'd like to discuss it specifically. The question we must ask is: for those valuation formulae that demand ROE as an input, are we able to plug in historical figures for this metric?

Three researchers — Patricia Dechow, Amy Hutton and Richard Sloan — conducted a study that covered a large sample of company data from 1976 to 1995. They found that on average companies with initially high ROEs experienced a decay rate of 38 per cent per year in the margin between their ROE and their cost of equity. Assuming their typical company has a cost of equity of 10 per cent and an initial ROE of 40 per cent, this fall would be to less than 29 per cent in the first year and to 21 per cent in the second. This means they found a strong tendency for ROE to move over time towards the cost of equity, which would see the share price fall towards book value.[140]

The 38 per cent decay rate quoted by these researchers is an average, and clearly it varies from company to company. And while an analyst might still choose to extrapolate high historical ROE figures, there must be justification that they will persist. It's useful to reflect on Graham's words regarding this: 'There must be plausible grounds for believing that this average or this trend is a dependable guide to the future.'

Enter the concept of sustainable competitive advantage, or 'moat'. It's why Buffett so dutifully searches moats out. This from his 2007 letter to Berkshire Hathaway shareholders: 'A truly great business must have an enduring "moat" that protects excellent returns on invested capital.'

To assist in the selection of companies more likely to maintain a high ROE, look for factors that bestow an enduring competitive advantage—such as a strong market position, consumer brand loyalty coupled with the ability to maintain a price premium, an ability to maintain lower operating costs than competitors, or advantageous licensing agreements. Without one or more of these advantages the barrier is low for new competitors to enter that business space. It's likely new competitors will continue to be attracted as long as the anticipated ROE exceeds the return they demand. New entrants and the increased price competition they bring will see falling revenues, reduced profit margins and lower ROE for all businesses operating in that sector.

This should not be taken as an argument against investing in companies with high ROEs. On the contrary, these are the very companies that should be sought out. However, it is those characterised by enduring ROE and that can be purchased at either a fair or cheap price that will generate wealth for their shareholders.

Additionally, look for companies operating in a business sector, or sectors, less vulnerable to the march of technology. In the same PBS interview I quoted in chapter 24, Charlie Rose read aloud the following Buffett quote:

> 'The Internet won't change chewing gum. When I look at the Internet I try to figure out how an industry or company can be hurt or changed by it and then I avoid it. Take Wrigleys. I don't think the Internet is going to change the way people chew gum.'

A CASE STUDY: FORGE GROUP

Now to a case study that was unravelling as I was writing this chapter. Forge Group is an Australian mining services company that rode high on the world mining boom fuelled by China's apparently insatiable appetite for iron ore and energy in the early 21st century. Forge's share price rose from a low of 15 cents in 2009 to a high of $7.06 in 2011, and over the following two years it hovered around the $5 to $7 mark. That represented a near 50-fold increase in its share price based on a fivefold increase in earnings.

The reason for the significant re-rating of its share price was that analysts had started to extrapolate the company's rapid change in fortune, and they were doing it in what they felt was a fairly conservative manner. The company was starting to deliver a new and consistently high return on equity of around 30 per cent. Annualised earnings had grown at an average rate of 37 per cent for a four-year period and the balance sheet appeared to be strong—there was a virtual absence of debt. What's more, there appeared to be plenty of new contracts in the pipeline for the company. And on a PE of less than seven times, even the most value-conscious of investors didn't appear to be going overboard on the share price. Certainly, based on historical metrics alone, this stock looked cheap.

Sailing along with its rosy metrics intact, the company requested a trading halt on 4 November 2013. Twenty-four days later the voluntary trading halt was lifted, and when trade recommenced Forge opened 91 per cent lower than its closing price before the halt. What happened?

The company had disclosed a $127 million profit write-down associated with two projects that seemed to be threatening the viability of the company. However, the bad news was closely followed by two positive announcements regarding new favourable future work contracts. Five weeks on and the share price was up 400 per cent from its November low.

But the renewed enthusiasm was short-lived. By February administrators were appointed and soon after the company was suspended from official quotation. Unlike the example of the Durant-Dort Carriage Company, the sector hadn't died, just the company. And what a roller-coaster it was for shareholders over the several months before it did.

To repeat Graham's words, for one to rely on historical metrics, 'There must be plausible grounds for believing that this average or this trend is a dependable guide to the future.'

How you best arrive at plausible grounds for this belief is up to you. For me it starts with companies that possess:

- a solid history of positive earnings
- earnings growth that is consistent rather than erratic

- revenue streams that don't rely on just a few customers
- products that are relatively immune to the economic cycle
- products that are more attractive than those offered by competitors, enabling favourable pricing.

I expect this is why Buffett is so attracted to consumer staple stocks such as Coke and Gillette—they tick every one of these five boxes. It's probably also why research undertaken by Wharton professor Jeremy Siegel demonstrates that the best returns have been delivered by companies possessing strong brand names, particularly in the consumer staples and pharmaceutical industries.[141]

In your search for numerical constants look for stable, class-leading companies in stable industries. Look for relative rather than absolute constants. Mean revert. Think long term, not short. And don't be influenced by current opinion or sentiment in your determination of what those constants should be.

Chapter summary

- Chosen rates of earnings growth should be conservative, in the low to middle single digits.
- Ben Graham recommended that defensive investors should seek companies that have demonstrated earnings growth over the previous 10 years of at least 33 per cent.
- Warren Buffett pays little for growth.
- A study found that on average companies with initially high ROE experienced a decay rate of 38 per cent per year in the margin between their ROE and their cost of equity.
- There must be plausible grounds to expect past results to be a reasonable guide to the future.
- You should seek companies that have a sustainable competitive advantage and that are less prone to falling victim to the march of technology.
- Use long-term averages rather than short-term trends.

27

THE HUMAN CONSTANT

We're searching for those extra factors that will help us plug the best numbers we can into our valuation formulae. We've found that 'absolute constants' don't exist, so let's continue looking for 'relative constants' as part of our search for an investing edge.

Ironically, the closest thing I've found to a constant in financial markets is also the one that causes the most volatility and inconsistency — human behaviour. It doesn't matter which decade or century you look at; the fact is that market participants react in a similar fashion given similar circumstances. I came to this conclusion years ago after an interminable amount of time spent reading books on economic and financial history.

It seems I'm not the only person to have come to this conclusion. The following is from the introduction of the 1954 edition of *The Intelligent Investor*, where Graham describes the 'rules' he'd been exposed to during his then 40-year Wall Street career: 'The rules that have failed relate mainly to types of securities; the ones that survive apply mainly to human nature and human conduct.'[142]

Let's consider how human nature and human conduct have been shaped.

IT'S ALL ABOUT HOW YOU THINK, STUPID!

The first time I went to New York was with my family. We visited the American Museum of Natural History. Fascinating. It has an exhibit called the Heilbrunn Cosmic Pathway, a 360-foot walkway spiralling downwards through a display that maps out 13 billion years of cosmic history. The Big Bang is at the top of the ramp, the present day at the bottom. As I was slowly winding my way down the exhibit, I could hear my family complaining from below, demanding I hurry up. Okay, so I was stopping to read every word the exhibit offered, but this stuff was interesting. And at the rate of 36 million years per foot of walkway, why the hurry?

I couldn't help but be overwhelmed by the proportions of the ramp. It hit me that I was being shown a very important fact: in evolutionary terms humans haven't been around very long. While the exhibit presented the universe as a time trail 360 feet long, the entire history of mankind was represented by the width of a single human hair at the very end. *Homo sapiens* is but a blink in the life of the cosmos.

Only for the last 50 000 years has Earth been home to a creature that, if dressed in a pinstriped suit, would resemble a modern-day stockbroker. Of that 50 000 years, stock markets have been around for only about 400. That's less than 1 per cent of human existence — definitely not long enough for Darwinian forces to sculpt our primitive brains into useful stock-trading accessories. Besides, why should the stock market influence the way we process information anyway? It's a poor evolutionary sieve. Successful investors have bigger bank accounts, but that doesn't mean they have bigger families!

The fact is, evolutionary forces aren't found on any stock exchange. Our brains were shaped in primeval swamps and savanna grasslands aeons ago. Our instincts were honed in an environment of physical risk, not financial risk.

The fight-or-flight response might have saved our ancestors from becoming a sabre-toothed tiger's dinner, but it's an impediment when it comes to investing. When financial markets collapse, panic initiates selling, which is pretty much the worst thing an investor can get involved in at the time. But this innate human response delivers an advantage to those investors and traders who can resist it. Jesse Livermore realised he could profit from this human frailty, as this popular quote of his shows:

> There is nothing new on Wall Street or in stock speculation. What has happened in the past will happen again and again and again. This is because human nature does not change, and it is human emotion that always gets in the way of human intelligence.

More than two centuries earlier, during the South Sea Bubble, the London attorney of a Dutch investor made the following observation of the activity on Exchange Alley: 'I had a fancy to go and look at the throngs...and this is how it struck me yesterday; it is like nothing so much as if all the lunatics had escaped out of the madhouse at once.'[143] The trick is to avoid becoming one of the lunatics who has escaped from the madhouse, which is easier said than done. A brief diversion from the financial markets will show what I mean.

Consider the true story of William Buckley, an English convict who was shipped out to Australia as part of the first European settlement in Victoria. The settlement was established in 1803 when around 400 settlers from England sailed into Port Phillip Bay aboard two ships, HMS *Calcutta*, a 52-gun man-of-war, and the *Ocean*, a transport ship. Buckley, then aged 23, was one of the 299 convicts in the party.

Dissatisfied with settlement life, Buckley escaped into the Australian bush. When he later saw the ships pull up anchor (they were sailing to Tasmania to establish a settlement in Hobart), he knew he was now the sole European left on the shores of Port Phillip Bay. He started living with the Aboriginal people, principally with the Barrabool, a small group of the Wathaurong tribe, around the Barwon River district. Buckley had no contact with Europeans from then until 1835, 32 years later, when he was 'discovered' by a European survey party. He was then reintegrated back into Australian/European society, where he remained until his death in 1856.*

A biography of Buckley, by John Morgan, was published in 1852. What's extraordinary about Buckley's story is that when he was found in 1835, after 32 years of cohabitation with the Aboriginal people, he had totally

---

*Buckley's incredible story of survival has given rise to the Australian phrase 'you've got Buckley's or none', meaning that what you are about to attempt to do has little chance of succeeding.

adopted their culture. He thought, behaved and spoke as they did. He even had to relearn English, despite having spent his first 23 years as an Englishman. That a mind can totally adapt to changes in its surroundings, that it can totally reconstruct its values and beliefs, was no less a surprise to Buckley himself. The following are his words:

> The reader may wonder, how it was possible for anyone like myself who had, in my earlier life, been associated with civilized beings, so to live; but I beg him to remember how many years I had led a different sort of existence, and how easy it is for the human being, as well as every other, to change his habits, taste, and may I add, feelings, when made the mere creator of circumstances. I look back now to that period of my life with inexpressible astonishment, considering it, as it were, altogether a dreaming delusion, and not reality. Perhaps there is no one living who can cast his mind back to so many years of his past life with such a multiplicity of extraordinary sensations, as have fallen to my lot to experience.[144]

His mind had been totally 'reprogrammed' to suit his new set of circumstances.

Buckley's story delivers a powerful message to investors. If we accept our susceptibility to groupthink, if we are able to admit that our vulnerability is so pervasive that we will likely fall prey to it without even being aware of it happening, then we can begin to understand that those who can maintain an independence of mind will have the greatest chance of investment success. You should always be seeking correctness, not consensus.

The Greek philosopher Socrates (470–399 BC) defined the framework for what is now termed the Socratic method. The Socratic method tells us that the correctness of a statement can be determined, not according to whether it is held by the majority, but according to whether it is incapable of being rationally contradicted. By the use of the Socratic method you need not second-guess whether the majority is correct or not. Simply ignore the crowd and determine for yourself what is the correct (or as near as possible to correct) answer. There is no doubt that Graham's approach to investing was aligned with the Socratic method. He clearly articulated this in *The Intelligent Investor*: 'You are neither right nor wrong because the crowd disagrees with you. You are right because your data and reasoning are right.'

How then must you think when assessing stocks? Answer: Like a businessperson who's looking for a great business but wants to pay as little as possible for it. Close your ears to the opinions and bids being made by all other parties involved.

How must you *not* think? Answer: Like nearly all other people.

Chapter summary

- One of the few consistencies in financial markets is how people behave when faced with similar sets of circumstances.

- Humans behave inappropriately when interacting with the financial markets because their instincts were shaped in an environment of physical risk, not financial risk.

- The fight-or-flight response causes many to sell at a time of stock market panic, the worst time to do so.

- Human beings are influenced strongly and unconsciously by groupthink.

- Investors who can think independently are at an advantage.

- You should always be seeking correctness, not consensus.

28

COIN-FLIPPING ORANG-UTANS (MY FIRST TRIPS TO OMAHA)

We're now approaching the end of the book. So what's the answer? The conclusion? The 'magic formula'? Surely someone must have worked it out after more than 400 years of stock market activity. The good news is that there appears to be a group of investors who have. Let me explain.

I have a friend who's an orthodontist. And no, Geoff isn't one of the investors I'm about to talk about, but he did tell me something 25 years ago that's relevant to the discussion. Orthodontists, as most people realise, are in the business of straightening crooked teeth. Both before and at the completion of treatment orthodontists take impressions and construct plaster models of the patient's teeth. These show the position of the teeth before and after treatment, demonstrating the success of the treatment. My friend told me that if an orthodontist wants to display their skill all they need do is put their 'plaster on the table'. So let me devote this final chapter to an investor who's certainly done this.

Now I'm conscious of how much I've already thrown the 'B' word around. But there is something you just can't deny: Warren Buffett is simply *the most successful investor we've ever seen*. And for that reason alone he needs to be included in any discussion on investment techniques and success. So let's start by taking a quick look at Buffett's investing record.

His best returns came during his early partnership years. In the 13 years between 1956 and 1969 his investment returns compounded at an average rate of 29.5 per cent per year. Over the same period the Dow compounded at 3.5 per cent. That meant Buffett multiplied the money of his long-term partners nearly 30 times while investors in the Dow increased theirs 1.5 times. His subsequent returns while at the helm of Berkshire Hathaway are easily established—they're laid out in the front of the Annual Report, where Berkshire's growth in book value and share price are both compared with the returns achieved from investing in the broad US index, the S&P 500. Since Berkshire doesn't pay a dividend, an accumulation of the S&P 500 is used for comparison (all dividends are added back into the return calculation). Berkshire's results under Buffett's stewardship up to 2014 are shown in table 28.1.

Table 28.1: Buffett vs the S&P Accumulation (1965–2014)

	Berkshire Hathaway	S&P 500 Accumulation
Compounded annual gain	21.6%	9.9%
Percentage gain overall	1 826 163%	11 196%

Expressed another way, $100 invested in the S&P 500 at the start of 1965 would have grown to $11 296 by the end of 2014 if all dividends had been reinvested. A $100 investment in Berkshire Hathaway would have grown to $1 826 263.

Want to call Buffett lucky? Go right ahead. There's the slimmest of chances you're right. But it's difficult to mount the case that he's had a 59-year lucky streak. And for those statisticians who've been calculating the odds, Buffett's 'luck' has progressively moved from a three to a four to a five sigma event. Five sigma is a statistical term derived from the normal distribution (bell) curve; it describes an extremely rare chance event. If luck explains his success, then he's moving so far down the tail of the bell curve that you now need a pair of binoculars to spot him. So let's address the luck issue before we move on.

HAS BUFFETT BEATEN THE MARKET THROUGH LUCK OR SKILL?

Financial journalist Carol Loomis has been a close friend of Buffett's for decades; they first met in 1967. At the time he was still a relatively unknown hedge fund manager in his thirties. Carol's husband, John

Loomis, had already met Buffett. John reported to his wife after that first meeting 'I think I've just met the smartest investor in the country.' From there Buffett went on to become the wealthiest man in the world. It would seem one mighty big coincidence for the two events not to have been associated—the early recognition of the skill and the subsequent outcome.

At Columbia University in 1984, in what is considered a classic Buffett speech, he answered the 'he's just been lucky' sceptics. Buffett's speech formed part of the commemoration of the 50th anniversary of the publishing of Graham and Dodd's *Security Analysis*. In delivering his speech, Buffett proposed a hypothetical national coin-flipping contest where 225 million Americans each waged a dollar in a one-on-one, instant-death contest. A successful flip on any day meant you progressed to the next day. Buffett stated that after 20 days of competition there would be 215 contestants remaining, each with a little over $1 million in accumulated earnings. At the end of the contest the last remaining contestant would hold the total $225 million. He added that a business school professor would argue the same result could be achieved if 225 million orang-utans engaged in the same exercise, so insinuating that Buffett's results could be put down to chance.

Up to that point Buffett's argument seemed to deny his skill, but he then presented a powerful reason why chance was unlikely to explain his success. He stated that he wasn't alone in his success, that there were plenty of other successful investors in the US, and if chance explained their success then their distribution would be random. That is, there would be no common link between them. But Buffett demonstrated a link: it was an intellectual one. He showed that a disproportionate number of successful investors came from a hypothetical village called 'Graham and Doddsville'. They were a group of investors unified by the fact they all practised Ben Graham's principles of value investing. It sunk the luck argument.

Let's explore further what these guys get up to, and in doing so include Buffett's long-time friend and business associate, Charlie Munger. Buffett and Munger first met in 1959 at a lunch organised by a mutual friend, Edwin Davis, at the exclusive Omaha Club. They quickly became friends. In 1965 Munger ceased practising law to start running his own investment partnership. Buffett and Munger consulted on a number of deals through the years, with the relationship developing into an informal partnership. Munger's place at Berkshire was cemented in 1978 when he became Vice-Chairman.

If you're a Munger follower you'll appreciate how logical his thought processes are. He suspects, questions and tests everything, and if an idea doesn't stand up to scrutiny then it's rejected. He's a voracious reader of science, mathematics, physics, history and biography. Fiction is off the reading list. He's a man who doesn't suffer fools. And for the last five decades this intelligent man of fact and logic has been there to pass judgement on Buffett's actions. No-one has been better qualified or better placed to do so. So I'm satisfied with Munger's conclusion that Buffett is an investor with few peers. Munger's ability to make that call is superior to anyone else's. And if you have a problem with this judgement, then don't call me, call Charlie. And good luck in arguing your case.

There's been no shortage of Buffett imitators. They usually start by reading a Buffett biography or two. Then they progress to watching Buffett interviews or reading books written by people claiming to have the inside running on how he values companies. They commit to memory a few pithy Buffett one-liners to guide them along their investment journey. They might even pin a 'Buffett Investing Rules Checklist' on the wall, a list of basic principles on how to identify market-beating stocks — ones possessing an economic moat, run by competent management and operating in business segments the investor understands.

It sounds easy, but never underestimate the effort, commitment and skill Buffett brings to the process. The full significance of this hit me when I went to Omaha to check things out for myself.

I attended my first Berkshire AGM in 2012. By then it had become a very big affair, attracting close to 35 000 people, but it hadn't always been that way. In his 1994 biography of Buffett, Andrew Kilpatrick writes, 'about 2,700 happy Berkshire pilgrims now journey to the event'.[145] Kilpatrick seemed impressed by how big the number had become by the early nineties.

During Buffett's early association with Berkshire, the annual meetings were a very tame affair. Back in 1962, when he first started acquiring Berkshire stock, Berkshire wasn't the massive conglomerate it is today. It was an ailing textile business based in New Bedford, Massachusetts. At that time the Berkshire meetings typically numbered about a dozen people.

As Buffett's influence on the company grew, he moved the meetings from New Bedford to a fourth-floor cafeteria at Berkshire's National Indemnity office in Omaha. And from there they progressively shifted to several Omaha sites. As the numbers grew, larger venues needed to be found. Today the AGM is held at Omaha's largest entertainment stadium, the 1.1 million square feet CenturyLink Center. But even that now fails to fit the bill. The facility seats nearly 19 000 people but 2015 saw a record attendance of over 40 000. That meant more than half the attendees (who had jetted in from 53 countries around the globe) were ushered into overflow rooms at CenturyLink's adjacent convention area and the Omaha Hilton across the street.

My first Berkshire meeting was a lot of fun. I did the usual things most attendees do. I flew into Omaha the day before. I attended the Saturday meeting and listened to Buffett and Munger philosophise about life and investing for several hours. I purchased the usual paraphernalia—T-shirts, See's candy and investment books. I bought my daughter some jewellery at Borsheim's on the Sunday after the meeting. Then I flew out on Monday morning. A great experience. But I didn't learn much.

One thing I knew for sure. I was definitely coming back in 2013, but this time I wanted to learn more. I'd heard about a course held at the University of Nebraska Omaha (UNO) during the week before the AGM. So I got googling. And there it was: the 'Genius of Buffett' course, organised, chaired and part presented by Buffett author Bob Miles. My credit card was out and I soon had my place. As an added bonus there was a two-day value investing conference immediately following Bob's three-day course, so I enrolled for that as well.

It's a long way from Melbourne, Australia, to Omaha, Nebraska. But when I landed at Eppley Airfield on that hot April afternoon in 2013, I had no time to feel tired. It was 5.45 pm local time and I was due to meet my fellow 'Genius of Buffett' attendees at the 'Dean's dinner' in 45 minutes' time. Finding a cab was easy, and 20 minutes later I was sliding my suitcase inside the door of my hotel room. I wandered down to reception to find out how to get to the Ponzu Sushi and Grill, where the dinner was being held. Since it was close to the hotel, I decided to walk. As I weaved my way through the Omaha backstreets, a couple chatting on their front porch broke their conversation to deliver me a welcoming wave. It made me feel good about Omaha.

Twenty minutes later I arrived perspiring and breathless at the restaurant. The surrounding district was a hive of construction activity. As I found out later, the area was called Aksarben Village, named after the Aksarben Racetrack, which, until eight years earlier, had stood on the site.*

Bob Miles welcomed me and introduced me to Dean Louis Pol, head of UNO's College of Business Administration. After a great dinner the dean and his wife, Janet, were kind enough to drive me back to my hotel in their convertible Mini. On the way they took me on a guided tour of UNO. Great hospitality again. Yep, this was shaping up to be a good week.

Bob Miles' course started in earnest the next morning. It was held at Mammel Hall, the College's new home. Appropriately the construction of this impressive complex was made possible by two generous donations of Berkshire-derived money — from the Bill and Ruth Scott Family Foundation and Carl and Joyce Mammel, all long-time Berkshire shareholders.

Bob had assembled a formidable group of presenters for his three-day course. All were people who were intimately connected with Buffett on a personal, business or family level. Here was a group of people who each had their own unique insight into what makes Buffett tick. Sure you get an idea from reading books, but the impact of that message is not the same as being face to face with people who really understand him.

What struck me listening to two of the early presentations (delivered by two of Berkshire's key management team) is how capable these guys were. Each was responsible for running one of Berkshire's 80-odd wholly owned companies. They weren't your typical highly paid corporate mercenaries there for a big salary or some lucrative options scheme. Each was passionate, knowledgeable, dedicated and experienced in their line of business. One of the two, Bob Batt, was the grandson of Rose Blumkin (known as 'Mrs B'), the founder of Nebraska Furniture Mart. This was no ordinary furniture store; it was the largest home furnishing store in North America. And Bob had been working there for the greater part of his life. The other presenter had been associated with Berkshire-owned insurance businesses for a period approaching three decades.

---

*Aksarben is Nebraska spelt backwards.

The reality was finally hitting home. Everything I'd read was true. *Buffett really does have extremely capable people heading Berkshire companies* — people he can trust, people he can leave to run the businesses as well as he could (no, *better* than he could). That's quite simply why he can and does leave his managers alone. The message is there: when selecting companies to invest in, quality management is essential.

So what is Buffett's role at Berkshire? He has several, the most important being to take the copious stream of cash these companies deliver and reinvest it. He's a skilled capital allocator. But in order to do his job well he also has to understand the businesses he buys into, and it's clear he does. The message I kept hearing from these CEOs about Buffett was, 'He's sharp. He understands how this business operates. The figures, the operations, the dynamics. Anytime I have a discussion with him on how things are going, he's on top of it.'

I'd read all this stuff in books, but sitting there hearing it direct from these guys brought it all sharply into focus. There was a level of mutual respect between Buffett and his managers I'd just never seen before.

And on that point, allow me a short diversion.

Have you read Walter Isaacson's biography of Steve Jobs? It leaves you in no doubt that Jobs was a powerful driving force behind innovation at Apple. It's an important consideration for any company trying to stay ahead of the curve in a dynamic and ever-changing business sector. At the time of writing Apple is easily the biggest company in the US but one cannot ignore a nagging nervousness that Jobs' premature death, in October 2011, may have impacted Apple's future, that without his creative direction maybe a competitor could do to Apple what Apple did to HP and Nokia.

The same could have been said about the Walt Disney Company when Walt died back in 1966. The company is still operating successfully today, but its continuing success has been mixed. Interestingly its fortunes were delivered a boost in the 1990s by its association with Pixar, a dynamic young computer animation company born from the computer division of George Lucas's film studio. Pixar's first film, *Toy Story*, was a box office success. And who was its new owner and CEO? None other than Steve Jobs.

So what's the take-home message? Capable leadership is always important, but where competition is fierce it's essential — so much so that its absence can potentially jeopardise a business's existence.

Let's get back to Omaha.

On day one of Bob Miles' course, Steve Jordon of the *Omaha World-Herald* was presenting. He flashed a childhood image of Buffett on the screen. It's the same photo that's reproduced on page two of Jordon's book. The image was taken on Christmas Day 1937, when Warren was just seven years old. It shows him standing on the footpath outside his home with his sisters Doris and Bertie, who are each clutching dolls. Warren is holding his favourite possession—a new nickel-plated coin-changer. He used the changer for storing and dispensing coins while making Coca-Cola and chewing gum sales. It demonstrates that by the age of seven Warren had already developed a fascination for business and money.

To me there's something significant about Buffett being seven in that photograph. It relates to the popular quote, 'Give me a child until he is seven and I will give you the man'. It's also interesting to relate it to the 1964 documentary *7 Up*, produced by Granada Television. It features 14 seven-year-old children, whose lives, expectations and ambitions are explored and documented. Since the first documentary was made, the lives of the same individuals have been tracked in successive documentaries produced every seven years. In 2012 the eighth was produced when they were 56 years old. The fascinating point this longitudinal study shows is that a person's characteristic traits, their innate skills and career expectations, are often firmly entrenched by the age of seven.

Buffett's lifetime passion for business, numbers and money is innate—clearly observable at a young age. What signals were you sending out at age seven? What were your hopes, expectations and passions? If you don't remember, ask those who might. It could provide some valuable insights into your own strengths and skills.

On now to the third and final day of Bob Miles' course. The two distinguished guest presenters that day were a person who'd worked with Buffett as his special assistant for several years, and a Buffett family member. Each had their unique insight into Buffett's life, and what they said that day finally delivered to me the essence of what the Buffett books never had—*why* he was so successful. After hearing what they had to say I knew it had nothing to do with luck.

Buffett's former special assistant presented first, and I knew what he was about to say would be both insightful and interesting. When he started working for Buffett there were only about 20 employees at the

Kiewit Plaza headquarters, most of whom were tax and administrative personnel. Since our presenter had worked on the investment side he had the opportunity to gain an intimate insight into how Buffett operates. I'd read that Buffett's time was principally spent reading and talking on the phone, but I'd always suspected the stories might have been exaggerated. Certainly that couldn't be all he did? If so, then this guy would know.

He described his time at Kiewit Plaza as a role with 'little direction'. He was given a desk to sit at but not told what to do. Occasionally he'd interact with Buffett, but there were long stretches when he didn't. Others in the office had better-defined work descriptions. For example, Buffett had a designated trader responsible for executing huge block trades at the best possible prices, and the rest of the staff were largely involved in administrative and accounting functions. So Buffett's new special assistant had to create his own fun.

I saw this presentation as an opportunity to gain insight into how Buffett derived a company's intrinsic value. I wanted to know how much time and effort Buffett put into performing a valuation. In particular, how did he come up with the all-important earnings projections? I felt this was the key — the ability to come up with future earnings estimates that were closer to the mark than the also-rans.

In my mind I prepared a question to ask at the end of the presentation. It seemed to me that Buffett favoured companies characterised by reliable earnings streams, consumer staples such as Coke and Gillette. Their relative insulation from the economic cycle meant less variation in projected earnings, and their economic moat meant they carried better levels of predictability. While none of this spelt out prediction or projection with a capital 'P', it certainly seemed better than taking a stab in the dark.

Indeed Ben Graham had indicated that some businesses were better suited to valuation than others. This from my 1954 edition of *The Intelligent Investor*: 'Valuation technique may be quite effective if applied, not indiscriminately, but at the right times and in the right places.'

I wanted to ask if this is why Buffett commonly chooses consumer staples as a preferred investment, and my opportunity came at the end of the 60-minute presentation. 'Any questions?' our presenter asked. Several hands shot up, and eventually he spotted mine. I asked, 'Does Buffett select the companies he reviews on the basis of the suitability of their financials to be plugged into valuation formulae?'

He just stared at me blankly. For several seconds you could have heard a pin drop. Eventually he responded, 'I don't understand your question.' I attempted to repeat it using different words, but it was all a waste of time. Eventually he chose to move on without providing an answer.

His inability to respond to my question was the answer itself. The reason for his blank stare had nothing to do with my Australian accent or my inability to express myself—he'd heard the question loud and clear. The simple truth was that he saw my question as placing far too much emphasis on the valuation calculation, as if it were the key to the whole process. It isn't. There's a lot more to the valuation process than the application of a formula. That bit happens right at the end of the process and takes up but a fraction of the time.

It reinforced that all the books I'd read on stock valuation were nothing more than red herrings. None of them held the key to success. They were overrated and excessively complex. Deep down I sort of knew it already—Graham had told us. But I'd always left the door of doubt slightly ajar. Maybe someone out there did have a better formula, and maybe that someone was Buffett. But now the insight I'd gained had slammed that door firmly shut, and in my mind I knew it would remain closed forever.

So let's shout it from the rooftops: 'IT'S NOT ALL ABOUT THE FORMULA!'

Fortunately our presenter reminded us, in just one sentence, what it *is* about. And here it is: It's about becoming a student of business models.

That's it. That's what Buffett's been doing for the past 60-plus years. He's been sitting, reading, studying and understanding businesses. And it makes perfect sense. What else are we buying when we buy shares but businesses?

People have always been interested in how Buffett spends his days. It's as if they could emulate his success if they spent their time doing the same thing. He was once asked by a shareholder at a Berkshire AGM what he typically does in a day. He replied that he mostly reads and talks on the phone, and added, 'That's what I do. Charlie, what do you do?' Here's how Charlie answered:

> That [question] reminds me very much of a friend of mine in World War II in a group that had nothing to do. A general once went up to my

friend's boss, we'll call him Captain Glotz. He said, 'Captain Glotz, what do you do?' His boss said, 'Not a damn thing.'

The general got madder and madder and turned to my friend and said, 'What do you do?'

My friend said, 'I help Captain Glotz.'

That's the best way to describe what I do at Berkshire.

The final special guest presentation was delivered on the afternoon of day three by a family member. We were told some amusing stories about early family life in the Buffett household, but the most powerful message delivered was of Warren Buffett's intense focus on investing. He was physically around his family but he was often disengaged, relying very much on Susie, his first wife, to attend to the family's emotional and physical needs. Following dinner Buffett would typically go upstairs to work, but he did make himself available to his family when called upon.[*]

Let's sum up with more from the 2012 PBS radio interview, which involved Charlie Rose, Warren Buffett and Carol Loomis:

Rose: Why has he had the record that he does? And you have said in a conversation with me he understands how to look at accounting statements and find the telling point. And it may be in a footnote.

Loomis: That's true.

Rose: So that he'll see opportunity and see the future.

Loomis: He will. He has an ability to do that that I think is matched by very few other investors. And he has this broad, extensive knowledge of business, and I think maybe I said this to you—so when something new comes up he has a frame of reference in which to place it. And then he adds this rationality that I really think just a handful of investors [have]. He doesn't let emotion take over when he's considering whether to buy. He goes at the decision in a very rational way and then the price goes down and he buys more whereas most people panic and sell when the price goes down.

So let's pose one final question that the discussion above begs: 'If people don't have the capacity or the time to invest as Buffett does, is there still a way to invest successfully?'

---

[*]Buffett did read to his children, help them with homework and joined them in playing with the family train set.

I'm pleased to report that the answer appears to be 'yes'. Plenty of other people have been successful in the endeavour, and after reading this book I hope you're one step closer to getting there yourself.

So in these final two paragraphs I'd like to summarise the essential ingredients to investing success.

Firstly, it's important that you question everything that you read and hear, because so much that's written and stated in the world of finance defies common reason. You will hear from many people who assign skill to outcomes that more likely happened simply by chance. You will also hear from people who confidently deliver statements that they have no way of knowing are correct. So don't accept what anyone says until it's passed cleanly through your own sieve of logic.

And, finally, I'd like to remind you of one of Warren Buffett's essential beliefs—that there are basically two skills stock investors require. One is to be able to value businesses. Many investors seem to forget they're acquiring parts of businesses when they buy stocks, but it's essential to understand how those businesses operate and what they are worth. Without this skill you run the risk of buying or selling at crazy prices. And the other is that it's essential to understand *how markets move*. Understanding how they can move is more important than understanding what's causing them to move (in fact it's rarely clear what is moving them). With an appreciation of how markets can move, the rational investor can stand confident while human emotion is throwing stock prices around. Gaining an understanding of how markets move means becoming a student of financial history. In reading about the follies of the past, you'll gain an edge over those who haven't because (hopefully) you'll be less likely to make the mistakes that others will be making.

Happy (and profitable) investing!

APPENDIX A:
WHY BOOK VALUE DIFFERS FROM ECONOMIC VALUE

Here are some of the reasons why book value differs from economic value:

- Plant and equipment are recorded at their purchase price less an allowance for depreciation. Inflation and technological advances often render this a poor measure of current market value. Book value typically understates the new replacement cost of plant and equipment for a going concern and overstates the sale price in the event of liquidation.

- Assets are depreciated at rates set by accounting standards. These rates often differ from economic reality.

- Real estate, when carried at historical cost, can fall well short of its market value over time. The significant write-downs undertaken by real estate investment trusts (REITs) in the wake of the subprime crisis and the GFC illustrate the potential for significant overvaluations to occur as well.

- The value of intangible assets, such as goodwill, are often misrepresented in the accounts. Goodwill can be internally generated through years of good customer service and product reliability (in the case of industrial companies that produce consumer and commercial products). That same goodwill can be acquired when one company buys another. Accounting standards require that goodwill is treated differently under each circumstance. Internally generated goodwill is not recorded in the accounts, while purchased goodwill is recorded as an asset by the acquirer. What's recorded is the amount by which the acquisition price exceeds the book value of the acquired company. Consider Coca-Cola (US), which possesses one of the most valuable brand names in the world. Accounting standards require that Coca-Cola doesn't recognise this internally generated goodwill in its books. But if Coca-Cola was acquired, the acquirer would record the goodwill as an asset, which in this case could well be in the order of $100 billion. It is exactly the same asset, but a different value is given to it depending on who owns it.

- For many companies, particularly those in service industries, human capital—the quality, skill and knowledge of the workforce (including management)—is of significant value. This is not reflected on the balance sheet.

APPENDIX B: DEBT ANALYSIS

When you invest in a company there are two important things you're looking for. Firstly, you don't want the company to go broke; secondly, you want it to deliver a good return. Both of these outcomes are influenced by how much debt a company carries on its balance sheet. So let's pose the question: how can you tell when a company has too much debt?

Debt can boost returns

Companies typically fund their operations by a mix of debt and equity. It's a bit like home ownership. If you own a house with a mortgage then the bank is funding part of the house (debt) and you are funding the rest (equity).

But that's where the analogy ends, because, unlike a mortgage, business debt isn't always a bad thing. Used prudently it can boost a company's return on equity (ROE), the return shareholders receive on their part of the funding equation. This is delivered when the return achieved on the debt capital is higher than the cost of the debt (the interest rate paid).

But it's important that management gets the debt/equity mix right, because too much debt can place a company in jeopardy when business conditions go sour. This is because, unlike shareholders, lenders demand to be paid in bad times as well as good.

Let's take a look at a commonly used metric used to measure the debt/ equity mix.

The debt to equity ratio

The debt to equity ratio quantifies the relative proportion of debt and equity used to fund a company's operations.

$$\text{Debt/equity ratio} = \frac{\text{Financial debt}}{\text{Equity}}$$

Another way to express this relationship is the percentage of total assets that is funded by debt. For example, if the debt to equity ratio is one, then it would be expressed (using the formula below) as debt representing 50 per cent of total capital.

$$\text{Gearing} = \frac{\text{Debt}}{\text{Debt} + \text{equity}} \times 100$$

Don't forget leases

Many leases are just a form of quasi-debt. This is particularly so with finance leases where the lessee enjoys the benefits and assumes all the risk of the property, plant or equipment. So when calculating gearing ratios it's appropriate to include them as debt.

Some analysts also like to include some off balance sheet liabilities in the calculation. Examples include operating leases and unpaid pensions, particularly when they are substantial in size.

Analysing the debt to equity ratio

What constitutes an acceptable level of debt varies from company to company, and its determination is a mix of analysis and judgement. Let's take a look at some important factors to consider.

1. Volatile revenue streams

Lenders demand that interest and principal payments are made on time and in full. But when a firm has a volatile revenue stream its ability to meet these regular payments is less certain. The problem is compounded when a business is burdened with high fixed costs—the costs of simply keeping the doors open even if it's not doing any business. So look out for red flags, such as where a company's debt materially exceeds that of its industry peers.

2. Concentration risk

When a large portion of the company's business is limited to a few customers, then it's prudent for it to carry less debt. Loss of an important customer will impact its revenue stream and jeopardise its capacity to service debt.

3. Start-ups and young companies

New companies with a limited track record should carry less debt. Their business models have yet to be fully tested and the reliability of their future revenue stream is often difficult to judge.

4. Debt structure (debt maturity)

The mix of long- and short-term debt employed by a company is important. Long-term assets are best funded out of equity and long-term borrowings, while working capital needs are best funded by bank overdraft and short-term borrowings.

Watch out for companies that rely heavily on the use of short-term debt, particularly those with a poor credit rating. These companies are faced with an ever-present need to keep rolling the debt over, and failure to do so could lead to failure of the business.

Maturities of borrowings should also be well spread. If the bulk of a company's borrowings fall due at a time when the availability of funds is limited (such as the recent post-GFC period), refinancing may prove difficult. With a chronological spread of maturities, the need to approach the capital markets for a large refinancing in a depressed period is reduced.

5. Debt structure (currency of debt)

Check for the currency of the debt. A company with overseas assets and/or revenue will often reduce its currency exposure by maintaining a similar level of debt in that currency. If this isn't the case, offshore borrowing is still okay if it's largely hedged/swapped back to its domestic currency. If neither is the case, then the company will likely be exposed to the risk of currency fluctuations.

6. Look out for loan covenants

A loan covenant is a clause in the lending contract requiring the borrower to refrain from doing certain things. For example, the borrower might have to maintain the ratio of total liabilities (borrowings and other liabilities) to total tangible assets at a certain percentage, say no higher than 60 per cent. It's very important that companies maintain such ratios. Even if a company is servicing its debt, the breach of such a covenant may lead to a 'technical breach' of the contract and potential recovery action by the lender.

So look out for loan covenants, study how onerous they are, and assess the likelihood of the company breaching them.

7. The level of secured borrowings in a company's balance sheet

Check the level of security that lenders are demanding. Where risks are high, lenders tend to demand more security. This provides an indication of the risk they have attached to that company.

8. Augment your analysis with other financial ratios

The debt to equity ratio should not be relied upon to the exclusion of other metrics. There are many others that can be used to judge the appropriateness of a company's debt. One that's commonly used is the interest coverage ratio, which shows how comfortably a company can meet its interest payments:

$$\text{Interest coverage ratio} = \frac{\text{EBIT}}{\text{Interest expense}}$$

(where EBIT is profit from ordinary activities before interest expense and income tax).

The higher the ratio, the better. But the ratio should be interpreted in a similar fashion to the debt to equity ratio. What represents an acceptable figure depends on a number of factors, including the nature of the company's business, the volatility of its revenues and the composition of its debt. However, as a guide, when an interest coverage ratio falls below two, concern should be raised.

9. The balance sheet is just a 'snapshot in time'

A criticism of the ratio approach is that ratios are static. They are correct at just one point in time (balance date), yet we are applying them to businesses that are dynamic, since the economic factors impacting businesses are ever changing.

Undertaking a debt capacity analysis goes some way towards addressing this issue. It poses a series of 'what if' questions. Take for example an Australian iron ore mining company. A debt capacity analysis would seek to quantify the impact on its ability to service debt under a variety of different scenarios. For example, what would happen if:

- the price of iron ore dropped 50 per cent?

- interest rates rose by 3 per cent?

- the Australian dollar appreciated by 20 per cent?

- the company's capacity to raise new equity was shut down?

10. Purchasing shares on margin

I want to finish this appendix on an important point: in an ideal world a company's debt structure should represent the optimal balance between risk and return for that company.

What then of investors who choose to buy the company's shares on margin—that is, with borrowed money? They are effectively throwing the whole risk/reward debt optimisation issue out the window, denying the judgement of the company's directors and re-establishing their own gearing level. And in the process they are dialling up the risks substantially, which is food for thought when you're next tempted to take out that margin loan to buy shares.

GLOSSARY

arbitrage—a risk-free return delivered by taking advantage of a price mismatch of the same security or commodity in two different markets. It typically involves synchronised buying and selling to take advantage of the price differential.

bank bill—a short-term transferable money market debt instrument with a defined expiry. In essence it's an IOU backed by a bank security.

book value—has various interpretations but in the sense it's used in this book it equals the total assets held by a company minus its total liabilities (as defined on its balance sheet). Can also be expressed as 'book value per share'.

buying on margin—borrowing to buy stocks and using the stocks themselves as security for the loan.

collateralised debt obligation (CDO)—a financial product that pools together cash-generating assets (e.g. mortgages, loans) and sells 'tranches' or parts of that pool to individual investors.

contrarian investor—one who explores the opposing view to the investing majority in a search for opportunity. Contrarian investors operate on the assumption that the majority is often wrong, particularly when emotions are running high at times of market extremes.

credit default swap (CDS)—an agreement that the seller of the CDS will financially compensate the buyer in the event of a loan default by a debtor.

derivative—a broad term covering a large number of financial contracts that derive their value from an underlying physical security. Examples include options and futures contracts.

equity/equities—synonymous term for 'share/s' or 'stock/s'.

fundamentalist—a person using a form of investment analysis that relies heavily on financial statements and industry-based data in determining the underlying value of an investment.

geometric rate of return—also referred to as the 'compound return', it is that single rate of return that, if applied to every unit of time in the period being considered, would deliver the overall investment return observed. It is typically expressed as an annual return.

government bond—a long-term debt instrument issued by a national government that delivers periodic interest payments (commonly six months) and returns the face value of the bond on the maturity date.

hedge fund—an investment fund administered by a professional management firm. Often, but not always, they are limited to high-net-worth individuals and employ a variety of investment techniques, including the use of financial derivatives and short selling.

index fund—a professionally managed fund that invests in the same stocks and in the same proportion as a major stock index. Its aim is therefore to match rather than to outperform the index.

large cap—a term used to describe listed companies that are large in size; 'cap' is short for 'market capitalisation', which is calculated by multiplying the total number of shares on issue by the current market price.

margin—collateral (money) that an investor has to deposit to cover part of an investment that has been financed largely by borrowing.

margin call—a call from the lender for an increase in collateral. When shares are purchased on margin, a margin call is triggered when the market price of the shares being used for security over the loan falls below a predetermined level.

marginal utility theory—a theory that considers the additional satisfaction delivered from consuming an additional unit of the item being studied. Alternatively it considers the loss felt from losing a unit of the item.

mortgage-backed security—an investment (security) backed by a mortgage over a property, or more commonly a pool of mortgages over multiple properties.

option markets—markets for the trading of options, such as the Chicago Board of Options Exchange. Options can also be bought and sold off-exchange though the over-the-counter market, where prices are struck directly between the buyer and seller with no intermediary.

price earnings (PE) ratio—a financial ratio commonly used by share investors as a measure of relative value. It is calculated by dividing the current share price by the most recently reported earnings per share (EPS).

return on equity (ROE)—measures the rate of return the company delivers on the book value or shareholders' equity. In other words, it measures the return shareholders are receiving on the money they have tied up in the company. It assists them in judging whether their return expectations are being met.

security/securities—a broad term covering any tradable financial asset (e.g. stocks, bonds, options).

self-managed superannuation fund (SMSF)—a superannuation fund that is managed by the beneficiaries of the fund rather than a professional third party.

share—an investment unit commonly referring to a part ownership in a corporation.

shorted—the act of short selling. Short selling describes when a financial security is sold without being owned. The seller aims to profit from the deal by buying the security at a later date (in order to fulfil their delivery obligation) after the security has fallen in price.

small cap—a commonly used term to describe listed companies that are small in size; 'cap' is short for 'market capitalisation', which is calculated by multiplying the total number of shares on issue by the current market price.

speculator—in times past, a term used to describe an investor. Now it is used exclusively to describe those prepared to take on greater risk, usually hoping to profit from favourable price movements delivered (typically) over short time periods.

SPI futures contract—a futures contract based on a benchmark stock index (in Australia this is the S&P/ASX 200 Index). It can be used either to hedge (insure) stock portfolios or as a speculative tool for trading on the price movement of the general stock index.

stock—synonymous term for 'share'.

technical analysis—a method of stock analysis that focuses on the study of share price movement and trading volume. The study of charts is a common theme.

trader—a person who buys and sells securities and commodities with the aim of profiting from favourable price movements. Traders are less concerned with returns delivered through dividend and interest income, and typically take a shorter-term view than investors.

treasury bond—a fixed-interest government debt security.

value investor—an investor who focuses their search on assets selling at below their true value. A strong case can be put forward that the word 'value' is redundant, since all investors should have this aim.

REFERENCES

1. Livermore, Jesse, *How to Trade in Stocks*, Duell, Sloan & Pearce, 1940.

2. Graham, Benjamin, *The Intelligent Investor*, 2nd edition, Harper & Brothers Publishers, 1954.

3. Graham, Benjamin, *The Intelligent Investor*, 4th edition, Harper & Row, 1973.

4. Livermore, Jesse, *How to Trade in Stocks*, Duell, Sloan & Pearce, 1940.

5. Kahneman, Daniel, *Thinking, Fast and Slow*, Allen Lane Penguin Books, 2011.

6. Allen, Larry, *The Global Financial System 1750–2000*, Reaktion Books, 2001.

7. Tetlock, Philip E., *Expert Political Judgment*, Princeton University Press, 2005.

8. Thomas, Gordon & Morgan-Witts, Max, *The Day the Bubble Burst*, Arrow Books, 1979.

9. Dent, Harry S. Jr., *The Next Great Bubble Boom*, Simon & Schuster, 2004.

10. Nelson, Samuel Armstrong, *The ABC of Stock Speculation*, Nelson's Wall Street Library Volume V, 1902.

11. Dent, Harry S. Jr., *The Next Great Bubble Boom*, Simon & Schuster, 2004.

12. Thomas, Gordon & Morgan-Witts, Max, *The Day the Bubble Burst*, Arrow Books, 1979.

13. Bernstein, Peter L., *Capital Ideas*, John Wiley & Sons, 2005.

14. Livermore, Jesse, *How to Trade in Stocks*, Duell, Sloan & Pearce, 1940.

15. Ibid.

16. Gibson, Thomas, *The Study of Fundamentals and their Bearing on Security Prices* (in *Investments and Speculation*), La Salle Extension University Chicago, 1910.

17. Hall, Henry, *How Money is Made in Security Investments*, 2nd edition, The De Vinne Press, 1907.

18. Sherrod, Julian, *Scapegoats*, Dallas, 1931.

19. Livermore, Jesse, *How to Trade in Stocks*, Duell, Sloan & Pearce, 1940.

20. Bachelier, Louis, *Théorie de la Spéculation*, Annales Scientifiques de l'École Normale Supérieure, 1900.

21. Working, Holbrook, 'A random-difference series for use in the analysis of time series', *Journal of the American Statistical Association*, XXIX, 1934.

22. Elliott, Ralph Nelson & Prechter, Robert R., Jr. (eds), *R.N. Elliott's Masterworks*, New Classics Library, 1994.

23. Kendall, Maurice G., 1953, 'The Analysis of Time Series, Part I: Prices', *Journal of the Royal Statistical Society,* vol. 96, pp. 11–25.

24. Hayes, Lynn, 'Ten Things You Should Know about Astrology', posting to Astrodynamics website, 2008.

25. Bishop, George W. Jr., *Charles H. Dow and the Dow Theory* (letter to the author, 1950), Appleton-Century-Crofts, New York, 1960.

26. Sether, Laura (ed.), *Dow Theory Unplugged: Charles Dow's Original Editorials & their Relevance Today*, W&A Publishing, 2009.

27. Ibid.

28. Hamilton, William Peter, *The Stock Market Barometer*, Harper & Brothers, 1922.

29. Extract from *Hearings before the Committee on Banking and Currency*, U.S. Senate, 84th Congress, U.S. Government Printing Office, March 11, 1955, 545.

30. Tobin, James, 'A General Equilibrium Approach to Monetary Theory', *Journal of Money, Credit and Banking*, vol. 1, no. 1 (Feb., 1969), pp. 15–29.

31. Smithers, Andrew & Wright, Stephen, *Valuing Wall Street*, McGraw-Hill, 2000.

32. *Fortune* magazine, 10 December 2001.

33. Coppock, E.S.C., 'The Madness of Crowds', *Barron's*, 15 October 1962.

34. Coppock, E.S.C., *Realistic Stock Market Speculation*, Trendex Research Corporation, 1972.

35. Ibid.

36. Dale, Richard, *The First Crash: Lessons from the South Sea Bubble*, Princeton University Press, 2004.

37. *The New York Times*, 3 October 1885.

38. Hirst, Francis W., *The Stock Exchange*, The University Press, Cambridge, USA, 1911.

39. Galbraith, John Kenneth, *A Short History of Financial Euphoria*, Penguin, 1990.

40. Bachelier, Louis, *Théorie de la Spéculation*, Annales Scientifiques de l'École Normale Supérieure, 1900.

41. Gibson, George, *The Stock Exchanges of London, Paris, and New York*, G.P. Putnam's Sons, 1889.

42. Rhea, Robert, *The Dow Theory*, Barron's, 1932.

43. Friedman, Milton & Friedman, Rose, *Two Lucky People: Memoirs*, University of Chicago Press, 1998.

44. Fama, Eugene F. & French, Kenneth R., 'Luck versus Skill in the Cross-Section of Mutual Fund Returns', *Journal of Finance*, 2010, vol. 65, issue 5: pp. 1915–47.

45. Fama, Eugene F., 'Random Walks in Stock Market Prices', *Journal of Business*, January 1965.

46. Black, Fischer, 'Noise', *Journal of Finance*, vol. 41, issue 3, Papers and Proceedings of the Forty-Fourth Annual Meeting of the American Finance Association, New York, December 20–30, 1985 (July 1986), pp. 529–43.

47. Samuelson, Paul A. 'Challenge to Judgment', *Journal of Portfolio Management*, 1974, vol. I (Fall), pp. 17–19.

48. Livermore, Jesse, *How to Trade in Stocks*, Duell, Sloan & Pearce, 1940.

49. Ibid.

50. Graham, Benjamin, *The Intelligent Investor*, 4th edition, Harper & Row, 1973.

51. Livermore, Jesse, *How to Trade in Stocks*, Duell, Sloan & Pearce, 1940.

52. Ibid.

53. Graham, Benjamin & Dodd, David, *Security Analysis*, McGraw-Hill Book Company, 1940.

54. Livermore, Jesse, *How to Trade in Stocks*, Duell, Sloan & Pearce, 1940.

55. Chambers, David & Dimson, Elroy, *John Maynard Keynes the Investment Innovator*, paper for Cambridge Judge Business School, 30 June 2013.

56. O'Shaughnessy, James P., *What Works on Wall Street*, McGraw-Hill, 2005.

57. Dreman, David, *Contrarian Investment Strategies: The Next Generation*, Simon & Schuster, 1998.

58. Henry, George Garr, *General Principles of Investment*, La Salle Extension University Chicago, 1910.

59. Arnott, Robert D. & Asness, Clifford S., 'Surprise! Higher Dividends = Higher Earnings Growth', *Financial Analysts Journal*, 2003, vol. 59, no. 1, pp. 70–87.

60. Zhou, Ping & Ruland, William, 'Dividend Payout and Future Earnings Growth', *Financial Analysts Journal*, 2006, vol. 62, no. 3, pp. 58–69.

61. O'Shaughnessy, James P., *What Works on Wall Street*, McGraw-Hill, 2005.

62. 'Remarks on the Celebrated Calculations of the Value of the South Sea Stock', *Flying-Post*, 9 April 1720, Kress-Goldsmith Microfilm Collection, London.

63. Ehrenberg, Richard, *Capital and Finance in the Age of the Renaissance*, (trans. H.M. Lucas, London 1928), p. 309.

64. Pisano, Leonardo, *Liber Abaci*, 1202 (reprinted Sigler, Laurence E., Fibonacci's *Liber Abaci*, Springer-Verlag New York, 2002).

65. Ibid.

66. de la Vega, Joseph, *Confusion de Confusiones*, 1688 (reprinted Fridson, Martin S., John Wiley & Sons, 1996).

67. Ibid.

68. Gelderblom, Oscar & Jonker, Joost, *Amsterdam as the Cradle of Modern Futures and Options Trading*, taken from *The Origins of Value*, Oxford University Press, 2005.

69. Hutcheson, Archibald, 'An Estimate of the Intrinsick Value of South Sea Stock', 11 June 1720 (from Dale, Richard, *The First Crash: Lessons from the South Sea Bubble*, Princeton University Press, 2004).

70. Anonymous pamphleteer, early 1720, cited in Carswell, John, *The South Sea Bubble*, The Cresset Press, 1960.

71. Buffett, Warren, Introduction to *The Intelligent Investor*, 4th edition, Harper & Row, 1973.

72. Anderson, Adam (1764) (from Dale, Richard, *The First Crash: Lessons from the South Sea Bubble*, Princeton University Press, 2004).

73. 'Remarks on the Celebrated Calculations of the Value of the South Sea Stock', *Flying-Post*, 9 April 1720, Kress-Goldsmith Microfilm Collection, London.

74. Mortimer, Thomas, *Everyman his Own Broker; or a Guide to Exchange Alley* 2nd edition, London: S. Hooper; with the 13th ed. published (1801).

75. Keynes, John Maynard, *The General Theory of Employment, Interest and Money*, Macmillan Cambridge University Press, 1936.

76. Gibson, Thomas, *The Pitfalls of Speculation*, The Moody Corporation, New York, 1906.

77. Dow, Charles, *The Wall Street Journal* editorial, 13 June 1901.

78. Graham, Benjamin, *The Intelligent Investor*, 2nd edition, Harper & Brothers, 1954.

79. Rittenhouse, L.J., *Buffett's Bites*, McGraw-Hill, 2010.

80. Hall, Henry, *How Money Is Made in Security Investments*, 2nd edition, The De Vinne Press, 1907.

81. Dow, Charles, *The Wall Street Journal* editorial, 15 February 1901.

82. Gibson, Thomas, *The Study of Fundamentals and their Bearing on Security Prices* (in *Investments and Speculation*), La Salle Extension University Chicago, 1910.

83. Houghton, John, *Collection for Improvement*, 20 July 1694.

84. Smith, Moses, *Plain Truths about Stock Speculation*, Brooklyn, NY, 1887.

85. Graham, Benjamin, *The Intelligent Investor*, 4th edition, Harper & Row, 1973.

86. Kelly, Fred C., *Why You Win or Lose. The Psychology of Speculation*, Houghton Mifflin, 1930.

87. de la Vega, Joseph, *Confusion de Confusiones*, 1688 (reprinted Fridson, Martin S., John Wiley & Sons, 1996).

88. Wyckoff, Richard D., *Wall Street Ventures & Adventures through Forty Years*, Harper & Brothers, 1930.

89. Fowler, William Worthington, *Ten Years in Wall Street or Revelations of Inside Life and Experience on Change*, Worthington, Dustin & Co., 1870.

90. Hall, Henry, *How Money Is Made in Security Investments*, 2nd edition, The De Vinne Press, 1907.

91. Carret, Philip L., *The Art of Speculation*, Barron's, New York, 1927.

92. Hirst, Francis W., *The Stock Exchange*, The University Press, Cambridge, USA, 1911.

93. Graham, Benjamin & Dodd, David, *Security Analysis*, McGraw-Hill Book Company, 1940.

94. Dow, Charles, *The Wall Street Journal* editorial, 22 March 1902.

95. Buffett, Warren, 'Letter to Berkshire Hathaway Shareholders', 2007.

96. Hirst, Francis W., *The Stock Exchange*, The University Press, Cambridge, USA, 1911.

97. Buffett, Warren, 'Letter to Berkshire Hathaway Shareholders', 1999.

98. Dow, Charles, *The Wall Street Journal* editorial, 2 May 1902.

99. Buffett, Warren, 'Letter to Berkshire Hathaway Shareholders', 1988.

100. Hirst, Francis W., *The Stock Exchange*, The University Press, Cambridge, USA, 1911.

101. Buffett, Warren, Introduction to *The Intelligent Investor*, 4th edition, Harper & Row, 1973.

102. Clews, Henry, *Fifty Years in Wall Street*, Irving Publishing Company, 1908.

103. Guenther, Louis, *Investments and Speculation*, La Salle Extension University, Chicago, 1910.

104. Smith, Matthew Hale, *Twenty Years among the Bulls and Bears of Wall Street*, J.B. Burr & Company, 1870.

105. Hirst, Francis W., *The Stock Exchange*, The University Press, Cambridge, USA, 1911.

106. Mortimer, Thomas, *Everyman his Own Broker; or a Guide to Exchange Alley*, 2nd edition, London: S. Hooper; with the 13th ed. published (1801).

107. 'Remarks on the Celebrated Calculations of the Value of the South Sea Stock', *Flying-Post*, 9 April 1720, Kress-Goldsmith Microfilm Collection, London.

108. Perino, Michael, *The Hellhound of Wall Street*, Penguin, 2010.

109. Guenther, Louis, *Investments and Speculation*, La Salle Extension University, Chicago, 1910.

110. Ibid.

111. Brandeis, Louis, *Other People's Money and How the Bankers Use It*, Frederick A. Stokes, New York, 1914.

112. Austin, K.L., 'Ivar Kreuger's Story in Light of Five Years', *The New York Times*, 7 March 1937.

113. Guenther, Louis, *Investments and Speculation*, La Salle Extension University, Chicago, 1910.

114. Sherrod, Julian, *Scapegoats*, Dallas, 1931.

115. Graham, Benjamin & Dodd, David, *Security Analysis*, McGraw-Hill Book Company, 1940.

116. Henry, George Garr, *General Principles of Investment*, La Salle Extension University, Chicago, 1910.

117. Schroeder, Alice, Darden School presentation, 2008.

118. Gibson, Thomas, *The Study of Fundamentals and their Bearing on Security Prices* (in *Investments and Speculation*), La Salle Extension University, Chicago, 1910.

119. Mackay, Charles, *Memoirs of Extraordinary Delusions*, Richard Bentley, New Burlington Street, 1841.

120. Harrison, Paul, 'Rational Equity Valuation at the Time of the South Sea Bubble', *History of Political Economy*, vol. 33, no. 2, 2001.

121. Kahneman, Daniel, *Thinking, Fast and Slow*, Allen Lane Penguin, 2011.

122. Williams, John Burr, *The Theory of Investment Value*, Harvard University Press, 1938.

123. Armstrong, William, *Stocks and Stock Jobbing in Wall Street*, New York Publishing Company, New York, 1848.

124. Wyckoff, Richard D., *Wall Street Ventures & Adventures through Forty Years*, Harper & Brothers, 1930.

125. Graham, Benjamin, *Review of John Burr Williams' The Theory of Investment Value* (Cambridge, Mass.: Harvard University Press, 1938), *Journal of Political Economy*, vol. 47, no. 2, April 1939, pp. 276–78.

126. Keynes, John Maynard, *The General Theory of Employment, Interest and Money*, Macmillan Cambridge University Press, 1936.

127. Little, Ian M.D. & Rayner, A.C., *Higgledy Piggledy Growth Again*, Basil Blackwell, 1966.

128. Hagstrom, Robert G., *The Warren Buffett Portfolio*, John Wiley & Sons, 1999.

129. Graham, Benjamin, *The Intelligent Investor*, 4th edition, Harper & Row, 1973.

130. Bernstein, Peter L., *Capital Ideas*, John Wiley & Sons, 2005.

131. Graham, Benjamin, From Special Report, *Medical Economics*, 20 September 1976.

132. de la Vega, Joseph, *Confusion de Confusiones*, 1688 (reprinted Fridson, Martin S., John Wiley & Sons, 1996).

133. Hall, Henry, *How Money Is Made in Security Investments*, 2nd edition, The De Vinne Press, 1907.

134. Marks, Howard, *The Most Important Thing*, Columbia Business School, 2011.

135. Graham, Benjamin, *The Intelligent Investor*, 2nd edition, Harper & Brothers, 1954.

136. Clews, Henry, *Fifty Years in Wall Street*, Irving Publishing Company, 1908.

137. Gordon, Myron, J., *The Investment, Financing and Valuation of the Corporation*, Richard D. Irwin Inc., 1962.

138. Little, Ian M.D. & Rayner, A.C., *Higgledy Piggledy Growth Again*, Basil Blackwell, 1966.

139. Sobel, Robert, *The Great Bull Market: Wall Street in the 1920s*, W.W. Norton & Company, 1968.

140. Dechow, Patricia M., Hutton, Amy P. & Sloan, Richard G., 'An Empirical Assessment of the Residual Income Valuation Model', *Journal of Accounting and Economics*, 1999, vol. 26, no. 1–3, pp. 1–34.

141. Siegel, Jeremy J. *The Future for Investors*, Crown Business (Random House), 2005.

142. Graham, Benjamin, *The Intelligent Investor*, Harper & Brothers, 1954.

143. Wilson, Charles, *Anglo Dutch Commerce & Finance in the 18th Century*, Cambridge University Press, 1941.

144. Morgan, John, *The Life and Adventures of William Buckley*, Archibald MacDougall, 1852.

145. Kilpatrick, Andrew, *Of Permanent Value—The Story of Warren Buffett*, AKPE, 1994.

BIBLIOGRAPHY

Allen, Larry, *The Global Financial System 1750–2000*, Reaktion Books, 2001.

Anderson, Adam (1764) (from Dale, Richard, *The First Crash: Lessons from the South Sea Bubble*, Princeton University Press, 2004).

Anonymous pamphleteer, early 1720, cited in Carswell, John, *The South Sea Bubble*, The Cresset Press, 1960.

Armstrong, William, *Stocks and Stock Jobbing in Wall Street*, New York Publishing Company, New York, 1848.

Arnott, Robert D. & Asness, Clifford S., 'Surprise! Higher Dividends = Higher Earnings Growth', *Financial Analysts Journal*, 2003, vol. 59, no. 1, pp. 70–87.

Austin, K.L., 'Ivar Kreuger's Story in Light of Five Years', *The New York Times*, 7 March 1937.

Bachelier, Louis, *Théorie de la Spéculation*, Annales Scientifiques de l'École Normale Supérieure, 1900.

Bernstein, Peter L., *Capital Ideas*, John Wiley & Sons, 2005.

Bishop, George W. Jr., *Charles H. Dow and the Dow Theory* (letter to the author, 1950), Appleton-Century-Crofts, New York, 1960.

Black, Fischer, 'Noise', *Journal of Finance*, vol. 41, issue 3, Papers and Proceedings of the Forty-Fourth Annual Meeting of the American Finance Association, New York, December 20–30, 1985 (July 1986), pp. 529–43.

Buffett, Warren, Introduction to *The Intelligent Investor*, 4th edition, Harper & Row, 1973.

Buffett, Warren, 'Letter to Berkshire Hathaway Shareholders', 1988.

Buffett, Warren, 'Letter to Berkshire Hathaway Shareholders', 1999.

Buffett, Warren, 'Letter to Berkshire Hathaway Shareholders', 2007.

Carret, Philip L., *The Art of Speculation*, Barron's, New York, 1927.

Chambers, David & Dimson, Elroy, *John Maynard Keynes the Investment Innovator*, paper for Cambridge Judge Business School, 30 June 2013.

Clews, Henry, *Fifty Years in Wall Street*, Irving Publishing Company, 1908.

Coppock, E.S.C., 'The Madness of Crowds', *Barron's*, 15 October 1962.

Dale, Richard, *The First Crash: Lessons from the South Sea Bubble*, Princeton University Press, 2004.

de la Vega, Joseph, *Confusion de Confusiones*, 1688 (reprinted Fridson, Martin S., John Wiley & Sons, 1996).

Dechow, Patricia M., Hutton, Amy P. & Sloan, Richard G., 'An Empirical Assessment of the Residual Income Valuation Model', *Journal of Accounting and Economics*, 1999, vol. 26, no. 1–3, pp. 1–34.

Dent, Harry S. Jr., *The Next Great Bubble Boom*, Simon & Schuster, 2004.

Dow, Charles, *The Wall Street Journal* editorial, 15 February 1901.

Dow, Charles, *The Wall Street Journal* editorial, 13 June 1901.

Dow, Charles, *The Wall Street Journal* editorial, 22 March 1902.

Dow, Charles, *The Wall Street Journal* editorial, 2 May 1902.

Dreman, David, *Contrarian Investment Strategies: The Next Generation*, Simon & Schuster, 1998.

Ehrenberg, Richard, *Capital and Finance in the Age of the Renaissance* (trans. H.M. Lucas, London 1928), p. 309.

Elliott, Ralph Nelson & Prechter, Robert R., Jr. (eds), *R.N. Elliott's Masterworks*, New Classics Library, 1994.

Extract from *Hearings before the Committee on Banking and Currency*, U.S. Senate, 84th Congress, U.S. Government Printing Office, March 11, 1955, 545.

Fama, Eugene F. & French, Kenneth R., 'Luck versus Skill in the Cross-Section of Mutual Fund Returns', *Journal of Finance*, 2010, vol. 65, issue 5: pp. 1915–47.

Fama, Eugene F., 'Random Walks in Stock Market Prices', *Journal of Business*, January 1965.

Fortune magazine, 10 December 2001.

Fowler, William Worthington, *Ten Years in Wall Street or Revelations of Inside Life and Experience on Change*, Worthington, Dustin & Co., 1870.

Friedman, Milton & Friedman, Rose, *Two Lucky People: Memoirs*, University of Chicago Press, 1998.

Galbraith, John Kenneth, *A Short History of Financial Euphoria*, Penguin, 1990.

Gelderblom, Oscar & Jonker, Joost, *Amsterdam as the Cradle of Modern Futures and Options Trading*, taken from *The Origins of Value*, Oxford University Press, 2005.

Gibson, George, *The Stock Exchanges of London, Paris, and New York*, G.P. Putnam's Sons, New York, 1889.

Gibson, Thomas, *The Pitfalls of Speculation*, The Moody Corporation, New York, 1906.

Gibson, Thomas, *The Study of Fundamentals and their Bearing on Security Prices* (in *Investments and Speculation*), La Salle Extension University, Chicago, 1910.

Gordon, Myron, J., *The Investment, Financing and Valuation of the Corporation*, Richard D. Irwin Inc., 1962.

Gordon, Myron, *The New York Times*, 3 October 1885.

Graham, Benjamin & Dodd, David, *Security Analysis*, McGraw-Hill Book Company, 1940.

Graham, Benjamin, From Special Report, *Medical Economics*, 20 September 1976.

Graham, Benjamin, Review of John Burr Williams' *The Theory of Investment Value* (Cambridge, Mass.: Harvard University Press, 1938), *Journal of Political Economy*, vol. 47, no. 2, April 1939, pp. 276–78.

Graham, Benjamin, *The Intelligent Investor*, 2nd edition, Harper & Brothers, 1954.

Graham, Benjamin, *The Intelligent Investor*, 4th edition, Harper & Row, 1973.

Guenther, Louis, *Investments and Speculation*, La Salle Extension University, Chicago, 1910.

Hagstrom, Robert G., *The Warren Buffett Portfolio*, John Wiley & Sons, 1999.

Hall, Henry, *How Money Is Made in Security Investments*, 2nd edition, The De Vinne Press, 1907.

Hamilton, William Peter, *The Stock Market Barometer*, Harper & Brothers, 1922.

Harrison, Paul, 'Rational Equity Valuation at the Time of the South Sea Bubble', *History of Political Economy*, vol. 33, no. 2, 2001.

Henry, George Garr, *General Principles of Investment*, La Salle Extension University Chicago, 1910.

Hirst, Francis W., *The Stock Exchange*, The University Press, Cambridge, USA, 1911.

Houghton, John, *Collection for Improvement*, 20 July 1694.

Hutcheson, Archibald, 'An Estimate of the Intrinsick Value of South Sea Stock', 11 June 1720 (from Dale, Richard, *The First Crash: Lessons from The South Sea Bubble*, Princeton University Press, 2004).

Kahneman, Daniel, *Thinking, Fast and Slow*, Allen Lane Penguin, 2011.

Kelly, Fred C., *Why You Win or Lose. The Psychology of Speculation*, Houghton Mifflin, 1930.

Keynes, John Maynard, *The General Theory of Employment, Interest and Money*, Macmillan Cambridge University Press, 1936.

Kilpatrick, Andrew, *Of Permanent Value—The Story of Warren Buffett*, AKPE, 1994.

Little, Ian M.D. & Rayner, A.C., *Higgledy Piggledy Growth Again*, Basil Blackwell, 1966.

Livermore, Jesse, *How to Trade in Stocks*, Duell, Sloan & Pearce, 1940.

Mackay, Charles, *Memoirs of Extraordinary Delusions*, Richard Bentley, New Burlington Street, 1841.

Marks, Howard, *The Most Important Thing*, Columbia Business School, 2011.

Morgan, John, *The Life and Adventures of William Buckley*, Archibald MacDougall, 1852.

Mortimer, Thomas, *Everyman his Own Broker; or a Guide to Exchange Alley*, 2nd edition, London: S. Hooper; with the 13th ed. published (1801).

Nelson, Samuel Armstrong, *The ABC of Stock Speculation*, Nelson's Wall Street Library Volume V, 1902.

O'Shaughnessy, James P., *What Works on Wall Street*, McGraw-Hill, 2005.

Perino, Michael, *The Hellhound of Wall Street*, Penguin, 2010.

Pisano, Leonardo, *Liber Abaci*, 1202 (reprinted Sigler, Laurence E., *Fibonacci's Liber Abaci*, Springer-Verlag New York, 2002).

'Remarks on the Celebrated Calculations of the Value of the South Sea Stock', *Flying-Post*, 9 April 1720, Kress-Goldsmith Microfilm Collection, London.

Rhea, Robert, *The Dow Theory*, Barron's, 1932.

Rittenhouse, L.J., *Buffett's Bites*, McGraw-Hill, 2010.

Samuelson, Paul A. 'Challenge to Judgment', *Journal of Portfolio Management*, 1974, vol. I (Fall), pp. 17–19.

Sether, Laura (ed.), *Dow Theory Unplugged: Charles Dow's Original Editorials & their Relevance Today*, W&A Publishing, 2009.

Sherrod, Julian, *Scapegoats*, Dallas, 1931.

Siegel, Jeremy J. *The Future for Investors*, Crown Business (Random House), 2005.

Smith, Matthew Hale, *Twenty Years among the Bulls and Bears of Wall Street*, J.B. Burr & Company, 1870.

Smith, Moses, *Plain Truths about Stock Speculation*, Brooklyn, NY, 1887.

Smithers, Andrew & Wright, Stephen, *Valuing Wall Street*, McGraw-Hill, 2000.

Sobel, Robert, *The Great Bull Market: Wall Street in the 1920s*, W.W. Norton & Company, 1968.

Tetlock, Philip E., *Expert Political Judgment*, Princeton University Press, 2005.

Thomas, Gordon & Morgan-Witts, Max, *The Day the Bubble Burst*, Arrow Books, 1979.

Tobin, James, 'A General Equilibrium Approach to Monetary Theory', *Journal of Money, Credit and Banking*, vol. 1, no. 1 (Feb., 1969), pp. 15–29.

Williams, John Burr, *The Theory of Investment Value*, Harvard University Press, 1938.

Wilson, Charles, *Anglo Dutch Commerce & Finance in the 18th Century*, Cambridge University Press, 1941.

Working, Holbrook, 'A random-difference series for use in the analysis of time series', *Journal of the American Statistical Association*, XXIX, 1934.

Wyckoff, Richard D., *Wall Street Ventures & Adventures through Forty Years*, Harper & Brothers, 1930.

Zhou, Ping & Ruland, William, 'Dividend Payout and Future Earnings Growth', *Financial Analysts Journal*, 2006, vol. 62, no. 3, pp. 58–69.

INDEX

Connect
with WILEY ▶▶▶

WILEY

Browse and purchase the full range of Wiley publications on our official website.

www.wiley.com

Check out the Wiley blog for news, articles and information from Wiley and our authors.

www.wileybizaus.com

Join the conversation on Twitter and keep up to date on the latest news and events in business.

@WileyBizAus

Sign up for Wiley newsletters to learn about our latest publications, upcoming events and conferences, and discounts available to our customers.

www.wiley.com/email

Wiley titles are also produced in e-book formats. Available from all good retailers.

WILEY

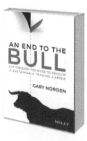

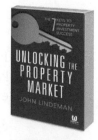